FIDELITY

NOTARY

JOURNAL

Official Single-View Record Book

FIDELITY

Fidelity means faithfulness to a person, cause, or belief, demonstrated by continuing loyalty and support. Therefore, this journal is titled "Fidelity" to remind you, a professional notary, of your commitment to loyally serve your state in this appointed role.

You are an official of integrity that's appointed by the state government to serve the public as an impartial witness in performing a variety of official fraud-deterrent acts related to the signing of important documents. Your duty is to screen the signer of important documents for their true identity, their willingness to sign without duress or intimidation, and their awareness of the contents of the document.

Our hope for the notary industry is that we find continued fulfillment in our service as we assist our communities and states faithfully. May every notarization be executed with precision and performed with devotion to the office of Notary Public.

NOTARY PUBLIC

Name: _____

Address: _____

_____

Phone: _____

Email: _____

Dates of Use: _____ to _____

This journal is the official property of a state appointed notary professional. Please contact the journal owner identified above or the Secretary of State for the state noted above if found.

ACKNOWLEDGMENT

An acknowledgment is a notarial act in which an individual, at a single time and place:

- Appears in person before the notary public and presents a document;

- Is personally known to the notary public or is identified by the notary through satisfactory evidence of identity; and

- Indicates to the notary public that the signature on the document was voluntarily affixed by the individual for the purposes stated within the document and, if applicable, that the individual had authority to sign in a particular representative capacity.

The emphasis, when a notary performs an acknowledgment, is on the free act and deed of the signer and the verification of their identity.

STEPS TO PERFORM AN ACKNOWLEDGMENT

Signers must personally appear on the date and in the place indicated on the notarial certificate.

1   Review the document to determine the document type and the notarial act to be performed.
2   Identify the signer through personal knowledge or an accepted form of identification.
3   Verify that the signature on the document is the signer's, either by watching them sign the document or if it has already been signed, by comparing the signature to the one on the signer's ID and the signature made by the signer in the notary's journal.
4   Have the signer verbally acknowledge that their signature was made competently and voluntarily.
5   Complete the notarial certificate. Sign the certificate, print your name, and affix your notary stamp. Complete the journal entry. [* Follow your state notary certificate guidelines]

JURAT

A jurat is a notarial act in which an individual, at a single time and place:

- Appears in person before the notary public and presents a document;

- Is personally known to the notary public or is identified by the notary through satisfactory evidence of identity;

- Signs the document in the presence of the notary public; and

- Takes an oath or affirmation before the notary public vouching for the truthfulness or accuracy of the signed document.

The emphasis, when a notary performs a jurat, is on the accuracy of the statements in the document and the signer's identity.

STEPS TO PERFORM A JURAT

Individual(s) must personally appear on the date and in the place indicated on the notarial certificate.

1   Review the document to determine the document type and the notarial act to be performed.
2   Identify the signer through personal knowledge or an accepted form of identification.
3   Have the signer verbally acknowledge they are signing the document competently and voluntarily.
4   Watch the signer affix their signature or mark to the document.
5   Administer the oath or affirmation aloud.
6   Complete the notarial certificate. Sign the certificate, print your name, and affix your notary stamp. Complete the journal entry. [* Follow your state notary certificate guidelines]

OATH AND AFFIRMATION

An oath is a notarial act, or part thereof, which is legally equivalent to an affirmation, in which an individual, at a single time and place:

- Appears in person before the notary public;

- Is personally known to the notary public or is identified by the notary through satisfactory evidence of identity; and

- Makes a vow of truthfulness or fidelity under the pains and penalties of perjury by invoking a deity or using any form of the word "swear."

An affirmation is a notarial act, or part thereof, that is legally equivalent to an oath in which an individual, at a single time and place:

- Appears in person before the notary public;

- Is personally known to the notary public or is identified by the notary through satisfactory evidence of identity; and

- Makes a vow of truthfulness or fidelity under the pains and penalties of perjury based on personal honor and without invoking a deity or using any form of the word "swear."

STEPS TO PERFORM AN OATH AND AFFIRMATION

The person must personally appear before the notary public.

- Identify the person through personal knowledge or an accepted form of identification.

- Administer the oath or affirmation by having the person raise their right hand and administer the oath or affirmation aloud.

- Complete the journal entry.

SIGNATURE WITNESSING

Signature witnessing is a notarial act in which an individual, at a single time and place:

- Appears in person before the notary public and presents a document;

- Is personally known to the notary public or is identified by the notary through satisfactory evidence of identity; and

- Signs the document in the presence of the notary public.

The emphasis, when a notary performs a signature witnessing, is to establish the document was signed on a specific date.

STEPS TO PERFORM A SIGNATURE WITNESSING

Signer must personally appear on the date and in the place indicated on the notarial certificate.

1. Review the document to determine the document type and the notarial act to be performed.

2. Identify the signer through personal knowledge or an accepted form of identification.

3. Have the signer verbally acknowledge that they are signing the document competently and voluntarily.

4. Watch the signer affix their signature or the mark to the document

5. Complete the notarial certificate. Sign the certificate, print your name, and affix your notary stamp. Complete the journal entry. [* Follow your state notary certificate guidelines]

Date		Time	AM	PM
1	**Full Name** ___ Signor ___ Witness _____ Address: _____	Verification Method DL PP Cred. Wit Other: _____ State: _____ Iss date: _____ Expiration: _____	Doc. Type ___ Paper ___ Electronic ___ Hybrid	Thumb Print
	Signature	Screening ___ Coherent ___ Consenting	Phone I Email	
2	**Full Name** ___ Signor ___ Witness _____ Address: _____	Verification Method DL PP Cred. Wit Other: _____ State: _____ Iss date: _____ Expiration: _____	Doc. Type ___ Paper ___ Electronic ___ Hybrid	Thumb Print
	Signature	Screening ___ Coherent ___ Consenting	Phone I Email	
3	**Full Name** ___ Signor ___ Witness _____ Address: _____	Verification Method DL PP Cred. Wit Other: _____ State: _____ Iss date: _____ Expiration: _____	Doc. Type ___ Paper ___ Electronic ___ Hybrid	Thumb Print
	Signature	Screening ___ Coherent ___ Consenting	Phone I Email	
4	**Full Name** ___ Signor ___ Witness _____ Address: _____	Verification Method DL PP Cred. Wit Other: _____ State: _____ Iss date: _____ Expiration: _____	Doc. Type ___ Paper ___ Electronic ___ Hybrid	Thumb Print
	Signature	Screening ___ Coherent ___ Consenting	Phone I Email	

Signing Location:	Observers:	Signing Service:	Fee:

Appointment Notes:
_____
_____
_____

Record of Signed Documents: Loan Documents

Borrower's Affidavit	__ Ack __ Jurat 1 2 3 4	Disbursement of Proceeds	__ Ack __ Jurat 1 2 3 4
Compliance Agreement	__ Ack __ Jurat 1 2 3 4	Errors & Omissions Agreement	__ Ack __ Jurat 1 2 3 4
Correction Agreement	__ Ack __ Jurat 1 2 3 4	Financial Affidavit	__ Ack __ Jurat 1 2 3 4
Indemnity Debt/Lien Affidavit	__ Ack __ Jurat 1 2 3 4	Grant Deed	__ Ack __ Jurat 1 2 3 4
Deed of Trust	__ Ack __ Jurat 1 2 3 4	Marital Status Affidavit	__ Ack __ Jurat 1 2 3 4
Mortgage	__ Ack __ Jurat 1 2 3 4	Quit Claim Deed	__ Ack __ Jurat 1 2 3 4
Mortgagor's Affidavit	__ Ack __ Jurat 1 2 3 4	Signature/Name Affidavit	__ Ack __ Jurat 1 2 3 4
Occupancy Affidavit	__ Ack __ Jurat 1 2 3 4	Survey Affidavit	__ Ack __ Jurat 1 2 3 4
Owner's Affidavit	__ Ack __ Jurat 1 2 3 4	Warranty Deed	__ Ack __ Jurat 1 2 3 4
Payoff Affidavit	__ Ack __ Jurat 1 2 3 4	Other	__ Ack __ Jurat 1 2 3 4

Vehicle Docs:

Duplicate Title	__ Ack __ Jurat 1 2 3 4	Odometer/VIN Verification	__ Ack __ Jurat 1 2 3 4
Lien Release	__ Ack __ Jurat 1 2 3 4	Title Transfer	__ Ack __ Jurat 1 2 3 4

Wills/Trusts/ POA:

Living Trust	__ Ack __ Jurat 1 2 3 4	Power of Attorney	__ Ack __ Jurat 1 2 3 4
Last Will & Test	__ Ack __ Jurat 1 2 3 4	Trust Certification	__ Ack __ Jurat 1 2 3 4

Medical Docs:

Advance Healthcare Directive	__ Ack __ Jurat 1 2 3 4	HIPAA Release	__ Ack __ Jurat 1 2 3 4

Other Non-listed Docs:

Document Title: _____ Act Type 1 2 3 4	Document Title: _____ Act Type 1 2 3 4
Document Title: _____ Act Type 1 2 3 4	Document Title: _____ Act Type 1 2 3 4
Document Title: _____ Act Type 1 2 3 4	Document Title: _____ Act Type 1 2 3 4
Document Title: _____ Act Type 1 2 3 4	Document Title: _____ Act Type 1 2 3 4

Date			Time		AM	PM

| 1 | Full Name ___ Signor ___ Witness

_____

Address: _____ | | Verification Method
DL   PP   Cred. Wit
Other: _____
State: _____
Iss date: _____
Expiration: _____ | | Doc. Type

___ Paper
___ Electronic
___ Hybrid | Thumb Print |
| | Signature | | Screening
___ Coherent
___ Consenting | | Phone I Email | |

| 2 | Full Name ___ Signor ___ Witness

_____

Address: _____ | | Verification Method
DL   PP   Cred. Wit
Other: _____
State: _____
Iss date: _____
Expiration: _____ | | Doc. Type

___ Paper
___ Electronic
___ Hybrid | Thumb Print |
| | Signature | | Screening
___ Coherent
___ Consenting | | Phone I Email | |

| 3 | Full Name ___ Signor ___ Witness

_____

Address: _____ | | Verification Method
DL   PP   Cred. Wit
Other: _____
State: _____
Iss date: _____
Expiration: _____ | | Doc. Type

___ Paper
___ Electronic
___ Hybrid | Thumb Print |
| | Signature | | Screening
___ Coherent
___ Consenting | | Phone I Email | |

| 4 | Full Name ___ Signor ___ Witness

_____

Address: _____ | | Verification Method
DL   PP   Cred. Wit
Other: _____
State: _____
Iss date: _____
Expiration: _____ | | Doc. Type

___ Paper
___ Electronic
___ Hybrid | Thumb Print |
| | Signature | | Screening
___ Coherent
___ Consenting | | Phone I Email | |

Signing Location:	Observers:	Signing Service:	Fee:

Appointment Notes:

Record of Signed Documents: Loan Documents

Borrower's Affidavit	__ Ack __ Jurat 1 2 3 4	Disbursement of Proceeds	__ Ack __ Jurat 1 2 3 4
Compliance Agreement	__ Ack __ Jurat 1 2 3 4	Errors & Omissions Agreement	__ Ack __ Jurat 1 2 3 4
Correction Agreement	__ Ack __ Jurat 1 2 3 4	Financial Affidavit	__ Ack __ Jurat 1 2 3 4
Indemnity Debt/Lien Affidavit	__ Ack __ Jurat 1 2 3 4	Grant Deed	__ Ack __ Jurat 1 2 3 4
Deed of Trust	__ Ack __ Jurat 1 2 3 4	Marital Status Affidavit	__ Ack __ Jurat 1 2 3 4
Mortgage	__ Ack __ Jurat 1 2 3 4	Quit Claim Deed	__ Ack __ Jurat 1 2 3 4
Mortgagor's Affidavit	__ Ack __ Jurat 1 2 3 4	Signature/Name Affidavit	__ Ack __ Jurat 1 2 3 4
Occupancy Affidavit	__ Ack __ Jurat 1 2 3 4	Survey Affidavit	__ Ack __ Jurat 1 2 3 4
Owner's Affidavit	__ Ack __ Jurat 1 2 3 4	Warranty Deed	__ Ack __ Jurat 1 2 3 4
Payoff Affidavit	__ Ack __ Jurat 1 2 3 4	Other	__ Ack __ Jurat 1 2 3 4

Vehicle Docs:

Duplicate Title	__ Ack __ Jurat 1 2 3 4	Odometer/VIN Verification	__ Ack __ Jurat 1 2 3 4
Lien Release	__ Ack __ Jurat 1 2 3 4	Title Transfer	__ Ack __ Jurat 1 2 3 4

Wills/Trusts/ POA:

Living Trust	__ Ack __ Jurat 1 2 3 4	Power of Attorney	__ Ack __ Jurat 1 2 3 4
Last Will & Test	__ Ack __ Jurat 1 2 3 4	Trust Certification	__ Ack __ Jurat 1 2 3 4

Medical Docs:

Advance Healthcare Directive	__ Ack __ Jurat 1 2 3 4	HIPAA Release	__ Ack __ Jurat 1 2 3 4

Other Non-listed Docs:

Document Title: _____ Act Type 1 2 3 4	Document Title: _____ Act Type 1 2 3 4
Document Title: _____ Act Type 1 2 3 4	Document Title: _____ Act Type 1 2 3 4
Document Title: _____ Act Type 1 2 3 4	Document Title: _____ Act Type 1 2 3 4
Document Title: _____ Act Type 1 2 3 4	Document Title: _____ Act Type 1 2 3 4

Date		Time	AM	PM
	Full Name ___ Signor ___ Witness _____ Address: _____	Verification Method DL PP Cred. Wit Other: _____ State: _____ Iss date: _____ Expiration: _____	Doc. Type ___ Paper ___ Electronic ___ Hybrid	Thumb Print
1	Signature	Screening ___ Coherent ___ Consenting	Phone I Email	
	Full Name ___ Signor ___ Witness _____ Address: _____	Verification Method DL PP Cred. Wit Other: _____ State: _____ Iss date: _____ Expiration: _____	Doc. Type ___ Paper ___ Electronic ___ Hybrid	Thumb Print
2	Signature	Screening ___ Coherent ___ Consenting	Phone I Email	
	Full Name ___ Signor ___ Witness _____ Address: _____	Verification Method DL PP Cred. Wit Other: _____ State: _____ Iss date: _____ Expiration: _____	Doc. Type ___ Paper ___ Electronic ___ Hybrid	Thumb Print
3	Signature	Screening ___ Coherent ___ Consenting	Phone I Email	
	Full Name ___ Signor ___ Witness _____ Address: _____	Verification Method DL PP Cred. Wit Other: _____ State: _____ Iss date: _____ Expiration: _____	Doc. Type ___ Paper ___ Electronic ___ Hybrid	Thumb Print
4	Signature	Screening ___ Coherent ___ Consenting	Phone I Email	

Signing Location:	Observers:	Signing Service:	Fee:

Appointment Notes:

Record of Signed Documents: Loan Documents

Borrower's Affidavit	__ Ack __ Jurat 1 2 3 4	Disbursement of Proceeds	__ Ack __ Jurat 1 2 3 4
Compliance Agreement	__ Ack __ Jurat 1 2 3 4	Errors & Omissions Agreement	__ Ack __ Jurat 1 2 3 4
Correction Agreement	__ Ack __ Jurat 1 2 3 4	Financial Affidavit	__ Ack __ Jurat 1 2 3 4
Indemnity Debt/Lien Affidavit	__ Ack __ Jurat 1 2 3 4	Grant Deed	__ Ack __ Jurat 1 2 3 4
Deed of Trust	__ Ack __ Jurat 1 2 3 4	Marital Status Affidavit	__ Ack __ Jurat 1 2 3 4
Mortgage	__ Ack __ Jurat 1 2 3 4	Quit Claim Deed	__ Ack __ Jurat 1 2 3 4
Mortgagor's Affidavit	__ Ack __ Jurat 1 2 3 4	Signature/Name Affidavit	__ Ack __ Jurat 1 2 3 4
Occupancy Affidavit	__ Ack __ Jurat 1 2 3 4	Survey Affidavit	__ Ack __ Jurat 1 2 3 4
Owner's Affidavit	__ Ack __ Jurat 1 2 3 4	Warranty Deed	__ Ack __ Jurat 1 2 3 4
Payoff Affidavit	__ Ack __ Jurat 1 2 3 4	Other	__ Ack __ Jurat 1 2 3 4

Vehicle Docs:

Duplicate Title	__ Ack __ Jurat 1 2 3 4	Odometer/VIN Verification	__ Ack __ Jurat 1 2 3 4
Lien Release	__ Ack __ Jurat 1 2 3 4	Title Transfer	__ Ack __ Jurat 1 2 3 4

Wills/Trusts/ POA:

Living Trust	__ Ack __ Jurat 1 2 3 4	Power of Attorney	__ Ack __ Jurat 1 2 3 4
Last Will & Test	__ Ack __ Jurat 1 2 3 4	Trust Certification	__ Ack __ Jurat 1 2 3 4

Medical Docs:

Advance Healthcare Directive	__ Ack __ Jurat 1 2 3 4	HIPAA Release	__ Ack __ Jurat 1 2 3 4

Other Non-listed Docs:

Document Title: _____ Act Type 1 2 3 4		Document Title: _____ Act Type 1 2 3 4	
Document Title: _____ Act Type 1 2 3 4		Document Title: _____ Act Type 1 2 3 4	
Document Title: _____ Act Type 1 2 3 4		Document Title: _____ Act Type 1 2 3 4	
Document Title: _____ Act Type 1 2 3 4		Document Title: _____ Act Type 1 2 3 4	

Date			Time		AM	PM
1	Full Name ___ Signor ___ Witness _____ Address: _____		Verification Method DL PP Cred. Wit Other: _____ State: _____ Iss date: _____ Expiration: _____		Doc. Type ___ Paper ___ Electronic ___ Hybrid	Thumb Print
	Signature		Screening ___ Coherent ___ Consenting		Phone I Email	
2	Full Name ___ Signor ___ Witness _____ Address: _____		Verification Method DL PP Cred. Wit Other: _____ State: _____ Iss date: _____ Expiration: _____		Doc. Type ___ Paper ___ Electronic ___ Hybrid	Thumb Print
	Signature		Screening ___ Coherent ___ Consenting		Phone I Email	
3	Full Name ___ Signor ___ Witness _____ Address: _____		Verification Method DL PP Cred. Wit Other: _____ State: _____ Iss date: _____ Expiration: _____		Doc. Type ___ Paper ___ Electronic ___ Hybrid	Thumb Print
	Signature		Screening ___ Coherent ___ Consenting		Phone I Email	
4	Full Name ___ Signor ___ Witness _____ Address: _____		Verification Method DL PP Cred. Wit Other: _____ State: _____ Iss date: _____ Expiration: _____		Doc. Type ___ Paper ___ Electronic ___ Hybrid	Thumb Print
	Signature		Screening ___ Coherent ___ Consenting		Phone I Email	

Signing Location:	Observers:	Signing Service:	Fee:

Appointment Notes:

_____

_____

Record of Signed Documents: Loan Documents

Borrower's Affidavit	__ Ack __ Jurat 1 2 3 4	Disbursement of Proceeds	__ Ack __ Jurat 1 2 3 4
Compliance Agreement	__ Ack __ Jurat 1 2 3 4	Errors & Omissions Agreement	__ Ack __ Jurat 1 2 3 4
Correction Agreement	__ Ack __ Jurat 1 2 3 4	Financial Affidavit	__ Ack __ Jurat 1 2 3 4
Indemnity Debt/Lien Affidavit	__ Ack __ Jurat 1 2 3 4	Grant Deed	__ Ack __ Jurat 1 2 3 4
Deed of Trust	__ Ack __ Jurat 1 2 3 4	Marital Status Affidavit	__ Ack __ Jurat 1 2 3 4
Mortgage	__ Ack __ Jurat 1 2 3 4	Quit Claim Deed	__ Ack __ Jurat 1 2 3 4
Mortgagor's Affidavit	__ Ack __ Jurat 1 2 3 4	Signature/Name Affidavit	__ Ack __ Jurat 1 2 3 4
Occupancy Affidavit	__ Ack __ Jurat 1 2 3 4	Survey Affidavit	__ Ack __ Jurat 1 2 3 4
Owner's Affidavit	__ Ack __ Jurat 1 2 3 4	Warranty Deed	__ Ack __ Jurat 1 2 3 4
Payoff Affidavit	__ Ack __ Jurat 1 2 3 4	Other	__ Ack __ Jurat 1 2 3 4

Vehicle Docs:

Duplicate Title	__ Ack __ Jurat 1 2 3 4	Odometer/VIN Verification	__ Ack __ Jurat 1 2 3 4
Lien Release	__ Ack __ Jurat 1 2 3 4	Title Transfer	__ Ack __ Jurat 1 2 3 4

Wills/Trusts/ POA:

Living Trust	__ Ack __ Jurat 1 2 3 4	Power of Attorney	__ Ack __ Jurat 1 2 3 4
Last Will & Test	__ Ack __ Jurat 1 2 3 4	Trust Certification	__ Ack __ Jurat 1 2 3 4

Medical Docs:

Advance Healthcare Directive	__ Ack __ Jurat 1 2 3 4	HIPAA Release	__ Ack __ Jurat 1 2 3 4

Other Non-listed Docs:

Document Title: _____ Act Type 1 2 3 4	Document Title: _____ Act Type 1 2 3 4
Document Title: _____ Act Type 1 2 3 4	Document Title: _____ Act Type 1 2 3 4
Document Title: _____ Act Type 1 2 3 4	Document Title: _____ Act Type 1 2 3 4
Document Title: _____ Act Type 1 2 3 4	Document Title: _____ Act Type 1 2 3 4

Date			Time		AM	PM
1	Full Name ___ Signor ___ Witness _____ Address: _____		Verification Method DL PP Cred. Wit Other: _____ State: _____ Iss date: _____ Expiration: _____		Doc. Type ___ Paper ___ Electronic ___ Hybrid	Thumb Print
	Signature		Screening ___ Coherent ___ Consenting		Phone I Email	
2	Full Name ___ Signor ___ Witness _____ Address: _____		Verification Method DL PP Cred. Wit Other: _____ State: _____ Iss date: _____ Expiration: _____		Doc. Type ___ Paper ___ Electronic ___ Hybrid	Thumb Print
	Signature		Screening ___ Coherent ___ Consenting		Phone I Email	
3	Full Name ___ Signor ___ Witness _____ Address: _____		Verification Method DL PP Cred. Wit Other: _____ State: _____ Iss date: _____ Expiration: _____		Doc. Type ___ Paper ___ Electronic ___ Hybrid	Thumb Print
	Signature		Screening ___ Coherent ___ Consenting		Phone I Email	
4	Full Name ___ Signor ___ Witness _____ Address: _____		Verification Method DL PP Cred. Wit Other: _____ State: _____ Iss date: _____ Expiration: _____		Doc. Type ___ Paper ___ Electronic ___ Hybrid	Thumb Print
	Signature		Screening ___ Coherent ___ Consenting		Phone I Email	

Signing Location:	Observers:	Signing Service:	Fee:

Appointment Notes:

Record of Signed Documents: Loan Documents

Borrower's Affidavit	__ Ack __ Jurat 1 2 3 4	Disbursement of Proceeds	__ Ack __ Jurat 1 2 3 4
Compliance Agreement	__ Ack __ Jurat 1 2 3 4	Errors & Omissions Agreement	__ Ack __ Jurat 1 2 3 4
Correction Agreement	__ Ack __ Jurat 1 2 3 4	Financial Affidavit	__ Ack __ Jurat 1 2 3 4
Indemnity Debt/Lien Affidavit	__ Ack __ Jurat 1 2 3 4	Grant Deed	__ Ack __ Jurat 1 2 3 4
Deed of Trust	__ Ack __ Jurat 1 2 3 4	Marital Status Affidavit	__ Ack __ Jurat 1 2 3 4
Mortgage	__ Ack __ Jurat 1 2 3 4	Quit Claim Deed	__ Ack __ Jurat 1 2 3 4
Mortgagor's Affidavit	__ Ack __ Jurat 1 2 3 4	Signature/Name Affidavit	__ Ack __ Jurat 1 2 3 4
Occupancy Affidavit	__ Ack __ Jurat 1 2 3 4	Survey Affidavit	__ Ack __ Jurat 1 2 3 4
Owner's Affidavit	__ Ack __ Jurat 1 2 3 4	Warranty Deed	__ Ack __ Jurat 1 2 3 4
Payoff Affidavit	__ Ack __ Jurat 1 2 3 4	Other	__ Ack __ Jurat 1 2 3 4

Vehicle Docs:

Duplicate Title	__ Ack __ Jurat 1 2 3 4	Odometer/VIN Verification	__ Ack __ Jurat 1 2 3 4
Lien Release	__ Ack __ Jurat 1 2 3 4	Title Transfer	__ Ack __ Jurat 1 2 3 4

Wills/Trusts/ POA:

Living Trust	__ Ack __ Jurat 1 2 3 4	Power of Attorney	__ Ack __ Jurat 1 2 3 4
Last Will & Test	__ Ack __ Jurat 1 2 3 4	Trust Certification	__ Ack __ Jurat 1 2 3 4

Medical Docs:

Advance Healthcare Directive	__ Ack __ Jurat 1 2 3 4	HIPAA Release	__ Ack __ Jurat 1 2 3 4

Other Non-listed Docs:

Document Title: _____ Act Type 1 2 3 4	Document Title: _____ Act Type 1 2 3 4
Document Title: _____ Act Type 1 2 3 4	Document Title: _____ Act Type 1 2 3 4
Document Title: _____ Act Type 1 2 3 4	Document Title: _____ Act Type 1 2 3 4
Document Title: _____ Act Type 1 2 3 4	Document Title: _____ Act Type 1 2 3 4

Date			Time	AM	PM

	Full Name ___ Signor ___ Witness	Verification Method DL PP Cred. Wit Other: _____ State: _____ Iss date: _____ Expiration: _____	Doc. Type ___ Paper ___ Electronic ___ Hybrid	Thumb Print
1	Address: _____			
	Signature	Screening ___ Coherent ___ Consenting	Phone I Email	
	Full Name ___ Signor ___ Witness	Verification Method DL PP Cred. Wit Other: _____ State: _____ Iss date: _____ Expiration: _____	Doc. Type ___ Paper ___ Electronic ___ Hybrid	Thumb Print
2	Address: _____			
	Signature	Screening ___ Coherent ___ Consenting	Phone I Email	
	Full Name ___ Signor ___ Witness	Verification Method DL PP Cred. Wit Other: _____ State: _____ Iss date: _____ Expiration: _____	Doc. Type ___ Paper ___ Electronic ___ Hybrid	Thumb Print
3	Address: _____			
	Signature	Screening ___ Coherent ___ Consenting	Phone I Email	
	Full Name ___ Signor ___ Witness	Verification Method DL PP Cred. Wit Other: _____ State: _____ Iss date: _____ Expiration: _____	Doc. Type ___ Paper ___ Electronic ___ Hybrid	Thumb Print
4	Address: _____			
	Signature	Screening ___ Coherent ___ Consenting	Phone I Email	

Signing Location:	Observers:	Signing Service:	Fee:

Appointment Notes:

Record of Signed Documents: Loan Documents

Borrower's Affidavit	__ Ack __ Jurat 1 2 3 4	Disbursement of Proceeds	__ Ack __ Jurat 1 2 3 4
Compliance Agreement	__ Ack __ Jurat 1 2 3 4	Errors & Omissions Agreement	__ Ack __ Jurat 1 2 3 4
Correction Agreement	__ Ack __ Jurat 1 2 3 4	Financial Affidavit	__ Ack __ Jurat 1 2 3 4
Indemnity Debt/Lien Affidavit	__ Ack __ Jurat 1 2 3 4	Grant Deed	__ Ack __ Jurat 1 2 3 4
Deed of Trust	__ Ack __ Jurat 1 2 3 4	Marital Status Affidavit	__ Ack __ Jurat 1 2 3 4
Mortgage	__ Ack __ Jurat 1 2 3 4	Quit Claim Deed	__ Ack __ Jurat 1 2 3 4
Mortgagor's Affidavit	__ Ack __ Jurat 1 2 3 4	Signature/Name Affidavit	__ Ack __ Jurat 1 2 3 4
Occupancy Affidavit	__ Ack __ Jurat 1 2 3 4	Survey Affidavit	__ Ack __ Jurat 1 2 3 4
Owner's Affidavit	__ Ack __ Jurat 1 2 3 4	Warranty Deed	__ Ack __ Jurat 1 2 3 4
Payoff Affidavit	__ Ack __ Jurat 1 2 3 4	Other	__ Ack __ Jurat 1 2 3 4

Vehicle Docs:

Duplicate Title	__ Ack __ Jurat 1 2 3 4	Odometer/VIN Verification	__ Ack __ Jurat 1 2 3 4
Lien Release	__ Ack __ Jurat 1 2 3 4	Title Transfer	__ Ack __ Jurat 1 2 3 4

Wills/Trusts/ POA:

Living Trust	__ Ack __ Jurat 1 2 3 4	Power of Attorney	__ Ack __ Jurat 1 2 3 4
Last Will & Test	__ Ack __ Jurat 1 2 3 4	Trust Certification	__ Ack __ Jurat 1 2 3 4

Medical Docs:

Advance Healthcare Directive	__ Ack __ Jurat 1 2 3 4	HIPAA Release	__ Ack __ Jurat 1 2 3 4

Other Non-listed Docs:

Document Title: _____ Act Type 1 2 3 4		Document Title: _____ Act Type 1 2 3 4	
Document Title: _____ Act Type 1 2 3 4		Document Title: _____ Act Type 1 2 3 4	
Document Title: _____ Act Type 1 2 3 4		Document Title: _____ Act Type 1 2 3 4	
Document Title: _____ Act Type 1 2 3 4		Document Title: _____ Act Type 1 2 3 4	

Date		Time		AM	PM

1	Full Name ___ Signor ___ Witness _____ Address: _____	Verification Method DL PP Cred. Wit Other: _____ State: _____ Iss date: _____ Expiration: _____	Doc. Type ___ Paper ___ Electronic ___ Hybrid	Thumb Print
	Signature	Screening ___ Coherent ___ Consenting	Phone I Email	

2	Full Name ___ Signor ___ Witness _____ Address: _____	Verification Method DL PP Cred. Wit Other: _____ State: _____ Iss date: _____ Expiration: _____	Doc. Type ___ Paper ___ Electronic ___ Hybrid	Thumb Print
	Signature	Screening ___ Coherent ___ Consenting	Phone I Email	

3	Full Name ___ Signor ___ Witness _____ Address: _____	Verification Method DL PP Cred. Wit Other: _____ State: _____ Iss date: _____ Expiration: _____	Doc. Type ___ Paper ___ Electronic ___ Hybrid	Thumb Print
	Signature	Screening ___ Coherent ___ Consenting	Phone I Email	

4	Full Name ___ Signor ___ Witness _____ Address: _____	Verification Method DL PP Cred. Wit Other: _____ State: _____ Iss date: _____ Expiration: _____	Doc. Type ___ Paper ___ Electronic ___ Hybrid	Thumb Print
	Signature	Screening ___ Coherent ___ Consenting	Phone I Email	

Signing Location:	Observers:	Signing Service:	Fee:

Appointment Notes:

Record of Signed Documents: Loan Documents

Borrower's Affidavit	__ Ack __ Jurat 1 2 3 4	Disbursement of Proceeds	__ Ack __ Jurat 1 2 3 4
Compliance Agreement	__ Ack __ Jurat 1 2 3 4	Errors & Omissions Agreement	__ Ack __ Jurat 1 2 3 4
Correction Agreement	__ Ack __ Jurat 1 2 3 4	Financial Affidavit	__ Ack __ Jurat 1 2 3 4
Indemnity Debt/Lien Affidavit	__ Ack __ Jurat 1 2 3 4	Grant Deed	__ Ack __ Jurat 1 2 3 4
Deed of Trust	__ Ack __ Jurat 1 2 3 4	Marital Status Affidavit	__ Ack __ Jurat 1 2 3 4
Mortgage	__ Ack __ Jurat 1 2 3 4	Quit Claim Deed	__ Ack __ Jurat 1 2 3 4
Mortgagor's Affidavit	__ Ack __ Jurat 1 2 3 4	Signature/Name Affidavit	__ Ack __ Jurat 1 2 3 4
Occupancy Affidavit	__ Ack __ Jurat 1 2 3 4	Survey Affidavit	__ Ack __ Jurat 1 2 3 4
Owner's Affidavit	__ Ack __ Jurat 1 2 3 4	Warranty Deed	__ Ack __ Jurat 1 2 3 4
Payoff Affidavit	__ Ack __ Jurat 1 2 3 4	Other	__ Ack __ Jurat 1 2 3 4

Vehicle Docs:

Duplicate Title	__ Ack __ Jurat 1 2 3 4	Odometer/VIN Verification	__ Ack __ Jurat 1 2 3 4
Lien Release	__ Ack __ Jurat 1 2 3 4	Title Transfer	__ Ack __ Jurat 1 2 3 4

Wills/Trusts/ POA:

Living Trust	__ Ack __ Jurat 1 2 3 4	Power of Attorney	__ Ack __ Jurat 1 2 3 4
Last Will & Test	__ Ack __ Jurat 1 2 3 4	Trust Certification	__ Ack __ Jurat 1 2 3 4

Medical Docs:

Advance Healthcare Directive	__ Ack __ Jurat 1 2 3 4	HIPAA Release	__ Ack __ Jurat 1 2 3 4

Other Non-listed Docs:

Document Title: _____ Act Type 1 2 3 4	Document Title: _____ Act Type 1 2 3 4
Document Title: _____ Act Type 1 2 3 4	Document Title: _____ Act Type 1 2 3 4
Document Title: _____ Act Type 1 2 3 4	Document Title: _____ Act Type 1 2 3 4
Document Title: _____ Act Type 1 2 3 4	Document Title: _____ Act Type 1 2 3 4

Date		Time	AM	PM
	Full Name ___ Signor ___ Witness	Verification Method	Doc. Type	Thumb Print
1	_____ Address: _____	DL PP Cred. Wit Other: _____ State: _____ Iss date: _____ Expiration: _____	___ Paper ___ Electronic ___ Hybrid	
	Signature	Screening ___ Coherent ___ Consenting	Phone I Email	
	Full Name ___ Signor ___ Witness	Verification Method	Doc. Type	Thumb Print
2	_____ Address: _____	DL PP Cred. Wit Other: _____ State: _____ Iss date: _____ Expiration: _____	___ Paper ___ Electronic ___ Hybrid	
	Signature	Screening ___ Coherent ___ Consenting	Phone I Email	
	Full Name ___ Signor ___ Witness	Verification Method	Doc. Type	Thumb Print
3	_____ Address: _____	DL PP Cred. Wit Other: _____ State: _____ Iss date: _____ Expiration: _____	___ Paper ___ Electronic ___ Hybrid	
	Signature	Screening ___ Coherent ___ Consenting	Phone I Email	
	Full Name ___ Signor ___ Witness	Verification Method	Doc. Type	Thumb Print
4	_____ Address: _____	DL PP Cred. Wit Other: _____ State: _____ Iss date: _____ Expiration: _____	___ Paper ___ Electronic ___ Hybrid	
	Signature	Screening ___ Coherent ___ Consenting	Phone I Email	

Signing Location:	Observers:	Signing Service:	Fee:

Appointment Notes:

Record of Signed Documents: Loan Documents

Borrower's Affidavit	__ Ack __ Jurat 1 2 3 4	Disbursement of Proceeds	__ Ack __ Jurat 1 2 3 4
Compliance Agreement	__ Ack __ Jurat 1 2 3 4	Errors & Omissions Agreement	__ Ack __ Jurat 1 2 3 4
Correction Agreement	__ Ack __ Jurat 1 2 3 4	Financial Affidavit	__ Ack __ Jurat 1 2 3 4
Indemnity Debt/Lien Affidavit	__ Ack __ Jurat 1 2 3 4	Grant Deed	__ Ack __ Jurat 1 2 3 4
Deed of Trust	__ Ack __ Jurat 1 2 3 4	Marital Status Affidavit	__ Ack __ Jurat 1 2 3 4
Mortgage	__ Ack __ Jurat 1 2 3 4	Quit Claim Deed	__ Ack __ Jurat 1 2 3 4
Mortgagor's Affidavit	__ Ack __ Jurat 1 2 3 4	Signature/Name Affidavit	__ Ack __ Jurat 1 2 3 4
Occupancy Affidavit	__ Ack __ Jurat 1 2 3 4	Survey Affidavit	__ Ack __ Jurat 1 2 3 4
Owner's Affidavit	__ Ack __ Jurat 1 2 3 4	Warranty Deed	__ Ack __ Jurat 1 2 3 4
Payoff Affidavit	__ Ack __ Jurat 1 2 3 4	Other	__ Ack __ Jurat 1 2 3 4

Vehicle Docs:

Duplicate Title	__ Ack __ Jurat 1 2 3 4	Odometer/VIN Verification	__ Ack __ Jurat 1 2 3 4
Lien Release	__ Ack __ Jurat 1 2 3 4	Title Transfer	__ Ack __ Jurat 1 2 3 4

Wills/Trusts/ POA:

Living Trust	__ Ack __ Jurat 1 2 3 4	Power of Attorney	__ Ack __ Jurat 1 2 3 4
Last Will & Test	__ Ack __ Jurat 1 2 3 4	Trust Certification	__ Ack __ Jurat 1 2 3 4

Medical Docs:

Advance Healthcare Directive	__ Ack __ Jurat 1 2 3 4	HIPAA Release	__ Ack __ Jurat 1 2 3 4

Other Non-listed Docs:

Document Title: _____ Act Type 1 2 3 4	Document Title: _____ Act Type 1 2 3 4
Document Title: _____ Act Type 1 2 3 4	Document Title: _____ Act Type 1 2 3 4
Document Title: _____ Act Type 1 2 3 4	Document Title: _____ Act Type 1 2 3 4
Document Title: _____ Act Type 1 2 3 4	Document Title: _____ Act Type 1 2 3 4

Date			Time	AM	PM
1	Full Name ___ Signor ___ Witness _____ Address: _____		Verification Method DL PP Cred. Wit Other: _____ State: _____ Iss date: _____ Expiration: _____	Doc. Type ___ Paper ___ Electronic ___ Hybrid	Thumb Print
	Signature		Screening ___ Coherent ___ Consenting	Phone I Email	
2	Full Name ___ Signor ___ Witness _____ Address: _____		Verification Method DL PP Cred. Wit Other: _____ State: _____ Iss date: _____ Expiration: _____	Doc. Type ___ Paper ___ Electronic ___ Hybrid	Thumb Print
	Signature		Screening ___ Coherent ___ Consenting	Phone I Email	
3	Full Name ___ Signor ___ Witness _____ Address: _____		Verification Method DL PP Cred. Wit Other: _____ State: _____ Iss date: _____ Expiration: _____	Doc. Type ___ Paper ___ Electronic ___ Hybrid	Thumb Print
	Signature		Screening ___ Coherent ___ Consenting	Phone I Email	
4	Full Name ___ Signor ___ Witness _____ Address: _____		Verification Method DL PP Cred. Wit Other: _____ State: _____ Iss date: _____ Expiration: _____	Doc. Type ___ Paper ___ Electronic ___ Hybrid	Thumb Print
	Signature		Screening ___ Coherent ___ Consenting	Phone I Email	

Signing Location:	Observers:	Signing Service:	Fee:

Appointment Notes:

Record of Signed Documents: Loan Documents

Borrower's Affidavit	__ Ack __ Jurat 1 2 3 4	Disbursement of Proceeds	__ Ack __ Jurat 1 2 3 4
Compliance Agreement	__ Ack __ Jurat 1 2 3 4	Errors & Omissions Agreement	__ Ack __ Jurat 1 2 3 4
Correction Agreement	__ Ack __ Jurat 1 2 3 4	Financial Affidavit	__ Ack __ Jurat 1 2 3 4
Indemnity Debt/Lien Affidavit	__ Ack __ Jurat 1 2 3 4	Grant Deed	__ Ack __ Jurat 1 2 3 4
Deed of Trust	__ Ack __ Jurat 1 2 3 4	Marital Status Affidavit	__ Ack __ Jurat 1 2 3 4
Mortgage	__ Ack __ Jurat 1 2 3 4	Quit Claim Deed	__ Ack __ Jurat 1 2 3 4
Mortgagor's Affidavit	__ Ack __ Jurat 1 2 3 4	Signature/Name Affidavit	__ Ack __ Jurat 1 2 3 4
Occupancy Affidavit	__ Ack __ Jurat 1 2 3 4	Survey Affidavit	__ Ack __ Jurat 1 2 3 4
Owner's Affidavit	__ Ack __ Jurat 1 2 3 4	Warranty Deed	__ Ack __ Jurat 1 2 3 4
Payoff Affidavit	__ Ack __ Jurat 1 2 3 4	Other	__ Ack __ Jurat 1 2 3 4

Vehicle Docs:

Duplicate Title	__ Ack __ Jurat 1 2 3 4	Odometer/VIN Verification	__ Ack __ Jurat 1 2 3 4
Lien Release	__ Ack __ Jurat 1 2 3 4	Title Transfer	__ Ack __ Jurat 1 2 3 4

Wills/Trusts/ POA:

Living Trust	__ Ack __ Jurat 1 2 3 4	Power of Attorney	__ Ack __ Jurat 1 2 3 4
Last Will & Test	__ Ack __ Jurat 1 2 3 4	Trust Certification	__ Ack __ Jurat 1 2 3 4

Medical Docs:

Advance Healthcare Directive	__ Ack __ Jurat 1 2 3 4	HIPAA Release	__ Ack __ Jurat 1 2 3 4

Other Non-listed Docs:

Document Title: _____ Act Type 1 2 3 4		Document Title: _____ Act Type 1 2 3 4	
Document Title: _____ Act Type 1 2 3 4		Document Title: _____ Act Type 1 2 3 4	
Document Title: _____ Act Type 1 2 3 4		Document Title: _____ Act Type 1 2 3 4	
Document Title: _____ Act Type 1 2 3 4		Document Title: _____ Act Type 1 2 3 4	

Date		Time	AM	PM

	Full Name ___ Signor ___ Witness	Verification Method	Doc. Type	Thumb Print
1	_____ Address: _____	DL PP Cred. Wit Other: _____ State: _____ Iss date: _____ Expiration: _____	___ Paper ___ Electronic ___ Hybrid	
	Signature	Screening ___ Coherent ___ Consenting	Phone I Email	

	Full Name ___ Signor ___ Witness	Verification Method	Doc. Type	Thumb Print
2	_____ Address: _____	DL PP Cred. Wit Other: _____ State: _____ Iss date: _____ Expiration: _____	___ Paper ___ Electronic ___ Hybrid	
	Signature	Screening ___ Coherent ___ Consenting	Phone I Email	

	Full Name ___ Signor ___ Witness	Verification Method	Doc. Type	Thumb Print
3	_____ Address: _____	DL PP Cred. Wit Other: _____ State: _____ Iss date: _____ Expiration: _____	___ Paper ___ Electronic ___ Hybrid	
	Signature	Screening ___ Coherent ___ Consenting	Phone I Email	

	Full Name ___ Signor ___ Witness	Verification Method	Doc. Type	Thumb Print
4	_____ Address: _____	DL PP Cred. Wit Other: _____ State: _____ Iss date: _____ Expiration: _____	___ Paper ___ Electronic ___ Hybrid	
	Signature	Screening ___ Coherent ___ Consenting	Phone I Email	

Signing Location:	Observers:	Signing Service:	Fee:

Appointment Notes:

Record of Signed Documents: Loan Documents

Borrower's Affidavit	__ Ack __ Jurat 1 2 3 4	Disbursement of Proceeds	__ Ack __ Jurat 1 2 3 4
Compliance Agreement	__ Ack __ Jurat 1 2 3 4	Errors & Omissions Agreement	__ Ack __ Jurat 1 2 3 4
Correction Agreement	__ Ack __ Jurat 1 2 3 4	Financial Affidavit	__ Ack __ Jurat 1 2 3 4
Indemnity Debt/Lien Affidavit	__ Ack __ Jurat 1 2 3 4	Grant Deed	__ Ack __ Jurat 1 2 3 4
Deed of Trust	__ Ack __ Jurat 1 2 3 4	Marital Status Affidavit	__ Ack __ Jurat 1 2 3 4
Mortgage	__ Ack __ Jurat 1 2 3 4	Quit Claim Deed	__ Ack __ Jurat 1 2 3 4
Mortgagor's Affidavit	__ Ack __ Jurat 1 2 3 4	Signature/Name Affidavit	__ Ack __ Jurat 1 2 3 4
Occupancy Affidavit	__ Ack __ Jurat 1 2 3 4	Survey Affidavit	__ Ack __ Jurat 1 2 3 4
Owner's Affidavit	__ Ack __ Jurat 1 2 3 4	Warranty Deed	__ Ack __ Jurat 1 2 3 4
Payoff Affidavit	__ Ack __ Jurat 1 2 3 4	Other	__ Ack __ Jurat 1 2 3 4

Vehicle Docs:

Duplicate Title	__ Ack __ Jurat 1 2 3 4	Odometer/VIN Verification	__ Ack __ Jurat 1 2 3 4
Lien Release	__ Ack __ Jurat 1 2 3 4	Title Transfer	__ Ack __ Jurat 1 2 3 4

Wills/Trusts/ POA:

Living Trust	__ Ack __ Jurat 1 2 3 4	Power of Attorney	__ Ack __ Jurat 1 2 3 4
Last Will & Test	__ Ack __ Jurat 1 2 3 4	Trust Certification	__ Ack __ Jurat 1 2 3 4

Medical Docs:

Advance Healthcare Directive	__ Ack __ Jurat 1 2 3 4	HIPAA Release	__ Ack __ Jurat 1 2 3 4

Other Non-listed Docs:

Document Title: _____ Act Type 1 2 3 4		Document Title: _____ Act Type 1 2 3 4	
Document Title: _____ Act Type 1 2 3 4		Document Title: _____ Act Type 1 2 3 4	
Document Title: _____ Act Type 1 2 3 4		Document Title: _____ Act Type 1 2 3 4	
Document Title: _____ Act Type 1 2 3 4		Document Title: _____ Act Type 1 2 3 4	

Date		Time	AM	PM

1	Full Name ___ Signor ___ Witness _____ Address: _____	Verification Method DL PP Cred. Wit Other: _____ State: _____ Iss date: _____ Expiration: _____	Doc. Type ___ Paper ___ Electronic ___ Hybrid	Thumb Print
	Signature	Screening ___ Coherent ___ Consenting	Phone I Email	
2	Full Name ___ Signor ___ Witness _____ Address: _____	Verification Method DL PP Cred. Wit Other: _____ State: _____ Iss date: _____ Expiration: _____	Doc. Type ___ Paper ___ Electronic ___ Hybrid	Thumb Print
	Signature	Screening ___ Coherent ___ Consenting	Phone I Email	
3	Full Name ___ Signor ___ Witness _____ Address: _____	Verification Method DL PP Cred. Wit Other: _____ State: _____ Iss date: _____ Expiration: _____	Doc. Type ___ Paper ___ Electronic ___ Hybrid	Thumb Print
	Signature	Screening ___ Coherent ___ Consenting	Phone I Email	
4	Full Name ___ Signor ___ Witness _____ Address: _____	Verification Method DL PP Cred. Wit Other: _____ State: _____ Iss date: _____ Expiration: _____	Doc. Type ___ Paper ___ Electronic ___ Hybrid	Thumb Print
	Signature	Screening ___ Coherent ___ Consenting	Phone I Email	

Signing Location:	Observers:	Signing Service:	Fee:

Appointment Notes:

Record of Signed Documents: Loan Documents

Borrower's Affidavit	__ Ack __ Jurat 1 2 3 4	Disbursement of Proceeds	__ Ack __ Jurat 1 2 3 4
Compliance Agreement	__ Ack __ Jurat 1 2 3 4	Errors & Omissions Agreement	__ Ack __ Jurat 1 2 3 4
Correction Agreement	__ Ack __ Jurat 1 2 3 4	Financial Affidavit	__ Ack __ Jurat 1 2 3 4
Indemnity Debt/Lien Affidavit	__ Ack __ Jurat 1 2 3 4	Grant Deed	__ Ack __ Jurat 1 2 3 4
Deed of Trust	__ Ack __ Jurat 1 2 3 4	Marital Status Affidavit	__ Ack __ Jurat 1 2 3 4
Mortgage	__ Ack __ Jurat 1 2 3 4	Quit Claim Deed	__ Ack __ Jurat 1 2 3 4
Mortgagor's Affidavit	__ Ack __ Jurat 1 2 3 4	Signature/Name Affidavit	__ Ack __ Jurat 1 2 3 4
Occupancy Affidavit	__ Ack __ Jurat 1 2 3 4	Survey Affidavit	__ Ack __ Jurat 1 2 3 4
Owner's Affidavit	__ Ack __ Jurat 1 2 3 4	Warranty Deed	__ Ack __ Jurat 1 2 3 4
Payoff Affidavit	__ Ack __ Jurat 1 2 3 4	Other	__ Ack __ Jurat 1 2 3 4

Vehicle Docs:

Duplicate Title	__ Ack __ Jurat 1 2 3 4	Odometer/VIN Verification	__ Ack __ Jurat 1 2 3 4
Lien Release	__ Ack __ Jurat 1 2 3 4	Title Transfer	__ Ack __ Jurat 1 2 3 4

Wills/Trusts/ POA:

Living Trust	__ Ack __ Jurat 1 2 3 4	Power of Attorney	__ Ack __ Jurat 1 2 3 4
Last Will & Test	__ Ack __ Jurat 1 2 3 4	Trust Certification	__ Ack __ Jurat 1 2 3 4

Medical Docs:

Advance Healthcare Directive	__ Ack __ Jurat 1 2 3 4	HIPAA Release	__ Ack __ Jurat 1 2 3 4

Other Non-listed Docs:

Document Title: _____ Act Type 1 2 3 4	Document Title: _____ Act Type 1 2 3 4
Document Title: _____ Act Type 1 2 3 4	Document Title: _____ Act Type 1 2 3 4
Document Title: _____ Act Type 1 2 3 4	Document Title: _____ Act Type 1 2 3 4
Document Title: _____ Act Type 1 2 3 4	Document Title: _____ Act Type 1 2 3 4

Date			Time		AM	PM

1	Full Name ___ Signor ___ Witness _____ Address: _____	Verification Method DL PP Cred. Wit Other: _____ State: _____ Iss date: _____ Expiration: _____	Doc. Type ___ Paper ___ Electronic ___ Hybrid	Thumb Print	
	Signature	Screening ___ Coherent ___ Consenting	Phone I Email		
2	Full Name ___ Signor ___ Witness _____ Address: _____	Verification Method DL PP Cred. Wit Other: _____ State: _____ Iss date: _____ Expiration: _____	Doc. Type ___ Paper ___ Electronic ___ Hybrid	Thumb Print	
	Signature	Screening ___ Coherent ___ Consenting	Phone I Email		
3	Full Name ___ Signor ___ Witness _____ Address: _____	Verification Method DL PP Cred. Wit Other: _____ State: _____ Iss date: _____ Expiration: _____	Doc. Type ___ Paper ___ Electronic ___ Hybrid	Thumb Print	
	Signature	Screening ___ Coherent ___ Consenting	Phone I Email		
4	Full Name ___ Signor ___ Witness _____ Address: _____	Verification Method DL PP Cred. Wit Other: _____ State: _____ Iss date: _____ Expiration: _____	Doc. Type ___ Paper ___ Electronic ___ Hybrid	Thumb Print	
	Signature	Screening ___ Coherent ___ Consenting	Phone I Email		

Signing Location:	Observers:	Signing Service:	Fee:

Appointment Notes:

_____

_____

Record of Signed Documents: Loan Documents

Borrower's Affidavit	__ Ack __ Jurat 1 2 3 4	Disbursement of Proceeds	__ Ack __ Jurat 1 2 3 4
Compliance Agreement	__ Ack __ Jurat 1 2 3 4	Errors & Omissions Agreement	__ Ack __ Jurat 1 2 3 4
Correction Agreement	__ Ack __ Jurat 1 2 3 4	Financial Affidavit	__ Ack __ Jurat 1 2 3 4
Indemnity Debt/Lien Affidavit	__ Ack __ Jurat 1 2 3 4	Grant Deed	__ Ack __ Jurat 1 2 3 4
Deed of Trust	__ Ack __ Jurat 1 2 3 4	Marital Status Affidavit	__ Ack __ Jurat 1 2 3 4
Mortgage	__ Ack __ Jurat 1 2 3 4	Quit Claim Deed	__ Ack __ Jurat 1 2 3 4
Mortgagor's Affidavit	__ Ack __ Jurat 1 2 3 4	Signature/Name Affidavit	__ Ack __ Jurat 1 2 3 4
Occupancy Affidavit	__ Ack __ Jurat 1 2 3 4	Survey Affidavit	__ Ack __ Jurat 1 2 3 4
Owner's Affidavit	__ Ack __ Jurat 1 2 3 4	Warranty Deed	__ Ack __ Jurat 1 2 3 4
Payoff Affidavit	__ Ack __ Jurat 1 2 3 4	Other	__ Ack __ Jurat 1 2 3 4

Vehicle Docs:

Duplicate Title	__ Ack __ Jurat 1 2 3 4	Odometer/VIN Verification	__ Ack __ Jurat 1 2 3 4
Lien Release	__ Ack __ Jurat 1 2 3 4	Title Transfer	__ Ack __ Jurat 1 2 3 4

Wills/Trusts/ POA:

Living Trust	__ Ack __ Jurat 1 2 3 4	Power of Attorney	__ Ack __ Jurat 1 2 3 4
Last Will & Test	__ Ack __ Jurat 1 2 3 4	Trust Certification	__ Ack __ Jurat 1 2 3 4

Medical Docs:

Advance Healthcare Directive	__ Ack __ Jurat 1 2 3 4	HIPAA Release	__ Ack __ Jurat 1 2 3 4

Other Non-listed Docs:

Document Title: _____ Act Type 1 2 3 4	Document Title: _____ Act Type 1 2 3 4
Document Title: _____ Act Type 1 2 3 4	Document Title: _____ Act Type 1 2 3 4
Document Title: _____ Act Type 1 2 3 4	Document Title: _____ Act Type 1 2 3 4
Document Title: _____ Act Type 1 2 3 4	Document Title: _____ Act Type 1 2 3 4

Date		Time	AM	PM
1	**Full Name** ___ Signor ___ Witness _____ Address: _____	Verification Method DL PP Cred. Wit Other: _____ State: _____ Iss date: _____ Expiration: _____	Doc. Type ___ Paper ___ Electronic ___ Hybrid	Thumb Print
	Signature	Screening ___ Coherent ___ Consenting	Phone I Email	
2	**Full Name** ___ Signor ___ Witness _____ Address: _____	Verification Method DL PP Cred. Wit Other: _____ State: _____ Iss date: _____ Expiration: _____	Doc. Type ___ Paper ___ Electronic ___ Hybrid	Thumb Print
	Signature	Screening ___ Coherent ___ Consenting	Phone I Email	
3	**Full Name** ___ Signor ___ Witness _____ Address: _____	Verification Method DL PP Cred. Wit Other: _____ State: _____ Iss date: _____ Expiration: _____	Doc. Type ___ Paper ___ Electronic ___ Hybrid	Thumb Print
	Signature	Screening ___ Coherent ___ Consenting	Phone I Email	
4	**Full Name** ___ Signor ___ Witness _____ Address: _____	Verification Method DL PP Cred. Wit Other: _____ State: _____ Iss date: _____ Expiration: _____	Doc. Type ___ Paper ___ Electronic ___ Hybrid	Thumb Print
	Signature	Screening ___ Coherent ___ Consenting	Phone I Email	

Signing Location:	Observers:	Signing Service:	Fee:

Appointment Notes:

_____

_____

Record of Signed Documents: Loan Documents

Borrower's Affidavit	__ Ack __ Jurat 1 2 3 4	Disbursement of Proceeds	__ Ack __ Jurat 1 2 3 4
Compliance Agreement	__ Ack __ Jurat 1 2 3 4	Errors & Omissions Agreement	__ Ack __ Jurat 1 2 3 4
Correction Agreement	__ Ack __ Jurat 1 2 3 4	Financial Affidavit	__ Ack __ Jurat 1 2 3 4
Indemnity Debt/Lien Affidavit	__ Ack __ Jurat 1 2 3 4	Grant Deed	__ Ack __ Jurat 1 2 3 4
Deed of Trust	__ Ack __ Jurat 1 2 3 4	Marital Status Affidavit	__ Ack __ Jurat 1 2 3 4
Mortgage	__ Ack __ Jurat 1 2 3 4	Quit Claim Deed	__ Ack __ Jurat 1 2 3 4
Mortgagor's Affidavit	__ Ack __ Jurat 1 2 3 4	Signature/Name Affidavit	__ Ack __ Jurat 1 2 3 4
Occupancy Affidavit	__ Ack __ Jurat 1 2 3 4	Survey Affidavit	__ Ack __ Jurat 1 2 3 4
Owner's Affidavit	__ Ack __ Jurat 1 2 3 4	Warranty Deed	__ Ack __ Jurat 1 2 3 4
Payoff Affidavit	__ Ack __ Jurat 1 2 3 4	Other	__ Ack __ Jurat 1 2 3 4

Vehicle Docs:

Duplicate Title	__ Ack __ Jurat 1 2 3 4	Odometer/VIN Verification	__ Ack __ Jurat 1 2 3 4
Lien Release	__ Ack __ Jurat 1 2 3 4	Title Transfer	__ Ack __ Jurat 1 2 3 4

Wills/Trusts/ POA:

Living Trust	__ Ack __ Jurat 1 2 3 4	Power of Attorney	__ Ack __ Jurat 1 2 3 4
Last Will & Test	__ Ack __ Jurat 1 2 3 4	Trust Certification	__ Ack __ Jurat 1 2 3 4

Medical Docs:

Advance Healthcare Directive	__ Ack __ Jurat 1 2 3 4	HIPAA Release	__ Ack __ Jurat 1 2 3 4

Other Non-listed Docs:

Document Title: _____ Act Type 1 2 3 4	Document Title: _____ Act Type 1 2 3 4
Document Title: _____ Act Type 1 2 3 4	Document Title: _____ Act Type 1 2 3 4
Document Title: _____ Act Type 1 2 3 4	Document Title: _____ Act Type 1 2 3 4
Document Title: _____ Act Type 1 2 3 4	Document Title: _____ Act Type 1 2 3 4

Date		Time		AM	PM
1	Full Name ___ Signor ___ Witness _____ Address: _____	Verification Method DL PP Cred. Wit Other: _____ State: _____ Iss date: _____ Expiration: _____		Doc. Type ___ Paper ___ Electronic ___ Hybrid	Thumb Print
	Signature	Screening ___ Coherent ___ Consenting		Phone I Email	
2	Full Name ___ Signor ___ Witness _____ Address: _____	Verification Method DL PP Cred. Wit Other: _____ State: _____ Iss date: _____ Expiration: _____		Doc. Type ___ Paper ___ Electronic ___ Hybrid	Thumb Print
	Signature	Screening ___ Coherent ___ Consenting		Phone I Email	
3	Full Name ___ Signor ___ Witness _____ Address: _____	Verification Method DL PP Cred. Wit Other: _____ State: _____ Iss date: _____ Expiration: _____		Doc. Type ___ Paper ___ Electronic ___ Hybrid	Thumb Print
	Signature	Screening ___ Coherent ___ Consenting		Phone I Email	
4	Full Name ___ Signor ___ Witness _____ Address: _____	Verification Method DL PP Cred. Wit Other: _____ State: _____ Iss date: _____ Expiration: _____		Doc. Type ___ Paper ___ Electronic ___ Hybrid	Thumb Print
	Signature	Screening ___ Coherent ___ Consenting		Phone I Email	

Signing Location:	Observers:	Signing Service:	Fee:

Appointment Notes:

Record of Signed Documents: Loan Documents

Borrower's Affidavit	__ Ack __ Jurat 1 2 3 4	Disbursement of Proceeds	__ Ack __ Jurat 1 2 3 4
Compliance Agreement	__ Ack __ Jurat 1 2 3 4	Errors & Omissions Agreement	__ Ack __ Jurat 1 2 3 4
Correction Agreement	__ Ack __ Jurat 1 2 3 4	Financial Affidavit	__ Ack __ Jurat 1 2 3 4
Indemnity Debt/Lien Affidavit	__ Ack __ Jurat 1 2 3 4	Grant Deed	__ Ack __ Jurat 1 2 3 4
Deed of Trust	__ Ack __ Jurat 1 2 3 4	Marital Status Affidavit	__ Ack __ Jurat 1 2 3 4
Mortgage	__ Ack __ Jurat 1 2 3 4	Quit Claim Deed	__ Ack __ Jurat 1 2 3 4
Mortgagor's Affidavit	__ Ack __ Jurat 1 2 3 4	Signature/Name Affidavit	__ Ack __ Jurat 1 2 3 4
Occupancy Affidavit	__ Ack __ Jurat 1 2 3 4	Survey Affidavit	__ Ack __ Jurat 1 2 3 4
Owner's Affidavit	__ Ack __ Jurat 1 2 3 4	Warranty Deed	__ Ack __ Jurat 1 2 3 4
Payoff Affidavit	__ Ack __ Jurat 1 2 3 4	Other	__ Ack __ Jurat 1 2 3 4

Vehicle Docs:

Duplicate Title	__ Ack __ Jurat 1 2 3 4	Odometer/VIN Verification	__ Ack __ Jurat 1 2 3 4
Lien Release	__ Ack __ Jurat 1 2 3 4	Title Transfer	__ Ack __ Jurat 1 2 3 4

Wills/Trusts/ POA:

Living Trust	__ Ack __ Jurat 1 2 3 4	Power of Attorney	__ Ack __ Jurat 1 2 3 4
Last Will & Test	__ Ack __ Jurat 1 2 3 4	Trust Certification	__ Ack __ Jurat 1 2 3 4

Medical Docs:

Advance Healthcare Directive	__ Ack __ Jurat 1 2 3 4	HIPAA Release	__ Ack __ Jurat 1 2 3 4

Other Non-listed Docs:

Document Title: _____ Act Type 1 2 3 4		Document Title: _____ Act Type 1 2 3 4	
Document Title: _____ Act Type 1 2 3 4		Document Title: _____ Act Type 1 2 3 4	
Document Title: _____ Act Type 1 2 3 4		Document Title: _____ Act Type 1 2 3 4	
Document Title: _____ Act Type 1 2 3 4		Document Title: _____ Act Type 1 2 3 4	

Date			Time	AM	PM

1	Full Name ___ Signor ___ Witness _____ Address: _____	Verification Method DL PP Cred. Wit Other: _____ State: _____ Iss date: _____ Expiration: _____	Doc. Type ___ Paper ___ Electronic ___ Hybrid	Thumb Print
	Signature	Screening ___ Coherent ___ Consenting	Phone I Email	

2	Full Name ___ Signor ___ Witness _____ Address: _____	Verification Method DL PP Cred. Wit Other: _____ State: _____ Iss date: _____ Expiration: _____	Doc. Type ___ Paper ___ Electronic ___ Hybrid	Thumb Print
	Signature	Screening ___ Coherent ___ Consenting	Phone I Email	

3	Full Name ___ Signor ___ Witness _____ Address: _____	Verification Method DL PP Cred. Wit Other: _____ State: _____ Iss date: _____ Expiration: _____	Doc. Type ___ Paper ___ Electronic ___ Hybrid	Thumb Print
	Signature	Screening ___ Coherent ___ Consenting	Phone I Email	

4	Full Name ___ Signor ___ Witness _____ Address: _____	Verification Method DL PP Cred. Wit Other: _____ State: _____ Iss date: _____ Expiration: _____	Doc. Type ___ Paper ___ Electronic ___ Hybrid	Thumb Print
	Signature	Screening ___ Coherent ___ Consenting	Phone I Email	

Signing Location:	Observers:	Signing Service:	Fee:

Appointment Notes:

Record of Signed Documents: Loan Documents

Borrower's Affidavit	__ Ack __ Jurat 1 2 3 4	Disbursement of Proceeds	__ Ack __ Jurat 1 2 3 4
Compliance Agreement	__ Ack __ Jurat 1 2 3 4	Errors & Omissions Agreement	__ Ack __ Jurat 1 2 3 4
Correction Agreement	__ Ack __ Jurat 1 2 3 4	Financial Affidavit	__ Ack __ Jurat 1 2 3 4
Indemnity Debt/Lien Affidavit	__ Ack __ Jurat 1 2 3 4	Grant Deed	__ Ack __ Jurat 1 2 3 4
Deed of Trust	__ Ack __ Jurat 1 2 3 4	Marital Status Affidavit	__ Ack __ Jurat 1 2 3 4
Mortgage	__ Ack __ Jurat 1 2 3 4	Quit Claim Deed	__ Ack __ Jurat 1 2 3 4
Mortgagor's Affidavit	__ Ack __ Jurat 1 2 3 4	Signature/Name Affidavit	__ Ack __ Jurat 1 2 3 4
Occupancy Affidavit	__ Ack __ Jurat 1 2 3 4	Survey Affidavit	__ Ack __ Jurat 1 2 3 4
Owner's Affidavit	__ Ack __ Jurat 1 2 3 4	Warranty Deed	__ Ack __ Jurat 1 2 3 4
Payoff Affidavit	__ Ack __ Jurat 1 2 3 4	Other	__ Ack __ Jurat 1 2 3 4

Vehicle Docs:

Duplicate Title	__ Ack __ Jurat 1 2 3 4	Odometer/VIN Verification	__ Ack __ Jurat 1 2 3 4
Lien Release	__ Ack __ Jurat 1 2 3 4	Title Transfer	__ Ack __ Jurat 1 2 3 4

Wills/Trusts/ POA:

Living Trust	__ Ack __ Jurat 1 2 3 4	Power of Attorney	__ Ack __ Jurat 1 2 3 4
Last Will & Test	__ Ack __ Jurat 1 2 3 4	Trust Certification	__ Ack __ Jurat 1 2 3 4

Medical Docs:

Advance Healthcare Directive	__ Ack __ Jurat 1 2 3 4	HIPAA Release	__ Ack __ Jurat 1 2 3 4

Other Non-listed Docs:

Document Title: _____ Act Type 1 2 3 4	Document Title: _____ Act Type 1 2 3 4
Document Title: _____ Act Type 1 2 3 4	Document Title: _____ Act Type 1 2 3 4
Document Title: _____ Act Type 1 2 3 4	Document Title: _____ Act Type 1 2 3 4
Document Title: _____ Act Type 1 2 3 4	Document Title: _____ Act Type 1 2 3 4

Date		Time	AM	PM
1	**Full Name** ___ Signor ___ Witness _____ Address: _____	**Verification Method** DL PP Cred. Wit Other: _____ State: _____ Iss date: _____ Expiration: _____	**Doc. Type** ___ Paper ___ Electronic ___ Hybrid	**Thumb Print**
	Signature	**Screening** ___ Coherent ___ Consenting	**Phone I Email**	
2	**Full Name** ___ Signor ___ Witness _____ Address: _____	**Verification Method** DL PP Cred. Wit Other: _____ State: _____ Iss date: _____ Expiration: _____	**Doc. Type** ___ Paper ___ Electronic ___ Hybrid	**Thumb Print**
	Signature	**Screening** ___ Coherent ___ Consenting	**Phone I Email**	
3	**Full Name** ___ Signor ___ Witness _____ Address: _____	**Verification Method** DL PP Cred. Wit Other: _____ State: _____ Iss date: _____ Expiration: _____	**Doc. Type** ___ Paper ___ Electronic ___ Hybrid	**Thumb Print**
	Signature	**Screening** ___ Coherent ___ Consenting	**Phone I Email**	
4	**Full Name** ___ Signor ___ Witness _____ Address: _____	**Verification Method** DL PP Cred. Wit Other: _____ State: _____ Iss date: _____ Expiration: _____	**Doc. Type** ___ Paper ___ Electronic ___ Hybrid	**Thumb Print**
	Signature	**Screening** ___ Coherent ___ Consenting	**Phone I Email**	

Signing Location:	Observers:	Signing Service:	Fee:

Appointment Notes:

_____

_____

Record of Signed Documents: Loan Documents

Borrower's Affidavit	__ Ack __ Jurat 1 2 3 4	Disbursement of Proceeds	__ Ack __ Jurat 1 2 3 4
Compliance Agreement	__ Ack __ Jurat 1 2 3 4	Errors & Omissions Agreement	__ Ack __ Jurat 1 2 3 4
Correction Agreement	__ Ack __ Jurat 1 2 3 4	Financial Affidavit	__ Ack __ Jurat 1 2 3 4
Indemnity Debt/Lien Affidavit	__ Ack __ Jurat 1 2 3 4	Grant Deed	__ Ack __ Jurat 1 2 3 4
Deed of Trust	__ Ack __ Jurat 1 2 3 4	Marital Status Affidavit	__ Ack __ Jurat 1 2 3 4
Mortgage	__ Ack __ Jurat 1 2 3 4	Quit Claim Deed	__ Ack __ Jurat 1 2 3 4
Mortgagor's Affidavit	__ Ack __ Jurat 1 2 3 4	Signature/Name Affidavit	__ Ack __ Jurat 1 2 3 4
Occupancy Affidavit	__ Ack __ Jurat 1 2 3 4	Survey Affidavit	__ Ack __ Jurat 1 2 3 4
Owner's Affidavit	__ Ack __ Jurat 1 2 3 4	Warranty Deed	__ Ack __ Jurat 1 2 3 4
Payoff Affidavit	__ Ack __ Jurat 1 2 3 4	Other	__ Ack __ Jurat 1 2 3 4

Vehicle Docs:

Duplicate Title	__ Ack __ Jurat 1 2 3 4	Odometer/VIN Verification	__ Ack __ Jurat 1 2 3 4
Lien Release	__ Ack __ Jurat 1 2 3 4	Title Transfer	__ Ack __ Jurat 1 2 3 4

Wills/Trusts/ POA:

Living Trust	__ Ack __ Jurat 1 2 3 4	Power of Attorney	__ Ack __ Jurat 1 2 3 4
Last Will & Test	__ Ack __ Jurat 1 2 3 4	Trust Certification	__ Ack __ Jurat 1 2 3 4

Medical Docs:

Advance Healthcare Directive	__ Ack __ Jurat 1 2 3 4	HIPAA Release	__ Ack __ Jurat 1 2 3 4

Other Non-listed Docs:

Document Title: _____ Act Type 1 2 3 4		Document Title: _____ Act Type 1 2 3 4	
Document Title: _____ Act Type 1 2 3 4		Document Title: _____ Act Type 1 2 3 4	
Document Title: _____ Act Type 1 2 3 4		Document Title: _____ Act Type 1 2 3 4	
Document Title: _____ Act Type 1 2 3 4		Document Title: _____ Act Type 1 2 3 4	

Date		Time	AM	PM
1	Full Name ___ Signor ___ Witness _____ Address: _____	Verification Method DL PP Cred. Wit Other: _____ State: _____ Iss date: _____ Expiration: _____	Doc. Type ___ Paper ___ Electronic ___ Hybrid	Thumb Print
	Signature	Screening ___ Coherent ___ Consenting	Phone I Email	
2	Full Name ___ Signor ___ Witness _____ Address: _____	Verification Method DL PP Cred. Wit Other: _____ State: _____ Iss date: _____ Expiration: _____	Doc. Type ___ Paper ___ Electronic ___ Hybrid	Thumb Print
	Signature	Screening ___ Coherent ___ Consenting	Phone I Email	
3	Full Name ___ Signor ___ Witness _____ Address: _____	Verification Method DL PP Cred. Wit Other: _____ State: _____ Iss date: _____ Expiration: _____	Doc. Type ___ Paper ___ Electronic ___ Hybrid	Thumb Print
	Signature	Screening ___ Coherent ___ Consenting	Phone I Email	
4	Full Name ___ Signor ___ Witness _____ Address: _____	Verification Method DL PP Cred. Wit Other: _____ State: _____ Iss date: _____ Expiration: _____	Doc. Type ___ Paper ___ Electronic ___ Hybrid	Thumb Print
	Signature	Screening ___ Coherent ___ Consenting	Phone I Email	

Signing Location:	Observers:	Signing Service:	Fee:

Appointment Notes:

Record of Signed Documents: Loan Documents

Document	Act		Document	Act
Borrower's Affidavit	__ Ack __ Jurat 1 2 3 4		Disbursement of Proceeds	__ Ack __ Jurat 1 2 3 4
Compliance Agreement	__ Ack __ Jurat 1 2 3 4		Errors & Omissions Agreement	__ Ack __ Jurat 1 2 3 4
Correction Agreement	__ Ack __ Jurat 1 2 3 4		Financial Affidavit	__ Ack __ Jurat 1 2 3 4
Indemnity Debt/Lien Affidavit	__ Ack __ Jurat 1 2 3 4		Grant Deed	__ Ack __ Jurat 1 2 3 4
Deed of Trust	__ Ack __ Jurat 1 2 3 4		Marital Status Affidavit	__ Ack __ Jurat 1 2 3 4
Mortgage	__ Ack __ Jurat 1 2 3 4		Quit Claim Deed	__ Ack __ Jurat 1 2 3 4
Mortgagor's Affidavit	__ Ack __ Jurat 1 2 3 4		Signature/Name Affidavit	__ Ack __ Jurat 1 2 3 4
Occupancy Affidavit	__ Ack __ Jurat 1 2 3 4		Survey Affidavit	__ Ack __ Jurat 1 2 3 4
Owner's Affidavit	__ Ack __ Jurat 1 2 3 4		Warranty Deed	__ Ack __ Jurat 1 2 3 4
Payoff Affidavit	__ Ack __ Jurat 1 2 3 4		Other	__ Ack __ Jurat 1 2 3 4

Vehicle Docs:

Document	Act		Document	Act
Duplicate Title	__ Ack __ Jurat 1 2 3 4		Odometer/VIN Verification	__ Ack __ Jurat 1 2 3 4
Lien Release	__ Ack __ Jurat 1 2 3 4		Title Transfer	__ Ack __ Jurat 1 2 3 4

Wills/Trusts/ POA:

Document	Act		Document	Act
Living Trust	__ Ack __ Jurat 1 2 3 4		Power of Attorney	__ Ack __ Jurat 1 2 3 4
Last Will & Test	__ Ack __ Jurat 1 2 3 4		Trust Certification	__ Ack __ Jurat 1 2 3 4

Medical Docs:

Document	Act		Document	Act
Advance Healthcare Directive	__ Ack __ Jurat 1 2 3 4		HIPAA Release	__ Ack __ Jurat 1 2 3 4

Other Non-listed Docs:

Document Title:				Act Type	Document Title:				Act Type
1	2	3	4		1	2	3	4	
Document Title:				Act Type	Document Title:				Act Type
1	2	3	4		1	2	3	4	
Document Title:				Act Type	Document Title:				Act Type
1	2	3	4		1	2	3	4	
Document Title:				Act Type	Document Title:				Act Type
1	2	3	4		1	2	3	4	

Date				Time	AM	PM

	Full Name ___ Signor ___ Witness	Verification Method DL PP Cred. Wit Other: _____ State: _____ Iss date: _____ Expiration: _____	Doc. Type ___ Paper ___ Electronic ___ Hybrid	Thumb Print
1	Signature	Screening ___ Coherent ___ Consenting	Phone I Email	
	Full Name ___ Signor ___ Witness	Verification Method DL PP Cred. Wit Other: _____ State: _____ Iss date: _____ Expiration: _____	Doc. Type ___ Paper ___ Electronic ___ Hybrid	Thumb Print
2	Signature	Screening ___ Coherent ___ Consenting	Phone I Email	
	Full Name ___ Signor ___ Witness	Verification Method DL PP Cred. Wit Other: _____ State: _____ Iss date: _____ Expiration: _____	Doc. Type ___ Paper ___ Electronic ___ Hybrid	Thumb Print
3	Signature	Screening ___ Coherent ___ Consenting	Phone I Email	
	Full Name ___ Signor ___ Witness	Verification Method DL PP Cred. Wit Other: _____ State: _____ Iss date: _____ Expiration: _____	Doc. Type ___ Paper ___ Electronic ___ Hybrid	Thumb Print
4	Signature	Screening ___ Coherent ___ Consenting	Phone I Email	

Signing Location:	Observers:	Signing Service:	Fee:

Appointment Notes:

Record of Signed Documents: Loan Documents

Borrower's Affidavit	__ Ack __ Jurat 1 2 3 4	Disbursement of Proceeds	__ Ack __ Jurat 1 2 3 4
Compliance Agreement	__ Ack __ Jurat 1 2 3 4	Errors & Omissions Agreement	__ Ack __ Jurat 1 2 3 4
Correction Agreement	__ Ack __ Jurat 1 2 3 4	Financial Affidavit	__ Ack __ Jurat 1 2 3 4
Indemnity Debt/Lien Affidavit	__ Ack __ Jurat 1 2 3 4	Grant Deed	__ Ack __ Jurat 1 2 3 4
Deed of Trust	__ Ack __ Jurat 1 2 3 4	Marital Status Affidavit	__ Ack __ Jurat 1 2 3 4
Mortgage	__ Ack __ Jurat 1 2 3 4	Quit Claim Deed	__ Ack __ Jurat 1 2 3 4
Mortgagor's Affidavit	__ Ack __ Jurat 1 2 3 4	Signature/Name Affidavit	__ Ack __ Jurat 1 2 3 4
Occupancy Affidavit	__ Ack __ Jurat 1 2 3 4	Survey Affidavit	__ Ack __ Jurat 1 2 3 4
Owner's Affidavit	__ Ack __ Jurat 1 2 3 4	Warranty Deed	__ Ack __ Jurat 1 2 3 4
Payoff Affidavit	__ Ack __ Jurat 1 2 3 4	Other	__ Ack __ Jurat 1 2 3 4

Vehicle Docs:

Duplicate Title	__ Ack __ Jurat 1 2 3 4	Odometer/VIN Verification	__ Ack __ Jurat 1 2 3 4
Lien Release	__ Ack __ Jurat 1 2 3 4	Title Transfer	__ Ack __ Jurat 1 2 3 4

Wills/Trusts/ POA:

Living Trust	__ Ack __ Jurat 1 2 3 4	Power of Attorney	__ Ack __ Jurat 1 2 3 4
Last Will & Test	__ Ack __ Jurat 1 2 3 4	Trust Certification	__ Ack __ Jurat 1 2 3 4

Medical Docs:

Advance Healthcare Directive	__ Ack __ Jurat 1 2 3 4	HIPAA Release	__ Ack __ Jurat 1 2 3 4

Other Non-listed Docs:

Document Title: _____ Act Type 1 2 3 4		Document Title: _____ Act Type 1 2 3 4	
Document Title: _____ Act Type 1 2 3 4		Document Title: _____ Act Type 1 2 3 4	
Document Title: _____ Act Type 1 2 3 4		Document Title: _____ Act Type 1 2 3 4	
Document Title: _____ Act Type 1 2 3 4		Document Title: _____ Act Type 1 2 3 4	

Date			Time		AM	PM

	Full Name ___ Signor ___ Witness	Verification Method DL PP Cred. Wit Other: _____ State: _____ Iss date: _____ Expiration: _____	Doc. Type ___ Paper ___ Electronic ___ Hybrid	Thumb Print
1	_____ Address: _____			
	Signature	Screening ___ Coherent ___ Consenting	Phone I Email	

	Full Name ___ Signor ___ Witness	Verification Method DL PP Cred. Wit Other: _____ State: _____ Iss date: _____ Expiration: _____	Doc. Type ___ Paper ___ Electronic ___ Hybrid	Thumb Print
2	_____ Address: _____			
	Signature	Screening ___ Coherent ___ Consenting	Phone I Email	

	Full Name ___ Signor ___ Witness	Verification Method DL PP Cred. Wit Other: _____ State: _____ Iss date: _____ Expiration: _____	Doc. Type ___ Paper ___ Electronic ___ Hybrid	Thumb Print
3	_____ Address: _____			
	Signature	Screening ___ Coherent ___ Consenting	Phone I Email	

	Full Name ___ Signor ___ Witness	Verification Method DL PP Cred. Wit Other: _____ State: _____ Iss date: _____ Expiration: _____	Doc. Type ___ Paper ___ Electronic ___ Hybrid	Thumb Print
4	_____ Address: _____			
	Signature	Screening ___ Coherent ___ Consenting	Phone I Email	

Signing Location:	Observers:	Signing Service:	Fee:

Appointment Notes:

Record of Signed Documents: Loan Documents

Borrower's Affidavit	__ Ack __ Jurat 1 2 3 4	Disbursement of Proceeds	__ Ack __ Jurat 1 2 3 4
Compliance Agreement	__ Ack __ Jurat 1 2 3 4	Errors & Omissions Agreement	__ Ack __ Jurat 1 2 3 4
Correction Agreement	__ Ack __ Jurat 1 2 3 4	Financial Affidavit	__ Ack __ Jurat 1 2 3 4
Indemnity Debt/Lien Affidavit	__ Ack __ Jurat 1 2 3 4	Grant Deed	__ Ack __ Jurat 1 2 3 4
Deed of Trust	__ Ack __ Jurat 1 2 3 4	Marital Status Affidavit	__ Ack __ Jurat 1 2 3 4
Mortgage	__ Ack __ Jurat 1 2 3 4	Quit Claim Deed	__ Ack __ Jurat 1 2 3 4
Mortgagor's Affidavit	__ Ack __ Jurat 1 2 3 4	Signature/Name Affidavit	__ Ack __ Jurat 1 2 3 4
Occupancy Affidavit	__ Ack __ Jurat 1 2 3 4	Survey Affidavit	__ Ack __ Jurat 1 2 3 4
Owner's Affidavit	__ Ack __ Jurat 1 2 3 4	Warranty Deed	__ Ack __ Jurat 1 2 3 4
Payoff Affidavit	__ Ack __ Jurat 1 2 3 4	Other	__ Ack __ Jurat 1 2 3 4

Vehicle Docs:

Duplicate Title	__ Ack __ Jurat 1 2 3 4	Odometer/VIN Verification	__ Ack __ Jurat 1 2 3 4
Lien Release	__ Ack __ Jurat 1 2 3 4	Title Transfer	__ Ack __ Jurat 1 2 3 4

Wills/Trusts/ POA:

Living Trust	__ Ack __ Jurat 1 2 3 4	Power of Attorney	__ Ack __ Jurat 1 2 3 4
Last Will & Test	__ Ack __ Jurat 1 2 3 4	Trust Certification	__ Ack __ Jurat 1 2 3 4

Medical Docs:

Advance Healthcare Directive	__ Ack __ Jurat 1 2 3 4	HIPAA Release	__ Ack __ Jurat 1 2 3 4

Other Non-listed Docs:

Document Title: _____ Act Type 1 2 3 4	Document Title: _____ Act Type 1 2 3 4
Document Title: _____ Act Type 1 2 3 4	Document Title: _____ Act Type 1 2 3 4
Document Title: _____ Act Type 1 2 3 4	Document Title: _____ Act Type 1 2 3 4
Document Title: _____ Act Type 1 2 3 4	Document Title: _____ Act Type 1 2 3 4

Date			Time	AM	PM

| 1 | Full Name ___ Signor ___ Witness

_____

Address: _____ | Verification Method
DL   PP   Cred. Wit
Other: _____
State: _____
Iss date: _____
Expiration: _____ | Doc. Type

___ Paper
___ Electronic
___ Hybrid | Thumb Print |
| | Signature | Screening
___ Coherent
___ Consenting | Phone I Email | |

| 2 | Full Name ___ Signor ___ Witness

_____

Address: _____ | Verification Method
DL   PP   Cred. Wit
Other: _____
State: _____
Iss date: _____
Expiration: _____ | Doc. Type

___ Paper
___ Electronic
___ Hybrid | Thumb Print |
| | Signature | Screening
___ Coherent
___ Consenting | Phone I Email | |

| 3 | Full Name ___ Signor ___ Witness

_____

Address: _____ | Verification Method
DL   PP   Cred. Wit
Other: _____
State: _____
Iss date: _____
Expiration: _____ | Doc. Type

___ Paper
___ Electronic
___ Hybrid | Thumb Print |
| | Signature | Screening
___ Coherent
___ Consenting | Phone I Email | |

| 4 | Full Name ___ Signor ___ Witness

_____

Address: _____ | Verification Method
DL   PP   Cred. Wit
Other: _____
State: _____
Iss date: _____
Expiration: _____ | Doc. Type

___ Paper
___ Electronic
___ Hybrid | Thumb Print |
| | Signature | Screening
___ Coherent
___ Consenting | Phone I Email | |

Signing Location:	Observers:	Signing Service:	Fee:

Appointment Notes:

_____

_____

Record of Signed Documents: Loan Documents

Borrower's Affidavit	__ Ack __ Jurat 1 2 3 4	Disbursement of Proceeds	__ Ack __ Jurat 1 2 3 4
Compliance Agreement	__ Ack __ Jurat 1 2 3 4	Errors & Omissions Agreement	__ Ack __ Jurat 1 2 3 4
Correction Agreement	__ Ack __ Jurat 1 2 3 4	Financial Affidavit	__ Ack __ Jurat 1 2 3 4
Indemnity Debt/Lien Affidavit	__ Ack __ Jurat 1 2 3 4	Grant Deed	__ Ack __ Jurat 1 2 3 4
Deed of Trust	__ Ack __ Jurat 1 2 3 4	Marital Status Affidavit	__ Ack __ Jurat 1 2 3 4
Mortgage	__ Ack __ Jurat 1 2 3 4	Quit Claim Deed	__ Ack __ Jurat 1 2 3 4
Mortgagor's Affidavit	__ Ack __ Jurat 1 2 3 4	Signature/Name Affidavit	__ Ack __ Jurat 1 2 3 4
Occupancy Affidavit	__ Ack __ Jurat 1 2 3 4	Survey Affidavit	__ Ack __ Jurat 1 2 3 4
Owner's Affidavit	__ Ack __ Jurat 1 2 3 4	Warranty Deed	__ Ack __ Jurat 1 2 3 4
Payoff Affidavit	__ Ack __ Jurat 1 2 3 4	Other	__ Ack __ Jurat 1 2 3 4

Vehicle Docs:

Duplicate Title	__ Ack __ Jurat 1 2 3 4	Odometer/VIN Verification	__ Ack __ Jurat 1 2 3 4
Lien Release	__ Ack __ Jurat 1 2 3 4	Title Transfer	__ Ack __ Jurat 1 2 3 4

Wills/Trusts/ POA:

Living Trust	__ Ack __ Jurat 1 2 3 4	Power of Attorney	__ Ack __ Jurat 1 2 3 4
Last Will & Test	__ Ack __ Jurat 1 2 3 4	Trust Certification	__ Ack __ Jurat 1 2 3 4

Medical Docs:

Advance Healthcare Directive	__ Ack __ Jurat 1 2 3 4	HIPAA Release	__ Ack __ Jurat 1 2 3 4

Other Non-listed Docs:

Document Title: _____ Act Type 1 2 3 4		Document Title: _____ Act Type 1 2 3 4	
Document Title: _____ Act Type 1 2 3 4		Document Title: _____ Act Type 1 2 3 4	
Document Title: _____ Act Type 1 2 3 4		Document Title: _____ Act Type 1 2 3 4	
Document Title: _____ Act Type 1 2 3 4		Document Title: _____ Act Type 1 2 3 4	

Date			Time	AM	PM
1	Full Name ___ Signor ___ Witness		Verification Method DL PP Cred. Wit	Doc. Type	Thumb Print
			Other: _____	___ Paper	
			State: _____	___ Electronic	
	Address: _____		Iss date: _____	___ Hybrid	
			Expiration: _____		
	Signature		Screening ___ Coherent ___ Consenting	Phone I Email	
2	Full Name ___ Signor ___ Witness		Verification Method DL PP Cred. Wit	Doc. Type	Thumb Print
			Other: _____	___ Paper	
			State: _____	___ Electronic	
	Address: _____		Iss date: _____	___ Hybrid	
			Expiration: _____		
	Signature		Screening ___ Coherent ___ Consenting	Phone I Email	
3	Full Name ___ Signor ___ Witness		Verification Method DL PP Cred. Wit	Doc. Type	Thumb Print
			Other: _____	___ Paper	
			State: _____	___ Electronic	
	Address: _____		Iss date: _____	___ Hybrid	
			Expiration: _____		
	Signature		Screening ___ Coherent ___ Consenting	Phone I Email	
4	Full Name ___ Signor ___ Witness		Verification Method DL PP Cred. Wit	Doc. Type	Thumb Print
			Other: _____	___ Paper	
			State: _____	___ Electronic	
	Address: _____		Iss date: _____	___ Hybrid	
			Expiration: _____		
	Signature		Screening ___ Coherent ___ Consenting	Phone I Email	

Signing Location:	Observers:	Signing Service:	Fee:

Appointment Notes:

Record of Signed Documents: Loan Documents

Borrower's Affidavit	__ Ack __ Jurat 1 2 3 4	Disbursement of Proceeds	__ Ack __ Jurat 1 2 3 4
Compliance Agreement	__ Ack __ Jurat 1 2 3 4	Errors & Omissions Agreement	__ Ack __ Jurat 1 2 3 4
Correction Agreement	__ Ack __ Jurat 1 2 3 4	Financial Affidavit	__ Ack __ Jurat 1 2 3 4
Indemnity Debt/Lien Affidavit	__ Ack __ Jurat 1 2 3 4	Grant Deed	__ Ack __ Jurat 1 2 3 4
Deed of Trust	__ Ack __ Jurat 1 2 3 4	Marital Status Affidavit	__ Ack __ Jurat 1 2 3 4
Mortgage	__ Ack __ Jurat 1 2 3 4	Quit Claim Deed	__ Ack __ Jurat 1 2 3 4
Mortgagor's Affidavit	__ Ack __ Jurat 1 2 3 4	Signature/Name Affidavit	__ Ack __ Jurat 1 2 3 4
Occupancy Affidavit	__ Ack __ Jurat 1 2 3 4	Survey Affidavit	__ Ack __ Jurat 1 2 3 4
Owner's Affidavit	__ Ack __ Jurat 1 2 3 4	Warranty Deed	__ Ack __ Jurat 1 2 3 4
Payoff Affidavit	__ Ack __ Jurat 1 2 3 4	Other	__ Ack __ Jurat 1 2 3 4

Vehicle Docs:

Duplicate Title	__ Ack __ Jurat 1 2 3 4	Odometer/VIN Verification	__ Ack __ Jurat 1 2 3 4
Lien Release	__ Ack __ Jurat 1 2 3 4	Title Transfer	__ Ack __ Jurat 1 2 3 4

Wills/Trusts/ POA:

Living Trust	__ Ack __ Jurat 1 2 3 4	Power of Attorney	__ Ack __ Jurat 1 2 3 4
Last Will & Test	__ Ack __ Jurat 1 2 3 4	Trust Certification	__ Ack __ Jurat 1 2 3 4

Medical Docs:

Advance Healthcare Directive	__ Ack __ Jurat 1 2 3 4	HIPAA Release	__ Ack __ Jurat 1 2 3 4

Other Non-listed Docs:

Document Title: _____ Act Type 1 2 3 4	Document Title: _____ Act Type 1 2 3 4
Document Title: _____ Act Type 1 2 3 4	Document Title: _____ Act Type 1 2 3 4
Document Title: _____ Act Type 1 2 3 4	Document Title: _____ Act Type 1 2 3 4
Document Title: _____ Act Type 1 2 3 4	Document Title: _____ Act Type 1 2 3 4

Date		Time		AM	PM
1	**Full Name** ___ Signor ___ Witness _____ Address: _____	Verification Method DL PP Cred. Wit Other: _____ State: _____ Iss date: _____ Expiration: _____		Doc. Type ___ Paper ___ Electronic ___ Hybrid	Thumb Print
	Signature	Screening ___ Coherent ___ Consenting		Phone I Email	
2	**Full Name** ___ Signor ___ Witness _____ Address: _____	Verification Method DL PP Cred. Wit Other: _____ State: _____ Iss date: _____ Expiration: _____		Doc. Type ___ Paper ___ Electronic ___ Hybrid	Thumb Print
	Signature	Screening ___ Coherent ___ Consenting		Phone I Email	
3	**Full Name** ___ Signor ___ Witness _____ Address: _____	Verification Method DL PP Cred. Wit Other: _____ State: _____ Iss date: _____ Expiration: _____		Doc. Type ___ Paper ___ Electronic ___ Hybrid	Thumb Print
	Signature	Screening ___ Coherent ___ Consenting		Phone I Email	
4	**Full Name** ___ Signor ___ Witness _____ Address: _____	Verification Method DL PP Cred. Wit Other: _____ State: _____ Iss date: _____ Expiration: _____		Doc. Type ___ Paper ___ Electronic ___ Hybrid	Thumb Print
	Signature	Screening ___ Coherent ___ Consenting		Phone I Email	

Signing Location:	Observers:	Signing Service:	Fee:

Appointment Notes:

Record of Signed Documents: Loan Documents

Borrower's Affidavit	__ Ack __ Jurat 1 2 3 4	Disbursement of Proceeds	__ Ack __ Jurat 1 2 3 4
Compliance Agreement	__ Ack __ Jurat 1 2 3 4	Errors & Omissions Agreement	__ Ack __ Jurat 1 2 3 4
Correction Agreement	__ Ack __ Jurat 1 2 3 4	Financial Affidavit	__ Ack __ Jurat 1 2 3 4
Indemnity Debt/Lien Affidavit	__ Ack __ Jurat 1 2 3 4	Grant Deed	__ Ack __ Jurat 1 2 3 4
Deed of Trust	__ Ack __ Jurat 1 2 3 4	Marital Status Affidavit	__ Ack __ Jurat 1 2 3 4
Mortgage	__ Ack __ Jurat 1 2 3 4	Quit Claim Deed	__ Ack __ Jurat 1 2 3 4
Mortgagor's Affidavit	__ Ack __ Jurat 1 2 3 4	Signature/Name Affidavit	__ Ack __ Jurat 1 2 3 4
Occupancy Affidavit	__ Ack __ Jurat 1 2 3 4	Survey Affidavit	__ Ack __ Jurat 1 2 3 4
Owner's Affidavit	__ Ack __ Jurat 1 2 3 4	Warranty Deed	__ Ack __ Jurat 1 2 3 4
Payoff Affidavit	__ Ack __ Jurat 1 2 3 4	Other	__ Ack __ Jurat 1 2 3 4

Vehicle Docs:

Duplicate Title	__ Ack __ Jurat 1 2 3 4	Odometer/VIN Verification	__ Ack __ Jurat 1 2 3 4
Lien Release	__ Ack __ Jurat 1 2 3 4	Title Transfer	__ Ack __ Jurat 1 2 3 4

Wills/Trusts/ POA:

Living Trust	__ Ack __ Jurat 1 2 3 4	Power of Attorney	__ Ack __ Jurat 1 2 3 4
Last Will & Test	__ Ack __ Jurat 1 2 3 4	Trust Certification	__ Ack __ Jurat 1 2 3 4

Medical Docs:

Advance Healthcare Directive	__ Ack __ Jurat 1 2 3 4	HIPAA Release	__ Ack __ Jurat 1 2 3 4

Other Non-listed Docs:

Document Title: _____ Act Type 1 2 3 4		Document Title: _____ Act Type 1 2 3 4
Document Title: _____ Act Type 1 2 3 4		Document Title: _____ Act Type 1 2 3 4
Document Title: _____ Act Type 1 2 3 4		Document Title: _____ Act Type 1 2 3 4
Document Title: _____ Act Type 1 2 3 4		Document Title: _____ Act Type 1 2 3 4

Date		Time		AM	PM

| 1 | Full Name ___ Signor ___ Witness
_____
Address: _____ | Verification Method
DL   PP   Cred. Wit
Other: _____
State: _____
Iss date: _____
Expiration: _____ | Doc. Type

___ Paper
___ Electronic
___ Hybrid | Thumb Print |
| | Signature | Screening
___ Coherent
___ Consenting | Phone I Email | |

| 2 | Full Name ___ Signor ___ Witness
_____
Address: _____ | Verification Method
DL   PP   Cred. Wit
Other: _____
State: _____
Iss date: _____
Expiration: _____ | Doc. Type

___ Paper
___ Electronic
___ Hybrid | Thumb Print |
| | Signature | Screening
___ Coherent
___ Consenting | Phone I Email | |

| 3 | Full Name ___ Signor ___ Witness
_____
Address: _____ | Verification Method
DL   PP   Cred. Wit
Other: _____
State: _____
Iss date: _____
Expiration: _____ | Doc. Type

___ Paper
___ Electronic
___ Hybrid | Thumb Print |
| | Signature | Screening
___ Coherent
___ Consenting | Phone I Email | |

| 4 | Full Name ___ Signor ___ Witness
_____
Address: _____ | Verification Method
DL   PP   Cred. Wit
Other: _____
State: _____
Iss date: _____
Expiration: _____ | Doc. Type

___ Paper
___ Electronic
___ Hybrid | Thumb Print |
| | Signature | Screening
___ Coherent
___ Consenting | Phone I Email | |

Signing Location:	Observers:	Signing Service:	Fee:

Appointment Notes:

_____

_____

_____

Record of Signed Documents: Loan Documents

Borrower's Affidavit	__ Ack __ Jurat 1　2　3　4	Disbursement of Proceeds	__ Ack __ Jurat 1　2　3　4
Compliance Agreement	__ Ack __ Jurat 1　2　3　4	Errors & Omissions Agreement	__ Ack __ Jurat 1　2　3　4
Correction Agreement	__ Ack __ Jurat 1　2　3　4	Financial Affidavit	__ Ack __ Jurat 1　2　3　4
Indemnity Debt/Lien Affidavit	__ Ack __ Jurat 1　2　3　4	Grant Deed	__ Ack __ Jurat 1　2　3　4
Deed of Trust	__ Ack __ Jurat 1　2　3　4	Marital Status Affidavit	__ Ack __ Jurat 1　2　3　4
Mortgage	__ Ack __ Jurat 1　2　3　4	Quit Claim Deed	__ Ack __ Jurat 1　2　3　4
Mortgagor's Affidavit	__ Ack __ Jurat 1　2　3　4	Signature/Name Affidavit	__ Ack __ Jurat 1　2　3　4
Occupancy Affidavit	__ Ack __ Jurat 1　2　3　4	Survey Affidavit	__ Ack __ Jurat 1　2　3　4
Owner's Affidavit	__ Ack __ Jurat 1　2　3　4	Warranty Deed	__ Ack __ Jurat 1　2　3　4
Payoff Affidavit	__ Ack __ Jurat 1　2　3　4	Other	__ Ack __ Jurat 1　2　3　4

Vehicle Docs:

Duplicate Title	__ Ack __ Jurat 1　2　3　4	Odometer/VIN Verification	__ Ack __ Jurat 1　2　3　4
Lien Release	__ Ack __ Jurat 1　2　3　4	Title Transfer	__ Ack __ Jurat 1　2　3　4

Wills/Trusts/ POA:

Living Trust	__ Ack __ Jurat 1　2　3　4	Power of Attorney	__ Ack __ Jurat 1　2　3　4
Last Will & Test	__ Ack __ Jurat 1　2　3　4	Trust Certification	__ Ack __ Jurat 1　2　3　4

Medical Docs:

Advance Healthcare Directive	__ Ack __ Jurat 1　2　3　4	HIPAA Release	__ Ack __ Jurat 1　2　3　4

Other Non-listed Docs:

Document Title: _____ Act Type 1　　2　　3　　4		Document Title: _____ Act Type 1　　2　　3　　4	
Document Title: _____ Act Type 1　　2　　3　　4		Document Title: _____ Act Type 1　　2　　3　　4	
Document Title: _____ Act Type 1　　2　　3　　4		Document Title: _____ Act Type 1　　2　　3　　4	
Document Title: _____ Act Type 1　　2　　3　　4		Document Title: _____ Act Type 1　　2　　3　　4	

Date		Time		AM	PM
1	**Full Name** ___ Signor ___ Witness _____ Address: _____	**Verification Method** DL PP Cred. Wit Other: _____ State: _____ Iss date: _____ Expiration: _____	**Doc. Type** ___ Paper ___ Electronic ___ Hybrid	**Thumb Print**	
	Signature	**Screening** ___ Coherent ___ Consenting	**Phone l Email**		
2	**Full Name** ___ Signor ___ Witness _____ Address: _____	**Verification Method** DL PP Cred. Wit Other: _____ State: _____ Iss date: _____ Expiration: _____	**Doc. Type** ___ Paper ___ Electronic ___ Hybrid	**Thumb Print**	
	Signature	**Screening** ___ Coherent ___ Consenting	**Phone l Email**		
3	**Full Name** ___ Signor ___ Witness _____ Address: _____	**Verification Method** DL PP Cred. Wit Other: _____ State: _____ Iss date: _____ Expiration: _____	**Doc. Type** ___ Paper ___ Electronic ___ Hybrid	**Thumb Print**	
	Signature	**Screening** ___ Coherent ___ Consenting	**Phone l Email**		
4	**Full Name** ___ Signor ___ Witness _____ Address: _____	**Verification Method** DL PP Cred. Wit Other: _____ State: _____ Iss date: _____ Expiration: _____	**Doc. Type** ___ Paper ___ Electronic ___ Hybrid	**Thumb Print**	
	Signature	**Screening** ___ Coherent ___ Consenting	**Phone l Email**		

Signing Location:	Observers:	Signing Service:	Fee:

Appointment Notes:

Record of Signed Documents: Loan Documents

Borrower's Affidavit	__ Ack __ Jurat 1 2 3 4	Disbursement of Proceeds	__ Ack __ Jurat 1 2 3 4
Compliance Agreement	__ Ack __ Jurat 1 2 3 4	Errors & Omissions Agreement	__ Ack __ Jurat 1 2 3 4
Correction Agreement	__ Ack __ Jurat 1 2 3 4	Financial Affidavit	__ Ack __ Jurat 1 2 3 4
Indemnity Debt/Lien Affidavit	__ Ack __ Jurat 1 2 3 4	Grant Deed	__ Ack __ Jurat 1 2 3 4
Deed of Trust	__ Ack __ Jurat 1 2 3 4	Marital Status Affidavit	__ Ack __ Jurat 1 2 3 4
Mortgage	__ Ack __ Jurat 1 2 3 4	Quit Claim Deed	__ Ack __ Jurat 1 2 3 4
Mortgagor's Affidavit	__ Ack __ Jurat 1 2 3 4	Signature/Name Affidavit	__ Ack __ Jurat 1 2 3 4
Occupancy Affidavit	__ Ack __ Jurat 1 2 3 4	Survey Affidavit	__ Ack __ Jurat 1 2 3 4
Owner's Affidavit	__ Ack __ Jurat 1 2 3 4	Warranty Deed	__ Ack __ Jurat 1 2 3 4
Payoff Affidavit	__ Ack __ Jurat 1 2 3 4	Other	__ Ack __ Jurat 1 2 3 4

Vehicle Docs:

Duplicate Title	__ Ack __ Jurat 1 2 3 4	Odometer/VIN Verification	__ Ack __ Jurat 1 2 3 4
Lien Release	__ Ack __ Jurat 1 2 3 4	Title Transfer	__ Ack __ Jurat 1 2 3 4

Wills/Trusts/ POA:

Living Trust	__ Ack __ Jurat 1 2 3 4	Power of Attorney	__ Ack __ Jurat 1 2 3 4
Last Will & Test	__ Ack __ Jurat 1 2 3 4	Trust Certification	__ Ack __ Jurat 1 2 3 4

Medical Docs:

Advance Healthcare Directive	__ Ack __ Jurat 1 2 3 4	HIPAA Release	__ Ack __ Jurat 1 2 3 4

Other Non-listed Docs:

Document Title: _____ Act Type 1 2 3 4		Document Title: _____ Act Type 1 2 3 4	
Document Title: _____ Act Type 1 2 3 4		Document Title: _____ Act Type 1 2 3 4	
Document Title: _____ Act Type 1 2 3 4		Document Title: _____ Act Type 1 2 3 4	
Document Title: _____ Act Type 1 2 3 4		Document Title: _____ Act Type 1 2 3 4	

Date			Time		AM	PM

	Full Name ___ Signor ___ Witness	Verification Method DL PP Cred. Wit Other: _____ State: _____ Iss date: _____ Expiration: _____	Doc. Type ___ Paper ___ Electronic ___ Hybrid	Thumb Print
1	Address: _____			
	Signature	Screening ___ Coherent ___ Consenting	Phone I Email	

	Full Name ___ Signor ___ Witness	Verification Method DL PP Cred. Wit Other: _____ State: _____ Iss date: _____ Expiration: _____	Doc. Type ___ Paper ___ Electronic ___ Hybrid	Thumb Print
2	Address: _____			
	Signature	Screening ___ Coherent ___ Consenting	Phone I Email	

	Full Name ___ Signor ___ Witness	Verification Method DL PP Cred. Wit Other: _____ State: _____ Iss date: _____ Expiration: _____	Doc. Type ___ Paper ___ Electronic ___ Hybrid	Thumb Print
3	Address: _____			
	Signature	Screening ___ Coherent ___ Consenting	Phone I Email	

	Full Name ___ Signor ___ Witness	Verification Method DL PP Cred. Wit Other: _____ State: _____ Iss date: _____ Expiration: _____	Doc. Type ___ Paper ___ Electronic ___ Hybrid	Thumb Print
4	Address: _____			
	Signature	Screening ___ Coherent ___ Consenting	Phone I Email	

Signing Location:	Observers:	Signing Service:	Fee:

Appointment Notes:

Record of Signed Documents: Loan Documents

Borrower's Affidavit	__ Ack __ Jurat 1 2 3 4	Disbursement of Proceeds	__ Ack __ Jurat 1 2 3 4
Compliance Agreement	__ Ack __ Jurat 1 2 3 4	Errors & Omissions Agreement	__ Ack __ Jurat 1 2 3 4
Correction Agreement	__ Ack __ Jurat 1 2 3 4	Financial Affidavit	__ Ack __ Jurat 1 2 3 4
Indemnity Debt/Lien Affidavit	__ Ack __ Jurat 1 2 3 4	Grant Deed	__ Ack __ Jurat 1 2 3 4
Deed of Trust	__ Ack __ Jurat 1 2 3 4	Marital Status Affidavit	__ Ack __ Jurat 1 2 3 4
Mortgage	__ Ack __ Jurat 1 2 3 4	Quit Claim Deed	__ Ack __ Jurat 1 2 3 4
Mortgagor's Affidavit	__ Ack __ Jurat 1 2 3 4	Signature/Name Affidavit	__ Ack __ Jurat 1 2 3 4
Occupancy Affidavit	__ Ack __ Jurat 1 2 3 4	Survey Affidavit	__ Ack __ Jurat 1 2 3 4
Owner's Affidavit	__ Ack __ Jurat 1 2 3 4	Warranty Deed	__ Ack __ Jurat 1 2 3 4
Payoff Affidavit	__ Ack __ Jurat 1 2 3 4	Other	__ Ack __ Jurat 1 2 3 4

Vehicle Docs:

Duplicate Title	__ Ack __ Jurat 1 2 3 4	Odometer/VIN Verification	__ Ack __ Jurat 1 2 3 4
Lien Release	__ Ack __ Jurat 1 2 3 4	Title Transfer	__ Ack __ Jurat 1 2 3 4

Wills/Trusts/ POA:

Living Trust	__ Ack __ Jurat 1 2 3 4	Power of Attorney	__ Ack __ Jurat 1 2 3 4
Last Will & Test	__ Ack __ Jurat 1 2 3 4	Trust Certification	__ Ack __ Jurat 1 2 3 4

Medical Docs:

Advance Healthcare Directive	__ Ack __ Jurat 1 2 3 4	HIPAA Release	__ Ack __ Jurat 1 2 3 4

Other Non-listed Docs:

Document Title: _____ Act Type 1 2 3 4	Document Title: _____ Act Type 1 2 3 4
Document Title: _____ Act Type 1 2 3 4	Document Title: _____ Act Type 1 2 3 4
Document Title: _____ Act Type 1 2 3 4	Document Title: _____ Act Type 1 2 3 4
Document Title: _____ Act Type 1 2 3 4	Document Title: _____ Act Type 1 2 3 4

Date		Time	AM	PM

1	Full Name ___ Signor ___ Witness _____ Address: _____	Verification Method DL PP Cred. Wit Other: _____ State: _____ Iss date: _____ Expiration: _____	Doc. Type ___ Paper ___ Electronic ___ Hybrid	Thumb Print
	Signature	Screening ___ Coherent ___ Consenting	Phone | Email	
2	Full Name ___ Signor ___ Witness _____ Address: _____	Verification Method DL PP Cred. Wit Other: _____ State: _____ Iss date: _____ Expiration: _____	Doc. Type ___ Paper ___ Electronic ___ Hybrid	Thumb Print
	Signature	Screening ___ Coherent ___ Consenting	Phone | Email	
3	Full Name ___ Signor ___ Witness _____ Address: _____	Verification Method DL PP Cred. Wit Other: _____ State: _____ Iss date: _____ Expiration: _____	Doc. Type ___ Paper ___ Electronic ___ Hybrid	Thumb Print
	Signature	Screening ___ Coherent ___ Consenting	Phone | Email	
4	Full Name ___ Signor ___ Witness _____ Address: _____	Verification Method DL PP Cred. Wit Other: _____ State: _____ Iss date: _____ Expiration: _____	Doc. Type ___ Paper ___ Electronic ___ Hybrid	Thumb Print
	Signature	Screening ___ Coherent ___ Consenting	Phone | Email	

Signing Location:	Observers:	Signing Service:	Fee:

Appointment Notes:

Record of Signed Documents: Loan Documents

Borrower's Affidavit	__ Ack __ Jurat 1 2 3 4	Disbursement of Proceeds	__ Ack __ Jurat 1 2 3 4
Compliance Agreement	__ Ack __ Jurat 1 2 3 4	Errors & Omissions Agreement	__ Ack __ Jurat 1 2 3 4
Correction Agreement	__ Ack __ Jurat 1 2 3 4	Financial Affidavit	__ Ack __ Jurat 1 2 3 4
Indemnity Debt/Lien Affidavit	__ Ack __ Jurat 1 2 3 4	Grant Deed	__ Ack __ Jurat 1 2 3 4
Deed of Trust	__ Ack __ Jurat 1 2 3 4	Marital Status Affidavit	__ Ack __ Jurat 1 2 3 4
Mortgage	__ Ack __ Jurat 1 2 3 4	Quit Claim Deed	__ Ack __ Jurat 1 2 3 4
Mortgagor's Affidavit	__ Ack __ Jurat 1 2 3 4	Signature/Name Affidavit	__ Ack __ Jurat 1 2 3 4
Occupancy Affidavit	__ Ack __ Jurat 1 2 3 4	Survey Affidavit	__ Ack __ Jurat 1 2 3 4
Owner's Affidavit	__ Ack __ Jurat 1 2 3 4	Warranty Deed	__ Ack __ Jurat 1 2 3 4
Payoff Affidavit	__ Ack __ Jurat 1 2 3 4	Other	__ Ack __ Jurat 1 2 3 4

Vehicle Docs:

Duplicate Title	__ Ack __ Jurat 1 2 3 4	Odometer/VIN Verification	__ Ack __ Jurat 1 2 3 4
Lien Release	__ Ack __ Jurat 1 2 3 4	Title Transfer	__ Ack __ Jurat 1 2 3 4

Wills/Trusts/ POA:

Living Trust	__ Ack __ Jurat 1 2 3 4	Power of Attorney	__ Ack __ Jurat 1 2 3 4
Last Will & Test	__ Ack __ Jurat 1 2 3 4	Trust Certification	__ Ack __ Jurat 1 2 3 4

Medical Docs:

Advance Healthcare Directive	__ Ack __ Jurat 1 2 3 4	HIPAA Release	__ Ack __ Jurat 1 2 3 4

Other Non-listed Docs:

Document Title: _____ Act Type 1   2   3   4

Document Title: _____ Act Type 1   2   3   4

Document Title: _____ Act Type 1   2   3   4

Document Title: _____ Act Type 1   2   3   4

Document Title: _____ Act Type 1   2   3   4

Document Title: _____ Act Type 1   2   3   4

Document Title: _____ Act Type 1   2   3   4

Document Title: _____ Act Type 1   2   3   4

Date			Time	AM	PM

| 1 | Full Name ___ Signor ___ Witness

 _____

 Address: _____ | | Verification Method
 DL   PP   Cred. Wit
 Other: _____
 State: _____
 Iss date: _____
 Expiration: _____ | Doc. Type

 ___ Paper
 ___ Electronic
 ___ Hybrid | Thumb Print |
| | Signature | | Screening
 ___ Coherent
 ___ Consenting | Phone I Email | |

| 2 | Full Name ___ Signor ___ Witness

 _____

 Address: _____ | | Verification Method
 DL   PP   Cred. Wit
 Other: _____
 State: _____
 Iss date: _____
 Expiration: _____ | Doc. Type

 ___ Paper
 ___ Electronic
 ___ Hybrid | Thumb Print |
| | Signature | | Screening
 ___ Coherent
 ___ Consenting | Phone I Email | |

| 3 | Full Name ___ Signor ___ Witness

 _____

 Address: _____ | | Verification Method
 DL   PP   Cred. Wit
 Other: _____
 State: _____
 Iss date: _____
 Expiration: _____ | Doc. Type

 ___ Paper
 ___ Electronic
 ___ Hybrid | Thumb Print |
| | Signature | | Screening
 ___ Coherent
 ___ Consenting | Phone I Email | |

| 4 | Full Name ___ Signor ___ Witness

 _____

 Address: _____ | | Verification Method
 DL   PP   Cred. Wit
 Other: _____
 State: _____
 Iss date: _____
 Expiration: _____ | Doc. Type

 ___ Paper
 ___ Electronic
 ___ Hybrid | Thumb Print |
| | Signature | | Screening
 ___ Coherent
 ___ Consenting | Phone I Email | |

Signing Location:	Observers:	Signing Service:	Fee:

Appointment Notes:

Record of Signed Documents: Loan Documents

Borrower's Affidavit	__ Ack __ Jurat 1 2 3 4	Disbursement of Proceeds	__ Ack __ Jurat 1 2 3 4
Compliance Agreement	__ Ack __ Jurat 1 2 3 4	Errors & Omissions Agreement	__ Ack __ Jurat 1 2 3 4
Correction Agreement	__ Ack __ Jurat 1 2 3 4	Financial Affidavit	__ Ack __ Jurat 1 2 3 4
Indemnity Debt/Lien Affidavit	__ Ack __ Jurat 1 2 3 4	Grant Deed	__ Ack __ Jurat 1 2 3 4
Deed of Trust	__ Ack __ Jurat 1 2 3 4	Marital Status Affidavit	__ Ack __ Jurat 1 2 3 4
Mortgage	__ Ack __ Jurat 1 2 3 4	Quit Claim Deed	__ Ack __ Jurat 1 2 3 4
Mortgagor's Affidavit	__ Ack __ Jurat 1 2 3 4	Signature/Name Affidavit	__ Ack __ Jurat 1 2 3 4
Occupancy Affidavit	__ Ack __ Jurat 1 2 3 4	Survey Affidavit	__ Ack __ Jurat 1 2 3 4
Owner's Affidavit	__ Ack __ Jurat 1 2 3 4	Warranty Deed	__ Ack __ Jurat 1 2 3 4
Payoff Affidavit	__ Ack __ Jurat 1 2 3 4	Other	__ Ack __ Jurat 1 2 3 4

Vehicle Docs:

Duplicate Title	__ Ack __ Jurat 1 2 3 4	Odometer/VIN Verification	__ Ack __ Jurat 1 2 3 4
Lien Release	__ Ack __ Jurat 1 2 3 4	Title Transfer	__ Ack __ Jurat 1 2 3 4

Wills/Trusts/ POA:

Living Trust	__ Ack __ Jurat 1 2 3 4	Power of Attorney	__ Ack __ Jurat 1 2 3 4
Last Will & Test	__ Ack __ Jurat 1 2 3 4	Trust Certification	__ Ack __ Jurat 1 2 3 4

Medical Docs:

Advance Healthcare Directive	__ Ack __ Jurat 1 2 3 4	HIPAA Release	__ Ack __ Jurat 1 2 3 4

Other Non-listed Docs:

Document Title: _____ Act Type 1 2 3 4		Document Title: _____ Act Type 1 2 3 4	
Document Title: _____ Act Type 1 2 3 4		Document Title: _____ Act Type 1 2 3 4	
Document Title: _____ Act Type 1 2 3 4		Document Title: _____ Act Type 1 2 3 4	
Document Title: _____ Act Type 1 2 3 4		Document Title: _____ Act Type 1 2 3 4	

Date		Time	AM	PM
1	**Full Name** ___ Signor ___ Witness _____ Address: _____	Verification Method DL PP Cred. Wit Other: _____ State: _____ Iss date: _____ Expiration: _____	Doc. Type ___ Paper ___ Electronic ___ Hybrid	Thumb Print
	Signature	Screening ___ Coherent ___ Consenting	Phone I Email	
2	**Full Name** ___ Signor ___ Witness _____ Address: _____	Verification Method DL PP Cred. Wit Other: _____ State: _____ Iss date: _____ Expiration: _____	Doc. Type ___ Paper ___ Electronic ___ Hybrid	Thumb Print
	Signature	Screening ___ Coherent ___ Consenting	Phone I Email	
3	**Full Name** ___ Signor ___ Witness _____ Address: _____	Verification Method DL PP Cred. Wit Other: _____ State: _____ Iss date: _____ Expiration: _____	Doc. Type ___ Paper ___ Electronic ___ Hybrid	Thumb Print
	Signature	Screening ___ Coherent ___ Consenting	Phone I Email	
4	**Full Name** ___ Signor ___ Witness _____ Address: _____	Verification Method DL PP Cred. Wit Other: _____ State: _____ Iss date: _____ Expiration: _____	Doc. Type ___ Paper ___ Electronic ___ Hybrid	Thumb Print
	Signature	Screening ___ Coherent ___ Consenting	Phone I Email	

Signing Location:	Observers:	Signing Service:	Fee:

Appointment Notes:

Record of Signed Documents: Loan Documents

Borrower's Affidavit	__ Ack __ Jurat 1 2 3 4	Disbursement of Proceeds	__ Ack __ Jurat 1 2 3 4
Compliance Agreement	__ Ack __ Jurat 1 2 3 4	Errors & Omissions Agreement	__ Ack __ Jurat 1 2 3 4
Correction Agreement	__ Ack __ Jurat 1 2 3 4	Financial Affidavit	__ Ack __ Jurat 1 2 3 4
Indemnity Debt/Lien Affidavit	__ Ack __ Jurat 1 2 3 4	Grant Deed	__ Ack __ Jurat 1 2 3 4
Deed of Trust	__ Ack __ Jurat 1 2 3 4	Marital Status Affidavit	__ Ack __ Jurat 1 2 3 4
Mortgage	__ Ack __ Jurat 1 2 3 4	Quit Claim Deed	__ Ack __ Jurat 1 2 3 4
Mortgagor's Affidavit	__ Ack __ Jurat 1 2 3 4	Signature/Name Affidavit	__ Ack __ Jurat 1 2 3 4
Occupancy Affidavit	__ Ack __ Jurat 1 2 3 4	Survey Affidavit	__ Ack __ Jurat 1 2 3 4
Owner's Affidavit	__ Ack __ Jurat 1 2 3 4	Warranty Deed	__ Ack __ Jurat 1 2 3 4
Payoff Affidavit	__ Ack __ Jurat 1 2 3 4	Other	__ Ack __ Jurat 1 2 3 4

Vehicle Docs:

Duplicate Title	__ Ack __ Jurat 1 2 3 4	Odometer/VIN Verification	__ Ack __ Jurat 1 2 3 4
Lien Release	__ Ack __ Jurat 1 2 3 4	Title Transfer	__ Ack __ Jurat 1 2 3 4

Wills/Trusts/ POA:

Living Trust	__ Ack __ Jurat 1 2 3 4	Power of Attorney	__ Ack __ Jurat 1 2 3 4
Last Will & Test	__ Ack __ Jurat 1 2 3 4	Trust Certification	__ Ack __ Jurat 1 2 3 4

Medical Docs:

Advance Healthcare Directive	__ Ack __ Jurat 1 2 3 4	HIPAA Release	__ Ack __ Jurat 1 2 3 4

Other Non-listed Docs:

Document Title: _____ Act Type 1 2 3 4	Document Title: _____ Act Type 1 2 3 4
Document Title: _____ Act Type 1 2 3 4	Document Title: _____ Act Type 1 2 3 4
Document Title: _____ Act Type 1 2 3 4	Document Title: _____ Act Type 1 2 3 4
Document Title: _____ Act Type 1 2 3 4	Document Title: _____ Act Type 1 2 3 4

Date			Time	AM	PM
1	Full Name ___ Signor ___ Witness _____ Address: _____		Verification Method DL PP Cred. Wit Other: _____ State: _____ Iss date: _____ Expiration: _____	Doc. Type ___ Paper ___ Electronic ___ Hybrid	Thumb Print
	Signature		Screening ___ Coherent ___ Consenting	Phone I Email	
2	Full Name ___ Signor ___ Witness _____ Address: _____		Verification Method DL PP Cred. Wit Other: _____ State: _____ Iss date: _____ Expiration: _____	Doc. Type ___ Paper ___ Electronic ___ Hybrid	Thumb Print
	Signature		Screening ___ Coherent ___ Consenting	Phone I Email	
3	Full Name ___ Signor ___ Witness _____ Address: _____		Verification Method DL PP Cred. Wit Other: _____ State: _____ Iss date: _____ Expiration: _____	Doc. Type ___ Paper ___ Electronic ___ Hybrid	Thumb Print
	Signature		Screening ___ Coherent ___ Consenting	Phone I Email	
4	Full Name ___ Signor ___ Witness _____ Address: _____		Verification Method DL PP Cred. Wit Other: _____ State: _____ Iss date: _____ Expiration: _____	Doc. Type ___ Paper ___ Electronic ___ Hybrid	Thumb Print
	Signature		Screening ___ Coherent ___ Consenting	Phone I Email	

Signing Location:	Observers:	Signing Service:	Fee:

Appointment Notes:

Record of Signed Documents: Loan Documents

Borrower's Affidavit	__ Ack __ Jurat 1 2 3 4	Disbursement of Proceeds	__ Ack __ Jurat 1 2 3 4	
Compliance Agreement	__ Ack __ Jurat 1 2 3 4	Errors & Omissions Agreement	__ Ack __ Jurat 1 2 3 4	
Correction Agreement	__ Ack __ Jurat 1 2 3 4	Financial Affidavit	__ Ack __ Jurat 1 2 3 4	
Indemnity Debt/Lien Affidavit	__ Ack __ Jurat 1 2 3 4	Grant Deed	__ Ack __ Jurat 1 2 3 4	
Deed of Trust	__ Ack __ Jurat 1 2 3 4	Marital Status Affidavit	__ Ack __ Jurat 1 2 3 4	
Mortgage	__ Ack __ Jurat 1 2 3 4	Quit Claim Deed	__ Ack __ Jurat 1 2 3 4	
Mortgagor's Affidavit	__ Ack __ Jurat 1 2 3 4	Signature/Name Affidavit	__ Ack __ Jurat 1 2 3 4	
Occupancy Affidavit	__ Ack __ Jurat 1 2 3 4	Survey Affidavit	__ Ack __ Jurat 1 2 3 4	
Owner's Affidavit	__ Ack __ Jurat 1 2 3 4	Warranty Deed	__ Ack __ Jurat 1 2 3 4	
Payoff Affidavit	__ Ack __ Jurat 1 2 3 4	Other	__ Ack __ Jurat 1 2 3 4	

Vehicle Docs:

Duplicate Title	__ Ack __ Jurat 1 2 3 4	Odometer/VIN Verification	__ Ack __ Jurat 1 2 3 4
Lien Release	__ Ack __ Jurat 1 2 3 4	Title Transfer	__ Ack __ Jurat 1 2 3 4

Wills/Trusts/ POA:

Living Trust	__ Ack __ Jurat 1 2 3 4	Power of Attorney	__ Ack __ Jurat 1 2 3 4
Last Will & Test	__ Ack __ Jurat 1 2 3 4	Trust Certification	__ Ack __ Jurat 1 2 3 4

Medical Docs:

Advance Healthcare Directive	__ Ack __ Jurat 1 2 3 4	HIPAA Release	__ Ack __ Jurat 1 2 3 4

Other Non-listed Docs:

Document Title: _____ Act Type 1 2 3 4		Document Title: _____ Act Type 1 2 3 4	
Document Title: _____ Act Type 1 2 3 4		Document Title: _____ Act Type 1 2 3 4	
Document Title: _____ Act Type 1 2 3 4		Document Title: _____ Act Type 1 2 3 4	
Document Title: _____ Act Type 1 2 3 4		Document Title: _____ Act Type 1 2 3 4	

Date		Time	AM	PM

1	**Full Name** ___ Signor ___ Witness _____ Address: _____	**Verification Method** DL PP Cred. Wit Other: _____ State: _____ Iss date: _____ Expiration: _____	**Doc. Type** ___ Paper ___ Electronic ___ Hybrid	**Thumb Print**
	Signature	**Screening** ___ Coherent ___ Consenting	**Phone I Email**	
2	**Full Name** ___ Signor ___ Witness _____ Address: _____	**Verification Method** DL PP Cred. Wit Other: _____ State: _____ Iss date: _____ Expiration: _____	**Doc. Type** ___ Paper ___ Electronic ___ Hybrid	**Thumb Print**
	Signature	**Screening** ___ Coherent ___ Consenting	**Phone I Email**	
3	**Full Name** ___ Signor ___ Witness _____ Address: _____	**Verification Method** DL PP Cred. Wit Other: _____ State: _____ Iss date: _____ Expiration: _____	**Doc. Type** ___ Paper ___ Electronic ___ Hybrid	**Thumb Print**
	Signature	**Screening** ___ Coherent ___ Consenting	**Phone I Email**	
4	**Full Name** ___ Signor ___ Witness _____ Address: _____	**Verification Method** DL PP Cred. Wit Other: _____ State: _____ Iss date: _____ Expiration: _____	**Doc. Type** ___ Paper ___ Electronic ___ Hybrid	**Thumb Print**
	Signature	**Screening** ___ Coherent ___ Consenting	**Phone I Email**	

Signing Location:	Observers:	Signing Service:	Fee:

Appointment Notes:

Record of Signed Documents: Loan Documents

Borrower's Affidavit	__ Ack __ Jurat 1 2 3 4	Disbursement of Proceeds	__ Ack __ Jurat 1 2 3 4
Compliance Agreement	__ Ack __ Jurat 1 2 3 4	Errors & Omissions Agreement	__ Ack __ Jurat 1 2 3 4
Correction Agreement	__ Ack __ Jurat 1 2 3 4	Financial Affidavit	__ Ack __ Jurat 1 2 3 4
Indemnity Debt/Lien Affidavit	__ Ack __ Jurat 1 2 3 4	Grant Deed	__ Ack __ Jurat 1 2 3 4
Deed of Trust	__ Ack __ Jurat 1 2 3 4	Marital Status Affidavit	__ Ack __ Jurat 1 2 3 4
Mortgage	__ Ack __ Jurat 1 2 3 4	Quit Claim Deed	__ Ack __ Jurat 1 2 3 4
Mortgagor's Affidavit	__ Ack __ Jurat 1 2 3 4	Signature/Name Affidavit	__ Ack __ Jurat 1 2 3 4
Occupancy Affidavit	__ Ack __ Jurat 1 2 3 4	Survey Affidavit	__ Ack __ Jurat 1 2 3 4
Owner's Affidavit	__ Ack __ Jurat 1 2 3 4	Warranty Deed	__ Ack __ Jurat 1 2 3 4
Payoff Affidavit	__ Ack __ Jurat 1 2 3 4	Other	__ Ack __ Jurat 1 2 3 4

Vehicle Docs:

Duplicate Title	__ Ack __ Jurat 1 2 3 4	Odometer/VIN Verification	__ Ack __ Jurat 1 2 3 4
Lien Release	__ Ack __ Jurat 1 2 3 4	Title Transfer	__ Ack __ Jurat 1 2 3 4

Wills/Trusts/ POA:

Living Trust	__ Ack __ Jurat 1 2 3 4	Power of Attorney	__ Ack __ Jurat 1 2 3 4
Last Will & Test	__ Ack __ Jurat 1 2 3 4	Trust Certification	__ Ack __ Jurat 1 2 3 4

Medical Docs:

Advance Healthcare Directive	__ Ack __ Jurat 1 2 3 4	HIPAA Release	__ Ack __ Jurat 1 2 3 4

Other Non-listed Docs:

Document Title: _____ Act Type 1 2 3 4		Document Title: _____ Act Type 1 2 3 4	
Document Title: _____ Act Type 1 2 3 4		Document Title: _____ Act Type 1 2 3 4	
Document Title: _____ Act Type 1 2 3 4		Document Title: _____ Act Type 1 2 3 4	
Document Title: _____ Act Type 1 2 3 4		Document Title: _____ Act Type 1 2 3 4	

Date		Time		AM	PM

1	Full Name ___ Signor ___ Witness _____ Address: _____	Verification Method DL PP Cred. Wit Other: _____ State: _____ Iss date: _____ Expiration: _____	Doc. Type ___ Paper ___ Electronic ___ Hybrid	Thumb Print
	Signature	Screening ___ Coherent ___ Consenting	Phone I Email	

2	Full Name ___ Signor ___ Witness _____ Address: _____	Verification Method DL PP Cred. Wit Other: _____ State: _____ Iss date: _____ Expiration: _____	Doc. Type ___ Paper ___ Electronic ___ Hybrid	Thumb Print
	Signature	Screening ___ Coherent ___ Consenting	Phone I Email	

3	Full Name ___ Signor ___ Witness _____ Address: _____	Verification Method DL PP Cred. Wit Other: _____ State: _____ Iss date: _____ Expiration: _____	Doc. Type ___ Paper ___ Electronic ___ Hybrid	Thumb Print
	Signature	Screening ___ Coherent ___ Consenting	Phone I Email	

4	Full Name ___ Signor ___ Witness _____ Address: _____	Verification Method DL PP Cred. Wit Other: _____ State: _____ Iss date: _____ Expiration: _____	Doc. Type ___ Paper ___ Electronic ___ Hybrid	Thumb Print
	Signature	Screening ___ Coherent ___ Consenting	Phone I Email	

Signing Location:	Observers:	Signing Service:	Fee:

Appointment Notes:

Record of Signed Documents: Loan Documents

Document	Act		Document	Act
Borrower's Affidavit	__ Ack __ Jurat 1 2 3 4		Disbursement of Proceeds	__ Ack __ Jurat 1 2 3 4
Compliance Agreement	__ Ack __ Jurat 1 2 3 4		Errors & Omissions Agreement	__ Ack __ Jurat 1 2 3 4
Correction Agreement	__ Ack __ Jurat 1 2 3 4		Financial Affidavit	__ Ack __ Jurat 1 2 3 4
Indemnity Debt/Lien Affidavit	__ Ack __ Jurat 1 2 3 4		Grant Deed	__ Ack __ Jurat 1 2 3 4
Deed of Trust	__ Ack __ Jurat 1 2 3 4		Marital Status Affidavit	__ Ack __ Jurat 1 2 3 4
Mortgage	__ Ack __ Jurat 1 2 3 4		Quit Claim Deed	__ Ack __ Jurat 1 2 3 4
Mortgagor's Affidavit	__ Ack __ Jurat 1 2 3 4		Signature/Name Affidavit	__ Ack __ Jurat 1 2 3 4
Occupancy Affidavit	__ Ack __ Jurat 1 2 3 4		Survey Affidavit	__ Ack __ Jurat 1 2 3 4
Owner's Affidavit	__ Ack __ Jurat 1 2 3 4		Warranty Deed	__ Ack __ Jurat 1 2 3 4
Payoff Affidavit	__ Ack __ Jurat 1 2 3 4		Other	__ Ack __ Jurat 1 2 3 4

Vehicle Docs:

Document	Act		Document	Act
Duplicate Title	__ Ack __ Jurat 1 2 3 4		Odometer/VIN Verification	__ Ack __ Jurat 1 2 3 4
Lien Release	__ Ack __ Jurat 1 2 3 4		Title Transfer	__ Ack __ Jurat 1 2 3 4

Wills/Trusts/ POA:

Document	Act		Document	Act
Living Trust	__ Ack __ Jurat 1 2 3 4		Power of Attorney	__ Ack __ Jurat 1 2 3 4
Last Will & Test	__ Ack __ Jurat 1 2 3 4		Trust Certification	__ Ack __ Jurat 1 2 3 4

Medical Docs:

Document	Act		Document	Act
Advance Healthcare Directive	__ Ack __ Jurat 1 2 3 4		HIPAA Release	__ Ack __ Jurat 1 2 3 4

Other Non-listed Docs:

Document Title: _____ Act Type 1 2 3 4	Document Title: _____ Act Type 1 2 3 4
Document Title: _____ Act Type 1 2 3 4	Document Title: _____ Act Type 1 2 3 4
Document Title: _____ Act Type 1 2 3 4	Document Title: _____ Act Type 1 2 3 4
Document Title: _____ Act Type 1 2 3 4	Document Title: _____ Act Type 1 2 3 4

Date		Time	AM	PM
1	Full Name ___ Signor ___ Witness _____ Address: _____	Verification Method DL PP Cred. Wit Other: _____ State: _____ Iss date: _____ Expiration: _____	Doc. Type ___ Paper ___ Electronic ___ Hybrid	Thumb Print
	Signature	Screening ___ Coherent ___ Consenting	Phone I Email	
2	Full Name ___ Signor ___ Witness _____ Address: _____	Verification Method DL PP Cred. Wit Other: _____ State: _____ Iss date: _____ Expiration: _____	Doc. Type ___ Paper ___ Electronic ___ Hybrid	Thumb Print
	Signature	Screening ___ Coherent ___ Consenting	Phone I Email	
3	Full Name ___ Signor ___ Witness _____ Address: _____	Verification Method DL PP Cred. Wit Other: _____ State: _____ Iss date: _____ Expiration: _____	Doc. Type ___ Paper ___ Electronic ___ Hybrid	Thumb Print
	Signature	Screening ___ Coherent ___ Consenting	Phone I Email	
4	Full Name ___ Signor ___ Witness _____ Address: _____	Verification Method DL PP Cred. Wit Other: _____ State: _____ Iss date: _____ Expiration: _____	Doc. Type ___ Paper ___ Electronic ___ Hybrid	Thumb Print
	Signature	Screening ___ Coherent ___ Consenting	Phone I Email	

Signing Location:	Observers:	Signing Service:	Fee:

Appointment Notes:

Record of Signed Documents: Loan Documents

Borrower's Affidavit	__ Ack __ Jurat 1 2 3 4	Disbursement of Proceeds	__ Ack __ Jurat 1 2 3 4
Compliance Agreement	__ Ack __ Jurat 1 2 3 4	Errors & Omissions Agreement	__ Ack __ Jurat 1 2 3 4
Correction Agreement	__ Ack __ Jurat 1 2 3 4	Financial Affidavit	__ Ack __ Jurat 1 2 3 4
Indemnity Debt/Lien Affidavit	__ Ack __ Jurat 1 2 3 4	Grant Deed	__ Ack __ Jurat 1 2 3 4
Deed of Trust	__ Ack __ Jurat 1 2 3 4	Marital Status Affidavit	__ Ack __ Jurat 1 2 3 4
Mortgage	__ Ack __ Jurat 1 2 3 4	Quit Claim Deed	__ Ack __ Jurat 1 2 3 4
Mortgagor's Affidavit	__ Ack __ Jurat 1 2 3 4	Signature/Name Affidavit	__ Ack __ Jurat 1 2 3 4
Occupancy Affidavit	__ Ack __ Jurat 1 2 3 4	Survey Affidavit	__ Ack __ Jurat 1 2 3 4
Owner's Affidavit	__ Ack __ Jurat 1 2 3 4	Warranty Deed	__ Ack __ Jurat 1 2 3 4
Payoff Affidavit	__ Ack __ Jurat 1 2 3 4	Other	__ Ack __ Jurat 1 2 3 4

Vehicle Docs:

Duplicate Title	__ Ack __ Jurat 1 2 3 4	Odometer/VIN Verification	__ Ack __ Jurat 1 2 3 4
Lien Release	__ Ack __ Jurat 1 2 3 4	Title Transfer	__ Ack __ Jurat 1 2 3 4

Wills/Trusts/ POA:

Living Trust	__ Ack __ Jurat 1 2 3 4	Power of Attorney	__ Ack __ Jurat 1 2 3 4
Last Will & Test	__ Ack __ Jurat 1 2 3 4	Trust Certification	__ Ack __ Jurat 1 2 3 4

Medical Docs:

Advance Healthcare Directive	__ Ack __ Jurat 1 2 3 4	HIPAA Release	__ Ack __ Jurat 1 2 3 4

Other Non-listed Docs:

Document Title: _____ Act Type 1 2 3 4		Document Title: _____ Act Type 1 2 3 4	
Document Title: _____ Act Type 1 2 3 4		Document Title: _____ Act Type 1 2 3 4	
Document Title: _____ Act Type 1 2 3 4		Document Title: _____ Act Type 1 2 3 4	
Document Title: _____ Act Type 1 2 3 4		Document Title: _____ Act Type 1 2 3 4	

Date			Time		AM	PM
1	Full Name ___ Signor ___ Witness _____ Address: _____		Verification Method DL PP Cred. Wit Other: _____ State: _____ Iss date: _____ Expiration: _____		Doc. Type ___ Paper ___ Electronic ___ Hybrid	Thumb Print
	Signature		Screening ___ Coherent ___ Consenting		Phone I Email	
2	Full Name ___ Signor ___ Witness _____ Address: _____		Verification Method DL PP Cred. Wit Other: _____ State: _____ Iss date: _____ Expiration: _____		Doc. Type ___ Paper ___ Electronic ___ Hybrid	Thumb Print
	Signature		Screening ___ Coherent ___ Consenting		Phone I Email	
3	Full Name ___ Signor ___ Witness _____ Address: _____		Verification Method DL PP Cred. Wit Other: _____ State: _____ Iss date: _____ Expiration: _____		Doc. Type ___ Paper ___ Electronic ___ Hybrid	Thumb Print
	Signature		Screening ___ Coherent ___ Consenting		Phone I Email	
4	Full Name ___ Signor ___ Witness _____ Address: _____		Verification Method DL PP Cred. Wit Other: _____ State: _____ Iss date: _____ Expiration: _____		Doc. Type ___ Paper ___ Electronic ___ Hybrid	Thumb Print
	Signature		Screening ___ Coherent ___ Consenting		Phone I Email	

Signing Location:	Observers:	Signing Service:	Fee:

Appointment Notes:

_____

_____

Record of Signed Documents: Loan Documents

Borrower's Affidavit	__ Ack __ Jurat 1 2 3 4	Disbursement of Proceeds	__ Ack __ Jurat 1 2 3 4	
Compliance Agreement	__ Ack __ Jurat 1 2 3 4	Errors & Omissions Agreement	__ Ack __ Jurat 1 2 3 4	
Correction Agreement	__ Ack __ Jurat 1 2 3 4	Financial Affidavit	__ Ack __ Jurat 1 2 3 4	
Indemnity Debt/Lien Affidavit	__ Ack __ Jurat 1 2 3 4	Grant Deed	__ Ack __ Jurat 1 2 3 4	
Deed of Trust	__ Ack __ Jurat 1 2 3 4	Marital Status Affidavit	__ Ack __ Jurat 1 2 3 4	
Mortgage	__ Ack __ Jurat 1 2 3 4	Quit Claim Deed	__ Ack __ Jurat 1 2 3 4	
Mortgagor's Affidavit	__ Ack __ Jurat 1 2 3 4	Signature/Name Affidavit	__ Ack __ Jurat 1 2 3 4	
Occupancy Affidavit	__ Ack __ Jurat 1 2 3 4	Survey Affidavit	__ Ack __ Jurat 1 2 3 4	
Owner's Affidavit	__ Ack __ Jurat 1 2 3 4	Warranty Deed	__ Ack __ Jurat 1 2 3 4	
Payoff Affidavit	__ Ack __ Jurat 1 2 3 4	Other	__ Ack __ Jurat 1 2 3 4	

Vehicle Docs:

Duplicate Title	__ Ack __ Jurat 1 2 3 4	Odometer/VIN Verification	__ Ack __ Jurat 1 2 3 4	
Lien Release	__ Ack __ Jurat 1 2 3 4	Title Transfer	__ Ack __ Jurat 1 2 3 4	

Wills/Trusts/ POA:

Living Trust	__ Ack __ Jurat 1 2 3 4	Power of Attorney	__ Ack __ Jurat 1 2 3 4	
Last Will & Test	__ Ack __ Jurat 1 2 3 4	Trust Certification	__ Ack __ Jurat 1 2 3 4	

Medical Docs:

Advance Healthcare Directive	__ Ack __ Jurat 1 2 3 4	HIPAA Release	__ Ack __ Jurat 1 2 3 4	

Other Non-listed Docs:

Document Title: _____ Act Type 1 2 3 4	Document Title: _____ Act Type 1 2 3 4	
Document Title: _____ Act Type 1 2 3 4	Document Title: _____ Act Type 1 2 3 4	
Document Title: _____ Act Type 1 2 3 4	Document Title: _____ Act Type 1 2 3 4	
Document Title: _____ Act Type 1 2 3 4	Document Title: _____ Act Type 1 2 3 4	

Date			Time	AM	PM

1	Full Name ___ Signor ___ Witness _____ Address: _____		Verification Method DL PP Cred. Wit Other: _____ State: _____ Iss date: _____ Expiration: _____	Doc. Type ___ Paper ___ Electronic ___ Hybrid	Thumb Print
	Signature		Screening ___ Coherent ___ Consenting	Phone I Email	
2	Full Name ___ Signor ___ Witness _____ Address: _____		Verification Method DL PP Cred. Wit Other: _____ State: _____ Iss date: _____ Expiration: _____	Doc. Type ___ Paper ___ Electronic ___ Hybrid	Thumb Print
	Signature		Screening ___ Coherent ___ Consenting	Phone I Email	
3	Full Name ___ Signor ___ Witness _____ Address: _____		Verification Method DL PP Cred. Wit Other: _____ State: _____ Iss date: _____ Expiration: _____	Doc. Type ___ Paper ___ Electronic ___ Hybrid	Thumb Print
	Signature		Screening ___ Coherent ___ Consenting	Phone I Email	
4	Full Name ___ Signor ___ Witness _____ Address: _____		Verification Method DL PP Cred. Wit Other: _____ State: _____ Iss date: _____ Expiration: _____	Doc. Type ___ Paper ___ Electronic ___ Hybrid	Thumb Print
	Signature		Screening ___ Coherent ___ Consenting	Phone I Email	

Signing Location:	Observers:	Signing Service:	Fee:

Appointment Notes:

_____

Record of Signed Documents: Loan Documents

Borrower's Affidavit	__ Ack __ Jurat 1 2 3 4	Disbursement of Proceeds	__ Ack __ Jurat 1 2 3 4
Compliance Agreement	__ Ack __ Jurat 1 2 3 4	Errors & Omissions Agreement	__ Ack __ Jurat 1 2 3 4
Correction Agreement	__ Ack __ Jurat 1 2 3 4	Financial Affidavit	__ Ack __ Jurat 1 2 3 4
Indemnity Debt/Lien Affidavit	__ Ack __ Jurat 1 2 3 4	Grant Deed	__ Ack __ Jurat 1 2 3 4
Deed of Trust	__ Ack __ Jurat 1 2 3 4	Marital Status Affidavit	__ Ack __ Jurat 1 2 3 4
Mortgage	__ Ack __ Jurat 1 2 3 4	Quit Claim Deed	__ Ack __ Jurat 1 2 3 4
Mortgagor's Affidavit	__ Ack __ Jurat 1 2 3 4	Signature/Name Affidavit	__ Ack __ Jurat 1 2 3 4
Occupancy Affidavit	__ Ack __ Jurat 1 2 3 4	Survey Affidavit	__ Ack __ Jurat 1 2 3 4
Owner's Affidavit	__ Ack __ Jurat 1 2 3 4	Warranty Deed	__ Ack __ Jurat 1 2 3 4
Payoff Affidavit	__ Ack __ Jurat 1 2 3 4	Other	__ Ack __ Jurat 1 2 3 4

Vehicle Docs:

Duplicate Title	__ Ack __ Jurat 1 2 3 4	Odometer/VIN Verification	__ Ack __ Jurat 1 2 3 4
Lien Release	__ Ack __ Jurat 1 2 3 4	Title Transfer	__ Ack __ Jurat 1 2 3 4

Wills/Trusts/ POA:

Living Trust	__ Ack __ Jurat 1 2 3 4	Power of Attorney	__ Ack __ Jurat 1 2 3 4
Last Will & Test	__ Ack __ Jurat 1 2 3 4	Trust Certification	__ Ack __ Jurat 1 2 3 4

Medical Docs:

Advance Healthcare Directive	__ Ack __ Jurat 1 2 3 4	HIPAA Release	__ Ack __ Jurat 1 2 3 4

Other Non-listed Docs:

Document Title: _____ Act Type 1 2 3 4		Document Title: _____ Act Type 1 2 3 4	
Document Title: _____ Act Type 1 2 3 4		Document Title: _____ Act Type 1 2 3 4	
Document Title: _____ Act Type 1 2 3 4		Document Title: _____ Act Type 1 2 3 4	
Document Title: _____ Act Type 1 2 3 4		Document Title: _____ Act Type 1 2 3 4	

Date			Time		AM	PM
1	Full Name ___ Signor ___ Witness _____ Address: _____		Verification Method DL PP Cred. Wit Other: _____ State: _____ Iss date: _____ Expiration: _____		Doc. Type ___ Paper ___ Electronic ___ Hybrid	Thumb Print
	Signature		Screening ___ Coherent ___ Consenting		Phone I Email	
2	Full Name ___ Signor ___ Witness _____ Address: _____		Verification Method DL PP Cred. Wit Other: _____ State: _____ Iss date: _____ Expiration: _____		Doc. Type ___ Paper ___ Electronic ___ Hybrid	Thumb Print
	Signature		Screening ___ Coherent ___ Consenting		Phone I Email	
3	Full Name ___ Signor ___ Witness _____ Address: _____		Verification Method DL PP Cred. Wit Other: _____ State: _____ Iss date: _____ Expiration: _____		Doc. Type ___ Paper ___ Electronic ___ Hybrid	Thumb Print
	Signature		Screening ___ Coherent ___ Consenting		Phone I Email	
4	Full Name ___ Signor ___ Witness _____ Address: _____		Verification Method DL PP Cred. Wit Other: _____ State: _____ Iss date: _____ Expiration: _____		Doc. Type ___ Paper ___ Electronic ___ Hybrid	Thumb Print
	Signature		Screening ___ Coherent ___ Consenting		Phone I Email	

Signing Location:	Observers:	Signing Service:	Fee:

Appointment Notes:

_____

_____

Record of Signed Documents: Loan Documents

Borrower's Affidavit	__ Ack __ Jurat 1 2 3 4	Disbursement of Proceeds	__ Ack __ Jurat 1 2 3 4
Compliance Agreement	__ Ack __ Jurat 1 2 3 4	Errors & Omissions Agreement	__ Ack __ Jurat 1 2 3 4
Correction Agreement	__ Ack __ Jurat 1 2 3 4	Financial Affidavit	__ Ack __ Jurat 1 2 3 4
Indemnity Debt/Lien Affidavit	__ Ack __ Jurat 1 2 3 4	Grant Deed	__ Ack __ Jurat 1 2 3 4
Deed of Trust	__ Ack __ Jurat 1 2 3 4	Marital Status Affidavit	__ Ack __ Jurat 1 2 3 4
Mortgage	__ Ack __ Jurat 1 2 3 4	Quit Claim Deed	__ Ack __ Jurat 1 2 3 4
Mortgagor's Affidavit	__ Ack __ Jurat 1 2 3 4	Signature/Name Affidavit	__ Ack __ Jurat 1 2 3 4
Occupancy Affidavit	__ Ack __ Jurat 1 2 3 4	Survey Affidavit	__ Ack __ Jurat 1 2 3 4
Owner's Affidavit	__ Ack __ Jurat 1 2 3 4	Warranty Deed	__ Ack __ Jurat 1 2 3 4
Payoff Affidavit	__ Ack __ Jurat 1 2 3 4	Other	__ Ack __ Jurat 1 2 3 4

Vehicle Docs:

Duplicate Title	__ Ack __ Jurat 1 2 3 4	Odometer/VIN Verification	__ Ack __ Jurat 1 2 3 4
Lien Release	__ Ack __ Jurat 1 2 3 4	Title Transfer	__ Ack __ Jurat 1 2 3 4

Wills/Trusts/ POA:

Living Trust	__ Ack __ Jurat 1 2 3 4	Power of Attorney	__ Ack __ Jurat 1 2 3 4
Last Will & Test	__ Ack __ Jurat 1 2 3 4	Trust Certification	__ Ack __ Jurat 1 2 3 4

Medical Docs:

Advance Healthcare Directive	__ Ack __ Jurat 1 2 3 4	HIPAA Release	__ Ack __ Jurat 1 2 3 4

Other Non-listed Docs:

Document Title: _____ Act Type 1 2 3 4	Document Title: _____ Act Type 1 2 3 4
Document Title: _____ Act Type 1 2 3 4	Document Title: _____ Act Type 1 2 3 4
Document Title: _____ Act Type 1 2 3 4	Document Title: _____ Act Type 1 2 3 4
Document Title: _____ Act Type 1 2 3 4	Document Title: _____ Act Type 1 2 3 4

Date			Time	AM	PM
1	Full Name ___ Signor ___ Witness _____ Address: _____		Verification Method DL PP Cred. Wit Other: _____ State: _____ Iss date: _____ Expiration: _____	Doc. Type ___ Paper ___ Electronic ___ Hybrid	Thumb Print
	Signature		Screening ___ Coherent ___ Consenting	Phone I Email	
2	Full Name ___ Signor ___ Witness _____ Address: _____		Verification Method DL PP Cred. Wit Other: _____ State: _____ Iss date: _____ Expiration: _____	Doc. Type ___ Paper ___ Electronic ___ Hybrid	Thumb Print
	Signature		Screening ___ Coherent ___ Consenting	Phone I Email	
3	Full Name ___ Signor ___ Witness _____ Address: _____		Verification Method DL PP Cred. Wit Other: _____ State: _____ Iss date: _____ Expiration: _____	Doc. Type ___ Paper ___ Electronic ___ Hybrid	Thumb Print
	Signature		Screening ___ Coherent ___ Consenting	Phone I Email	
4	Full Name ___ Signor ___ Witness _____ Address: _____		Verification Method DL PP Cred. Wit Other: _____ State: _____ Iss date: _____ Expiration: _____	Doc. Type ___ Paper ___ Electronic ___ Hybrid	Thumb Print
	Signature		Screening ___ Coherent ___ Consenting	Phone I Email	

Signing Location:	Observers:	Signing Service:	Fee:

Appointment Notes:

_____

_____

Record of Signed Documents: Loan Documents

Borrower's Affidavit	__ Ack __ Jurat 1 2 3 4	Disbursement of Proceeds	__ Ack __ Jurat 1 2 3 4
Compliance Agreement	__ Ack __ Jurat 1 2 3 4	Errors & Omissions Agreement	__ Ack __ Jurat 1 2 3 4
Correction Agreement	__ Ack __ Jurat 1 2 3 4	Financial Affidavit	__ Ack __ Jurat 1 2 3 4
Indemnity Debt/Lien Affidavit	__ Ack __ Jurat 1 2 3 4	Grant Deed	__ Ack __ Jurat 1 2 3 4
Deed of Trust	__ Ack __ Jurat 1 2 3 4	Marital Status Affidavit	__ Ack __ Jurat 1 2 3 4
Mortgage	__ Ack __ Jurat 1 2 3 4	Quit Claim Deed	__ Ack __ Jurat 1 2 3 4
Mortgagor's Affidavit	__ Ack __ Jurat 1 2 3 4	Signature/Name Affidavit	__ Ack __ Jurat 1 2 3 4
Occupancy Affidavit	__ Ack __ Jurat 1 2 3 4	Survey Affidavit	__ Ack __ Jurat 1 2 3 4
Owner's Affidavit	__ Ack __ Jurat 1 2 3 4	Warranty Deed	__ Ack __ Jurat 1 2 3 4
Payoff Affidavit	__ Ack __ Jurat 1 2 3 4	Other	__ Ack __ Jurat 1 2 3 4

Vehicle Docs:

Duplicate Title	__ Ack __ Jurat 1 2 3 4	Odometer/VIN Verification	__ Ack __ Jurat 1 2 3 4
Lien Release	__ Ack __ Jurat 1 2 3 4	Title Transfer	__ Ack __ Jurat 1 2 3 4

Wills/Trusts/ POA:

Living Trust	__ Ack __ Jurat 1 2 3 4	Power of Attorney	__ Ack __ Jurat 1 2 3 4
Last Will & Test	__ Ack __ Jurat 1 2 3 4	Trust Certification	__ Ack __ Jurat 1 2 3 4

Medical Docs:

Advance Healthcare Directive	__ Ack __ Jurat 1 2 3 4	HIPAA Release	__ Ack __ Jurat 1 2 3 4

Other Non-listed Docs:

Document Title: _____ Act Type 1 2 3 4		Document Title: _____ Act Type 1 2 3 4	
Document Title: _____ Act Type 1 2 3 4		Document Title: _____ Act Type 1 2 3 4	
Document Title: _____ Act Type 1 2 3 4		Document Title: _____ Act Type 1 2 3 4	
Document Title: _____ Act Type 1 2 3 4		Document Title: _____ Act Type 1 2 3 4	

Date		Time	AM	PM

1

Full Name ___ Signor ___ Witness	Verification Method DL PP Cred. Wit Other: _____ State: _____ Iss date: _____ Expiration: _____	Doc. Type ___ Paper ___ Electronic ___ Hybrid	Thumb Print
Signature	Screening ___ Coherent ___ Consenting	Phone l Email	

2

Full Name ___ Signor ___ Witness	Verification Method DL PP Cred. Wit Other: _____ State: _____ Iss date: _____ Expiration: _____	Doc. Type ___ Paper ___ Electronic ___ Hybrid	Thumb Print
Signature	Screening ___ Coherent ___ Consenting	Phone l Email	

3

Full Name ___ Signor ___ Witness	Verification Method DL PP Cred. Wit Other: _____ State: _____ Iss date: _____ Expiration: _____	Doc. Type ___ Paper ___ Electronic ___ Hybrid	Thumb Print
Signature	Screening ___ Coherent ___ Consenting	Phone l Email	

4

Full Name ___ Signor ___ Witness	Verification Method DL PP Cred. Wit Other: _____ State: _____ Iss date: _____ Expiration: _____	Doc. Type ___ Paper ___ Electronic ___ Hybrid	Thumb Print
Signature	Screening ___ Coherent ___ Consenting	Phone l Email	

Signing Location:	Observers:	Signing Service:	Fee:

Appointment Notes:

Record of Signed Documents: Loan Documents

Borrower's Affidavit	__ Ack __ Jurat 1 2 3 4	Disbursement of Proceeds	__ Ack __ Jurat 1 2 3 4
Compliance Agreement	__ Ack __ Jurat 1 2 3 4	Errors & Omissions Agreement	__ Ack __ Jurat 1 2 3 4
Correction Agreement	__ Ack __ Jurat 1 2 3 4	Financial Affidavit	__ Ack __ Jurat 1 2 3 4
Indemnity Debt/Lien Affidavit	__ Ack __ Jurat 1 2 3 4	Grant Deed	__ Ack __ Jurat 1 2 3 4
Deed of Trust	__ Ack __ Jurat 1 2 3 4	Marital Status Affidavit	__ Ack __ Jurat 1 2 3 4
Mortgage	__ Ack __ Jurat 1 2 3 4	Quit Claim Deed	__ Ack __ Jurat 1 2 3 4
Mortgagor's Affidavit	__ Ack __ Jurat 1 2 3 4	Signature/Name Affidavit	__ Ack __ Jurat 1 2 3 4
Occupancy Affidavit	__ Ack __ Jurat 1 2 3 4	Survey Affidavit	__ Ack __ Jurat 1 2 3 4
Owner's Affidavit	__ Ack __ Jurat 1 2 3 4	Warranty Deed	__ Ack __ Jurat 1 2 3 4
Payoff Affidavit	__ Ack __ Jurat 1 2 3 4	Other	__ Ack __ Jurat 1 2 3 4

Vehicle Docs:

Duplicate Title	__ Ack __ Jurat 1 2 3 4	Odometer/VIN Verification	__ Ack __ Jurat 1 2 3 4
Lien Release	__ Ack __ Jurat 1 2 3 4	Title Transfer	__ Ack __ Jurat 1 2 3 4

Wills/Trusts/ POA:

Living Trust	__ Ack __ Jurat 1 2 3 4	Power of Attorney	__ Ack __ Jurat 1 2 3 4
Last Will & Test	__ Ack __ Jurat 1 2 3 4	Trust Certification	__ Ack __ Jurat 1 2 3 4

Medical Docs:

Advance Healthcare Directive	__ Ack __ Jurat 1 2 3 4	HIPAA Release	__ Ack __ Jurat 1 2 3 4

Other Non-listed Docs:

Document Title: _____ Act Type 1 2 3 4	Document Title: _____ Act Type 1 2 3 4
Document Title: _____ Act Type 1 2 3 4	Document Title: _____ Act Type 1 2 3 4
Document Title: _____ Act Type 1 2 3 4	Document Title: _____ Act Type 1 2 3 4
Document Title: _____ Act Type 1 2 3 4	Document Title: _____ Act Type 1 2 3 4

Date			Time		AM	PM
1	Full Name ___ Signor ___ Witness _____ Address: _____		Verification Method DL PP Cred. Wit Other: _____ State: _____ Iss date: _____ Expiration: _____		Doc. Type ___ Paper ___ Electronic ___ Hybrid	Thumb Print
	Signature		Screening ___ Coherent ___ Consenting		Phone I Email	
2	Full Name ___ Signor ___ Witness _____ Address: _____		Verification Method DL PP Cred. Wit Other: _____ State: _____ Iss date: _____ Expiration: _____		Doc. Type ___ Paper ___ Electronic ___ Hybrid	Thumb Print
	Signature		Screening ___ Coherent ___ Consenting		Phone I Email	
3	Full Name ___ Signor ___ Witness _____ Address: _____		Verification Method DL PP Cred. Wit Other: _____ State: _____ Iss date: _____ Expiration: _____		Doc. Type ___ Paper ___ Electronic ___ Hybrid	Thumb Print
	Signature		Screening ___ Coherent ___ Consenting		Phone I Email	
4	Full Name ___ Signor ___ Witness _____ Address: _____		Verification Method DL PP Cred. Wit Other: _____ State: _____ Iss date: _____ Expiration: _____		Doc. Type ___ Paper ___ Electronic ___ Hybrid	Thumb Print
	Signature		Screening ___ Coherent ___ Consenting		Phone I Email	

Signing Location:	Observers:	Signing Service:	Fee:

Appointment Notes:

Record of Signed Documents: Loan Documents

Borrower's Affidavit	__ Ack __ Jurat 1 2 3 4	Disbursement of Proceeds	__ Ack __ Jurat 1 2 3 4
Compliance Agreement	__ Ack __ Jurat 1 2 3 4	Errors & Omissions Agreement	__ Ack __ Jurat 1 2 3 4
Correction Agreement	__ Ack __ Jurat 1 2 3 4	Financial Affidavit	__ Ack __ Jurat 1 2 3 4
Indemnity Debt/Lien Affidavit	__ Ack __ Jurat 1 2 3 4	Grant Deed	__ Ack __ Jurat 1 2 3 4
Deed of Trust	__ Ack __ Jurat 1 2 3 4	Marital Status Affidavit	__ Ack __ Jurat 1 2 3 4
Mortgage	__ Ack __ Jurat 1 2 3 4	Quit Claim Deed	__ Ack __ Jurat 1 2 3 4
Mortgagor's Affidavit	__ Ack __ Jurat 1 2 3 4	Signature/Name Affidavit	__ Ack __ Jurat 1 2 3 4
Occupancy Affidavit	__ Ack __ Jurat 1 2 3 4	Survey Affidavit	__ Ack __ Jurat 1 2 3 4
Owner's Affidavit	__ Ack __ Jurat 1 2 3 4	Warranty Deed	__ Ack __ Jurat 1 2 3 4
Payoff Affidavit	__ Ack __ Jurat 1 2 3 4	Other	__ Ack __ Jurat 1 2 3 4

Vehicle Docs:

Duplicate Title	__ Ack __ Jurat 1 2 3 4	Odometer/VIN Verification	__ Ack __ Jurat 1 2 3 4
Lien Release	__ Ack __ Jurat 1 2 3 4	Title Transfer	__ Ack __ Jurat 1 2 3 4

Wills/Trusts/ POA:

Living Trust	__ Ack __ Jurat 1 2 3 4	Power of Attorney	__ Ack __ Jurat 1 2 3 4
Last Will & Test	__ Ack __ Jurat 1 2 3 4	Trust Certification	__ Ack __ Jurat 1 2 3 4

Medical Docs:

Advance Healthcare Directive	__ Ack __ Jurat 1 2 3 4	HIPAA Release	__ Ack __ Jurat 1 2 3 4

Other Non-listed Docs:

Document Title: _____ Act Type 1 2 3 4		Document Title: _____ Act Type 1 2 3 4
Document Title: _____ Act Type 1 2 3 4		Document Title: _____ Act Type 1 2 3 4
Document Title: _____ Act Type 1 2 3 4		Document Title: _____ Act Type 1 2 3 4
Document Title: _____ Act Type 1 2 3 4		Document Title: _____ Act Type 1 2 3 4

Date		Time		AM	PM
1	Full Name ___ Signor ___ Witness _____ Address: _____	Verification Method DL PP Cred. Wit Other: _____ State: _____ Iss date: _____ Expiration: _____	Doc. Type ___ Paper ___ Electronic ___ Hybrid	Thumb Print
	Signature	Screening ___ Coherent ___ Consenting	Phone I Email	
2	Full Name ___ Signor ___ Witness _____ Address: _____	Verification Method DL PP Cred. Wit Other: _____ State: _____ Iss date: _____ Expiration: _____	Doc. Type ___ Paper ___ Electronic ___ Hybrid	Thumb Print
	Signature	Screening ___ Coherent ___ Consenting	Phone I Email	
3	Full Name ___ Signor ___ Witness _____ Address: _____	Verification Method DL PP Cred. Wit Other: _____ State: _____ Iss date: _____ Expiration: _____	Doc. Type ___ Paper ___ Electronic ___ Hybrid	Thumb Print
	Signature	Screening ___ Coherent ___ Consenting	Phone I Email	
4	Full Name ___ Signor ___ Witness _____ Address: _____	Verification Method DL PP Cred. Wit Other: _____ State: _____ Iss date: _____ Expiration: _____	Doc. Type ___ Paper ___ Electronic ___ Hybrid	Thumb Print
	Signature	Screening ___ Coherent ___ Consenting	Phone I Email	

Signing Location:	Observers:	Signing Service:	Fee:

Appointment Notes:

Record of Signed Documents: Loan Documents

Borrower's Affidavit	__ Ack __ Jurat 1 2 3 4	Disbursement of Proceeds	__ Ack __ Jurat 1 2 3 4
Compliance Agreement	__ Ack __ Jurat 1 2 3 4	Errors & Omissions Agreement	__ Ack __ Jurat 1 2 3 4
Correction Agreement	__ Ack __ Jurat 1 2 3 4	Financial Affidavit	__ Ack __ Jurat 1 2 3 4
Indemnity Debt/Lien Affidavit	__ Ack __ Jurat 1 2 3 4	Grant Deed	__ Ack __ Jurat 1 2 3 4
Deed of Trust	__ Ack __ Jurat 1 2 3 4	Marital Status Affidavit	__ Ack __ Jurat 1 2 3 4
Mortgage	__ Ack __ Jurat 1 2 3 4	Quit Claim Deed	__ Ack __ Jurat 1 2 3 4
Mortgagor's Affidavit	__ Ack __ Jurat 1 2 3 4	Signature/Name Affidavit	__ Ack __ Jurat 1 2 3 4
Occupancy Affidavit	__ Ack __ Jurat 1 2 3 4	Survey Affidavit	__ Ack __ Jurat 1 2 3 4
Owner's Affidavit	__ Ack __ Jurat 1 2 3 4	Warranty Deed	__ Ack __ Jurat 1 2 3 4
Payoff Affidavit	__ Ack __ Jurat 1 2 3 4	Other	__ Ack __ Jurat 1 2 3 4

Vehicle Docs:

Duplicate Title	__ Ack __ Jurat 1 2 3 4	Odometer/VIN Verification	__ Ack __ Jurat 1 2 3 4
Lien Release	__ Ack __ Jurat 1 2 3 4	Title Transfer	__ Ack __ Jurat 1 2 3 4

Wills/Trusts/ POA:

Living Trust	__ Ack __ Jurat 1 2 3 4	Power of Attorney	__ Ack __ Jurat 1 2 3 4
Last Will & Test	__ Ack __ Jurat 1 2 3 4	Trust Certification	__ Ack __ Jurat 1 2 3 4

Medical Docs:

Advance Healthcare Directive	__ Ack __ Jurat 1 2 3 4	HIPAA Release	__ Ack __ Jurat 1 2 3 4

Other Non-listed Docs:

Document Title: _____ Act Type 1 2 3 4	Document Title: _____ Act Type 1 2 3 4
Document Title: _____ Act Type 1 2 3 4	Document Title: _____ Act Type 1 2 3 4
Document Title: _____ Act Type 1 2 3 4	Document Title: _____ Act Type 1 2 3 4
Document Title: _____ Act Type 1 2 3 4	Document Title: _____ Act Type 1 2 3 4

Date		Time	AM	PM
1	**Full Name** ___ Signor ___ Witness _____ **Address:** _____	**Verification Method** DL PP Cred. Wit Other: _____ State: _____ Iss date: _____ Expiration: _____	**Doc. Type** ___ Paper ___ Electronic ___ Hybrid	**Thumb Print**
1	**Signature**	**Screening** ___ Coherent ___ Consenting	**Phone I Email**	
2	**Full Name** ___ Signor ___ Witness _____ **Address:** _____	**Verification Method** DL PP Cred. Wit Other: _____ State: _____ Iss date: _____ Expiration: _____	**Doc. Type** ___ Paper ___ Electronic ___ Hybrid	**Thumb Print**
2	**Signature**	**Screening** ___ Coherent ___ Consenting	**Phone I Email**	
3	**Full Name** ___ Signor ___ Witness _____ **Address:** _____	**Verification Method** DL PP Cred. Wit Other: _____ State: _____ Iss date: _____ Expiration: _____	**Doc. Type** ___ Paper ___ Electronic ___ Hybrid	**Thumb Print**
3	**Signature**	**Screening** ___ Coherent ___ Consenting	**Phone I Email**	
4	**Full Name** ___ Signor ___ Witness _____ **Address:** _____	**Verification Method** DL PP Cred. Wit Other: _____ State: _____ Iss date: _____ Expiration: _____	**Doc. Type** ___ Paper ___ Electronic ___ Hybrid	**Thumb Print**
4	**Signature**	**Screening** ___ Coherent ___ Consenting	**Phone I Email**	

Signing Location:	Observers:	Signing Service:	Fee:

Appointment Notes:

_____

_____

Record of Signed Documents: Loan Documents

Borrower's Affidavit	__ Ack __ Jurat 1 2 3 4	Disbursement of Proceeds	__ Ack __ Jurat 1 2 3 4
Compliance Agreement	__ Ack __ Jurat 1 2 3 4	Errors & Omissions Agreement	__ Ack __ Jurat 1 2 3 4
Correction Agreement	__ Ack __ Jurat 1 2 3 4	Financial Affidavit	__ Ack __ Jurat 1 2 3 4
Indemnity Debt/Lien Affidavit	__ Ack __ Jurat 1 2 3 4	Grant Deed	__ Ack __ Jurat 1 2 3 4
Deed of Trust	__ Ack __ Jurat 1 2 3 4	Marital Status Affidavit	__ Ack __ Jurat 1 2 3 4
Mortgage	__ Ack __ Jurat 1 2 3 4	Quit Claim Deed	__ Ack __ Jurat 1 2 3 4
Mortgagor's Affidavit	__ Ack __ Jurat 1 2 3 4	Signature/Name Affidavit	__ Ack __ Jurat 1 2 3 4
Occupancy Affidavit	__ Ack __ Jurat 1 2 3 4	Survey Affidavit	__ Ack __ Jurat 1 2 3 4
Owner's Affidavit	__ Ack __ Jurat 1 2 3 4	Warranty Deed	__ Ack __ Jurat 1 2 3 4
Payoff Affidavit	__ Ack __ Jurat 1 2 3 4	Other	__ Ack __ Jurat 1 2 3 4

Vehicle Docs:

Duplicate Title	__ Ack __ Jurat 1 2 3 4	Odometer/VIN Verification	__ Ack __ Jurat 1 2 3 4
Lien Release	__ Ack __ Jurat 1 2 3 4	Title Transfer	__ Ack __ Jurat 1 2 3 4

Wills/Trusts/ POA:

Living Trust	__ Ack __ Jurat 1 2 3 4	Power of Attorney	__ Ack __ Jurat 1 2 3 4
Last Will & Test	__ Ack __ Jurat 1 2 3 4	Trust Certification	__ Ack __ Jurat 1 2 3 4

Medical Docs:

Advance Healthcare Directive	__ Ack __ Jurat 1 2 3 4	HIPAA Release	__ Ack __ Jurat 1 2 3 4

Other Non-listed Docs:

Document Title: _____ Act Type 1 2 3 4		Document Title: _____ Act Type 1 2 3 4	
Document Title: _____ Act Type 1 2 3 4		Document Title: _____ Act Type 1 2 3 4	
Document Title: _____ Act Type 1 2 3 4		Document Title: _____ Act Type 1 2 3 4	
Document Title: _____ Act Type 1 2 3 4		Document Title: _____ Act Type 1 2 3 4	

Date			Time		AM	PM

	Full Name ___ Signor ___ Witness	Verification Method DL PP Cred. Wit Other: _____ State: _____ Iss date: _____ Expiration: _____	Doc. Type ___ Paper ___ Electronic ___ Hybrid	Thumb Print
1	Address: _____			
	Signature	Screening ___ Coherent ___ Consenting	Phone I Email	

	Full Name ___ Signor ___ Witness	Verification Method DL PP Cred. Wit Other: _____ State: _____ Iss date: _____ Expiration: _____	Doc. Type ___ Paper ___ Electronic ___ Hybrid	Thumb Print
2	Address: _____			
	Signature	Screening ___ Coherent ___ Consenting	Phone I Email	

	Full Name ___ Signor ___ Witness	Verification Method DL PP Cred. Wit Other: _____ State: _____ Iss date: _____ Expiration: _____	Doc. Type ___ Paper ___ Electronic ___ Hybrid	Thumb Print
3	Address: _____			
	Signature	Screening ___ Coherent ___ Consenting	Phone I Email	

	Full Name ___ Signor ___ Witness	Verification Method DL PP Cred. Wit Other: _____ State: _____ Iss date: _____ Expiration: _____	Doc. Type ___ Paper ___ Electronic ___ Hybrid	Thumb Print
4	Address: _____			
	Signature	Screening ___ Coherent ___ Consenting	Phone I Email	

Signing Location:	Observers:	Signing Service:	Fee:

Appointment Notes:

Record of Signed Documents: Loan Documents

Borrower's Affidavit __ Ack __ Jurat 1 2 3 4	Disbursement of Proceeds __ Ack __ Jurat 1 2 3 4
Compliance Agreement __ Ack __ Jurat 1 2 3 4	Errors & Omissions Agreement __ Ack __ Jurat 1 2 3 4
Correction Agreement __ Ack __ Jurat 1 2 3 4	Financial Affidavit __ Ack __ Jurat 1 2 3 4
Indemnity Debt/Lien Affidavit __ Ack __ Jurat 1 2 3 4	Grant Deed __ Ack __ Jurat 1 2 3 4
Deed of Trust __ Ack __ Jurat 1 2 3 4	Marital Status Affidavit __ Ack __ Jurat 1 2 3 4
Mortgage __ Ack __ Jurat 1 2 3 4	Quit Claim Deed __ Ack __ Jurat 1 2 3 4
Mortgagor's Affidavit __ Ack __ Jurat 1 2 3 4	Signature/Name Affidavit __ Ack __ Jurat 1 2 3 4
Occupancy Affidavit __ Ack __ Jurat 1 2 3 4	Survey Affidavit __ Ack __ Jurat 1 2 3 4
Owner's Affidavit __ Ack __ Jurat 1 2 3 4	Warranty Deed __ Ack __ Jurat 1 2 3 4
Payoff Affidavit __ Ack __ Jurat 1 2 3 4	Other __ Ack __ Jurat 1 2 3 4

Vehicle Docs:

Duplicate Title __ Ack __ Jurat 1 2 3 4	Odometer/VIN Verification __ Ack __ Jurat 1 2 3 4
Lien Release __ Ack __ Jurat 1 2 3 4	Title Transfer __ Ack __ Jurat 1 2 3 4

Wills/Trusts/ POA:

Living Trust __ Ack __ Jurat 1 2 3 4	Power of Attorney __ Ack __ Jurat 1 2 3 4
Last Will & Test __ Ack __ Jurat 1 2 3 4	Trust Certification __ Ack __ Jurat 1 2 3 4

Medical Docs:

Advance Healthcare Directive __ Ack __ Jurat 1 2 3 4	HIPAA Release __ Ack __ Jurat 1 2 3 4

Other Non-listed Docs:

Document Title: _____ Act Type 1 2 3 4	Document Title: _____ Act Type 1 2 3 4
Document Title: _____ Act Type 1 2 3 4	Document Title: _____ Act Type 1 2 3 4
Document Title: _____ Act Type 1 2 3 4	Document Title: _____ Act Type 1 2 3 4
Document Title: _____ Act Type 1 2 3 4	Document Title: _____ Act Type 1 2 3 4

Date		Time	AM	PM

1	Full Name ___ Signor ___ Witness _____ Address: _____	Verification Method DL PP Cred. Wit Other: _____ State: _____ Iss date: _____ Expiration: _____	Doc. Type ___ Paper ___ Electronic ___ Hybrid	Thumb Print
	Signature	Screening ___ Coherent ___ Consenting	Phone I Email	
2	Full Name ___ Signor ___ Witness _____ Address: _____	Verification Method DL PP Cred. Wit Other: _____ State: _____ Iss date: _____ Expiration: _____	Doc. Type ___ Paper ___ Electronic ___ Hybrid	Thumb Print
	Signature	Screening ___ Coherent ___ Consenting	Phone I Email	
3	Full Name ___ Signor ___ Witness _____ Address: _____	Verification Method DL PP Cred. Wit Other: _____ State: _____ Iss date: _____ Expiration: _____	Doc. Type ___ Paper ___ Electronic ___ Hybrid	Thumb Print
	Signature	Screening ___ Coherent ___ Consenting	Phone I Email	
4	Full Name ___ Signor ___ Witness _____ Address: _____	Verification Method DL PP Cred. Wit Other: _____ State: _____ Iss date: _____ Expiration: _____	Doc. Type ___ Paper ___ Electronic ___ Hybrid	Thumb Print
	Signature	Screening ___ Coherent ___ Consenting	Phone I Email	

Signing Location:	Observers:	Signing Service:	Fee:

Appointment Notes:

Record of Signed Documents: Loan Documents

Borrower's Affidavit	__ Ack __ Jurat 1 2 3 4	Disbursement of Proceeds	__ Ack __ Jurat 1 2 3 4
Compliance Agreement	__ Ack __ Jurat 1 2 3 4	Errors & Omissions Agreement	__ Ack __ Jurat 1 2 3 4
Correction Agreement	__ Ack __ Jurat 1 2 3 4	Financial Affidavit	__ Ack __ Jurat 1 2 3 4
Indemnity Debt/Lien Affidavit	__ Ack __ Jurat 1 2 3 4	Grant Deed	__ Ack __ Jurat 1 2 3 4
Deed of Trust	__ Ack __ Jurat 1 2 3 4	Marital Status Affidavit	__ Ack __ Jurat 1 2 3 4
Mortgage	__ Ack __ Jurat 1 2 3 4	Quit Claim Deed	__ Ack __ Jurat 1 2 3 4
Mortgagor's Affidavit	__ Ack __ Jurat 1 2 3 4	Signature/Name Affidavit	__ Ack __ Jurat 1 2 3 4
Occupancy Affidavit	__ Ack __ Jurat 1 2 3 4	Survey Affidavit	__ Ack __ Jurat 1 2 3 4
Owner's Affidavit	__ Ack __ Jurat 1 2 3 4	Warranty Deed	__ Ack __ Jurat 1 2 3 4
Payoff Affidavit	__ Ack __ Jurat 1 2 3 4	Other	__ Ack __ Jurat 1 2 3 4

Vehicle Docs:

Duplicate Title	__ Ack __ Jurat 1 2 3 4	Odometer/VIN Verification	__ Ack __ Jurat 1 2 3 4
Lien Release	__ Ack __ Jurat 1 2 3 4	Title Transfer	__ Ack __ Jurat 1 2 3 4

Wills/Trusts/ POA:

Living Trust	__ Ack __ Jurat 1 2 3 4	Power of Attorney	__ Ack __ Jurat 1 2 3 4
Last Will & Test	__ Ack __ Jurat 1 2 3 4	Trust Certification	__ Ack __ Jurat 1 2 3 4

Medical Docs:

Advance Healthcare Directive	__ Ack __ Jurat 1 2 3 4	HIPAA Release	__ Ack __ Jurat 1 2 3 4

Other Non-listed Docs:

Document Title: _____ Act Type 1 2 3 4	Document Title: _____ Act Type 1 2 3 4
Document Title: _____ Act Type 1 2 3 4	Document Title: _____ Act Type 1 2 3 4
Document Title: _____ Act Type 1 2 3 4	Document Title: _____ Act Type 1 2 3 4
Document Title: _____ Act Type 1 2 3 4	Document Title: _____ Act Type 1 2 3 4

Date		Time	AM	PM
1	**Full Name** ___ Signor ___ Witness _____ Address: _____	**Verification Method** DL PP Cred. Wit Other: _____ State: _____ Iss date: _____ Expiration: _____	**Doc. Type** ___ Paper ___ Electronic ___ Hybrid	**Thumb Print**
	Signature	**Screening** ___ Coherent ___ Consenting	**Phone l Email**	
2	**Full Name** ___ Signor ___ Witness _____ Address: _____	**Verification Method** DL PP Cred. Wit Other: _____ State: _____ Iss date: _____ Expiration: _____	**Doc. Type** ___ Paper ___ Electronic ___ Hybrid	**Thumb Print**
	Signature	**Screening** ___ Coherent ___ Consenting	**Phone l Email**	
3	**Full Name** ___ Signor ___ Witness _____ Address: _____	**Verification Method** DL PP Cred. Wit Other: _____ State: _____ Iss date: _____ Expiration: _____	**Doc. Type** ___ Paper ___ Electronic ___ Hybrid	**Thumb Print**
	Signature	**Screening** ___ Coherent ___ Consenting	**Phone l Email**	
4	**Full Name** ___ Signor ___ Witness _____ Address: _____	**Verification Method** DL PP Cred. Wit Other: _____ State: _____ Iss date: _____ Expiration: _____	**Doc. Type** ___ Paper ___ Electronic ___ Hybrid	**Thumb Print**
	Signature	**Screening** ___ Coherent ___ Consenting	**Phone l Email**	

Signing Location:	Observers:	Signing Service:	Fee:

Appointment Notes:
_____
_____

Record of Signed Documents: Loan Documents

Borrower's Affidavit	__ Ack __ Jurat 1 2 3 4	Disbursement of Proceeds	__ Ack __ Jurat 1 2 3 4
Compliance Agreement	__ Ack __ Jurat 1 2 3 4	Errors & Omissions Agreement	__ Ack __ Jurat 1 2 3 4
Correction Agreement	__ Ack __ Jurat 1 2 3 4	Financial Affidavit	__ Ack __ Jurat 1 2 3 4
Indemnity Debt/Lien Affidavit	__ Ack __ Jurat 1 2 3 4	Grant Deed	__ Ack __ Jurat 1 2 3 4
Deed of Trust	__ Ack __ Jurat 1 2 3 4	Marital Status Affidavit	__ Ack __ Jurat 1 2 3 4
Mortgage	__ Ack __ Jurat 1 2 3 4	Quit Claim Deed	__ Ack __ Jurat 1 2 3 4
Mortgagor's Affidavit	__ Ack __ Jurat 1 2 3 4	Signature/Name Affidavit	__ Ack __ Jurat 1 2 3 4
Occupancy Affidavit	__ Ack __ Jurat 1 2 3 4	Survey Affidavit	__ Ack __ Jurat 1 2 3 4
Owner's Affidavit	__ Ack __ Jurat 1 2 3 4	Warranty Deed	__ Ack __ Jurat 1 2 3 4
Payoff Affidavit	__ Ack __ Jurat 1 2 3 4	Other	__ Ack __ Jurat 1 2 3 4

Vehicle Docs:

Duplicate Title	__ Ack __ Jurat 1 2 3 4	Odometer/VIN Verification	__ Ack __ Jurat 1 2 3 4
Lien Release	__ Ack __ Jurat 1 2 3 4	Title Transfer	__ Ack __ Jurat 1 2 3 4

Wills/Trusts/ POA:

Living Trust	__ Ack __ Jurat 1 2 3 4	Power of Attorney	__ Ack __ Jurat 1 2 3 4
Last Will & Test	__ Ack __ Jurat 1 2 3 4	Trust Certification	__ Ack __ Jurat 1 2 3 4

Medical Docs:

Advance Healthcare Directive	__ Ack __ Jurat 1 2 3 4	HIPAA Release	__ Ack __ Jurat 1 2 3 4

Other Non-listed Docs:

Document Title: _____ Act Type 1 2 3 4	Document Title: _____ Act Type 1 2 3 4
Document Title: _____ Act Type 1 2 3 4	Document Title: _____ Act Type 1 2 3 4
Document Title: _____ Act Type 1 2 3 4	Document Title: _____ Act Type 1 2 3 4
Document Title: _____ Act Type 1 2 3 4	Document Title: _____ Act Type 1 2 3 4

Date			Time	AM	PM

		Full Name ___ Signor ___ Witness	Verification Method DL PP Cred. Wit Other: _____ State: _____ Iss date: _____ Expiration: _____	Doc. Type ___ Paper ___ Electronic ___ Hybrid	Thumb Print
1		Address: _____			
		Signature	Screening ___ Coherent ___ Consenting	Phone I Email	
		Full Name ___ Signor ___ Witness	Verification Method DL PP Cred. Wit Other: _____ State: _____ Iss date: _____ Expiration: _____	Doc. Type ___ Paper ___ Electronic ___ Hybrid	Thumb Print
2		Address: _____			
		Signature	Screening ___ Coherent ___ Consenting	Phone I Email	
		Full Name ___ Signor ___ Witness	Verification Method DL PP Cred. Wit Other: _____ State: _____ Iss date: _____ Expiration: _____	Doc. Type ___ Paper ___ Electronic ___ Hybrid	Thumb Print
3		Address: _____			
		Signature	Screening ___ Coherent ___ Consenting	Phone I Email	
		Full Name ___ Signor ___ Witness	Verification Method DL PP Cred. Wit Other: _____ State: _____ Iss date: _____ Expiration: _____	Doc. Type ___ Paper ___ Electronic ___ Hybrid	Thumb Print
4		Address: _____			
		Signature	Screening ___ Coherent ___ Consenting	Phone I Email	

Signing Location:	Observers:	Signing Service:	Fee:

Appointment Notes:

Record of Signed Documents: Loan Documents

Borrower's Affidavit	__ Ack __ Jurat 1 2 3 4	Disbursement of Proceeds	__ Ack __ Jurat 1 2 3 4
Compliance Agreement	__ Ack __ Jurat 1 2 3 4	Errors & Omissions Agreement	__ Ack __ Jurat 1 2 3 4
Correction Agreement	__ Ack __ Jurat 1 2 3 4	Financial Affidavit	__ Ack __ Jurat 1 2 3 4
Indemnity Debt/Lien Affidavit	__ Ack __ Jurat 1 2 3 4	Grant Deed	__ Ack __ Jurat 1 2 3 4
Deed of Trust	__ Ack __ Jurat 1 2 3 4	Marital Status Affidavit	__ Ack __ Jurat 1 2 3 4
Mortgage	__ Ack __ Jurat 1 2 3 4	Quit Claim Deed	__ Ack __ Jurat 1 2 3 4
Mortgagor's Affidavit	__ Ack __ Jurat 1 2 3 4	Signature/Name Affidavit	__ Ack __ Jurat 1 2 3 4
Occupancy Affidavit	__ Ack __ Jurat 1 2 3 4	Survey Affidavit	__ Ack __ Jurat 1 2 3 4
Owner's Affidavit	__ Ack __ Jurat 1 2 3 4	Warranty Deed	__ Ack __ Jurat 1 2 3 4
Payoff Affidavit	__ Ack __ Jurat 1 2 3 4	Other	__ Ack __ Jurat 1 2 3 4

Vehicle Docs:

Duplicate Title	__ Ack __ Jurat 1 2 3 4	Odometer/VIN Verification	__ Ack __ Jurat 1 2 3 4
Lien Release	__ Ack __ Jurat 1 2 3 4	Title Transfer	__ Ack __ Jurat 1 2 3 4

Wills/Trusts/ POA:

Living Trust	__ Ack __ Jurat 1 2 3 4	Power of Attorney	__ Ack __ Jurat 1 2 3 4
Last Will & Test	__ Ack __ Jurat 1 2 3 4	Trust Certification	__ Ack __ Jurat 1 2 3 4

Medical Docs:

Advance Healthcare Directive	__ Ack __ Jurat 1 2 3 4	HIPAA Release	__ Ack __ Jurat 1 2 3 4

Other Non-listed Docs:

Document Title: _____ Act Type 1 2 3 4	Document Title: _____ Act Type 1 2 3 4
Document Title: _____ Act Type 1 2 3 4	Document Title: _____ Act Type 1 2 3 4
Document Title: _____ Act Type 1 2 3 4	Document Title: _____ Act Type 1 2 3 4
Document Title: _____ Act Type 1 2 3 4	Document Title: _____ Act Type 1 2 3 4

Date			Time	AM	PM
1	Full Name ___ Signor ___ Witness _____ Address: _____		Verification Method DL PP Cred. Wit Other: _____ State: _____ Iss date: _____ Expiration: _____	Doc. Type ___ Paper ___ Electronic ___ Hybrid	Thumb Print
1	Signature		Screening ___ Coherent ___ Consenting	Phone I Email	
2	Full Name ___ Signor ___ Witness _____ Address: _____		Verification Method DL PP Cred. Wit Other: _____ State: _____ Iss date: _____ Expiration: _____	Doc. Type ___ Paper ___ Electronic ___ Hybrid	Thumb Print
2	Signature		Screening ___ Coherent ___ Consenting	Phone I Email	
3	Full Name ___ Signor ___ Witness _____ Address: _____		Verification Method DL PP Cred. Wit Other: _____ State: _____ Iss date: _____ Expiration: _____	Doc. Type ___ Paper ___ Electronic ___ Hybrid	Thumb Print
3	Signature		Screening ___ Coherent ___ Consenting	Phone I Email	
4	Full Name ___ Signor ___ Witness _____ Address: _____		Verification Method DL PP Cred. Wit Other: _____ State: _____ Iss date: _____ Expiration: _____	Doc. Type ___ Paper ___ Electronic ___ Hybrid	Thumb Print
4	Signature		Screening ___ Coherent ___ Consenting	Phone I Email	

Signing Location:	Observers:	Signing Service:	Fee:

Appointment Notes:

Record of Signed Documents: Loan Documents

Borrower's Affidavit	__ Ack __ Jurat 1 2 3 4	Disbursement of Proceeds	__ Ack __ Jurat 1 2 3 4
Compliance Agreement	__ Ack __ Jurat 1 2 3 4	Errors & Omissions Agreement	__ Ack __ Jurat 1 2 3 4
Correction Agreement	__ Ack __ Jurat 1 2 3 4	Financial Affidavit	__ Ack __ Jurat 1 2 3 4
Indemnity Debt/Lien Affidavit	__ Ack __ Jurat 1 2 3 4	Grant Deed	__ Ack __ Jurat 1 2 3 4
Deed of Trust	__ Ack __ Jurat 1 2 3 4	Marital Status Affidavit	__ Ack __ Jurat 1 2 3 4
Mortgage	__ Ack __ Jurat 1 2 3 4	Quit Claim Deed	__ Ack __ Jurat 1 2 3 4
Mortgagor's Affidavit	__ Ack __ Jurat 1 2 3 4	Signature/Name Affidavit	__ Ack __ Jurat 1 2 3 4
Occupancy Affidavit	__ Ack __ Jurat 1 2 3 4	Survey Affidavit	__ Ack __ Jurat 1 2 3 4
Owner's Affidavit	__ Ack __ Jurat 1 2 3 4	Warranty Deed	__ Ack __ Jurat 1 2 3 4
Payoff Affidavit	__ Ack __ Jurat 1 2 3 4	Other	__ Ack __ Jurat 1 2 3 4

Vehicle Docs:

Duplicate Title	__ Ack __ Jurat 1 2 3 4	Odometer/VIN Verification	__ Ack __ Jurat 1 2 3 4
Lien Release	__ Ack __ Jurat 1 2 3 4	Title Transfer	__ Ack __ Jurat 1 2 3 4

Wills/Trusts/ POA:

Living Trust	__ Ack __ Jurat 1 2 3 4	Power of Attorney	__ Ack __ Jurat 1 2 3 4
Last Will & Test	__ Ack __ Jurat 1 2 3 4	Trust Certification	__ Ack __ Jurat 1 2 3 4

Medical Docs:

Advance Healthcare Directive	__ Ack __ Jurat 1 2 3 4	HIPAA Release	__ Ack __ Jurat 1 2 3 4

Other Non-listed Docs:

Document Title: _____ Act Type 1 2 3 4	Document Title: _____ Act Type 1 2 3 4
Document Title: _____ Act Type 1 2 3 4	Document Title: _____ Act Type 1 2 3 4
Document Title: _____ Act Type 1 2 3 4	Document Title: _____ Act Type 1 2 3 4
Document Title: _____ Act Type 1 2 3 4	Document Title: _____ Act Type 1 2 3 4

Date			Time	AM	PM
1	Full Name ___ Signor ___ Witness _____ Address: _____		Verification Method DL PP Cred. Wit Other: _____ State: _____ Iss date: _____ Expiration: _____	Doc. Type ___ Paper ___ Electronic ___ Hybrid	Thumb Print
	Signature		Screening ___ Coherent ___ Consenting	Phone I Email	
2	Full Name ___ Signor ___ Witness _____ Address: _____		Verification Method DL PP Cred. Wit Other: _____ State: _____ Iss date: _____ Expiration: _____	Doc. Type ___ Paper ___ Electronic ___ Hybrid	Thumb Print
	Signature		Screening ___ Coherent ___ Consenting	Phone I Email	
3	Full Name ___ Signor ___ Witness _____ Address: _____		Verification Method DL PP Cred. Wit Other: _____ State: _____ Iss date: _____ Expiration: _____	Doc. Type ___ Paper ___ Electronic ___ Hybrid	Thumb Print
	Signature		Screening ___ Coherent ___ Consenting	Phone I Email	
4	Full Name ___ Signor ___ Witness _____ Address: _____		Verification Method DL PP Cred. Wit Other: _____ State: _____ Iss date: _____ Expiration: _____	Doc. Type ___ Paper ___ Electronic ___ Hybrid	Thumb Print
	Signature		Screening ___ Coherent ___ Consenting	Phone I Email	

Signing Location:	Observers:	Signing Service:	Fee:

Appointment Notes:

Record of Signed Documents: Loan Documents

Borrower's Affidavit	__ Ack __ Jurat 1 2 3 4	Disbursement of Proceeds	__ Ack __ Jurat 1 2 3 4
Compliance Agreement	__ Ack __ Jurat 1 2 3 4	Errors & Omissions Agreement	__ Ack __ Jurat 1 2 3 4
Correction Agreement	__ Ack __ Jurat 1 2 3 4	Financial Affidavit	__ Ack __ Jurat 1 2 3 4
Indemnity Debt/Lien Affidavit	__ Ack __ Jurat 1 2 3 4	Grant Deed	__ Ack __ Jurat 1 2 3 4
Deed of Trust	__ Ack __ Jurat 1 2 3 4	Marital Status Affidavit	__ Ack __ Jurat 1 2 3 4
Mortgage	__ Ack __ Jurat 1 2 3 4	Quit Claim Deed	__ Ack __ Jurat 1 2 3 4
Mortgagor's Affidavit	__ Ack __ Jurat 1 2 3 4	Signature/Name Affidavit	__ Ack __ Jurat 1 2 3 4
Occupancy Affidavit	__ Ack __ Jurat 1 2 3 4	Survey Affidavit	__ Ack __ Jurat 1 2 3 4
Owner's Affidavit	__ Ack __ Jurat 1 2 3 4	Warranty Deed	__ Ack __ Jurat 1 2 3 4
Payoff Affidavit	__ Ack __ Jurat 1 2 3 4	Other	__ Ack __ Jurat 1 2 3 4

Vehicle Docs:

Duplicate Title	__ Ack __ Jurat 1 2 3 4	Odometer/VIN Verification	__ Ack __ Jurat 1 2 3 4
Lien Release	__ Ack __ Jurat 1 2 3 4	Title Transfer	__ Ack __ Jurat 1 2 3 4

Wills/Trusts/ POA:

Living Trust	__ Ack __ Jurat 1 2 3 4	Power of Attorney	__ Ack __ Jurat 1 2 3 4
Last Will & Test	__ Ack __ Jurat 1 2 3 4	Trust Certification	__ Ack __ Jurat 1 2 3 4

Medical Docs:

Advance Healthcare Directive	__ Ack __ Jurat 1 2 3 4	HIPAA Release	__ Ack __ Jurat 1 2 3 4

Other Non-listed Docs:

Document Title: _____ Act Type 1 2 3 4		Document Title: _____ Act Type 1 2 3 4	
Document Title: _____ Act Type 1 2 3 4		Document Title: _____ Act Type 1 2 3 4	
Document Title: _____ Act Type 1 2 3 4		Document Title: _____ Act Type 1 2 3 4	
Document Title: _____ Act Type 1 2 3 4		Document Title: _____ Act Type 1 2 3 4	

Date				Time		AM	PM

1

Full Name ___ Signor ___ Witness	Verification Method DL PP Cred. Wit Other: _____ State: _____ Iss date: _____ Expiration: _____	Doc. Type ___ Paper ___ Electronic ___ Hybrid	Thumb Print
_____ Address: _____			
Signature	Screening ___ Coherent ___ Consenting	Phone I Email	

2

Full Name ___ Signor ___ Witness	Verification Method DL PP Cred. Wit Other: _____ State: _____ Iss date: _____ Expiration: _____	Doc. Type ___ Paper ___ Electronic ___ Hybrid	Thumb Print
_____ Address: _____			
Signature	Screening ___ Coherent ___ Consenting	Phone I Email	

3

Full Name ___ Signor ___ Witness	Verification Method DL PP Cred. Wit Other: _____ State: _____ Iss date: _____ Expiration: _____	Doc. Type ___ Paper ___ Electronic ___ Hybrid	Thumb Print
_____ Address: _____			
Signature	Screening ___ Coherent ___ Consenting	Phone I Email	

4

Full Name ___ Signor ___ Witness	Verification Method DL PP Cred. Wit Other: _____ State: _____ Iss date: _____ Expiration: _____	Doc. Type ___ Paper ___ Electronic ___ Hybrid	Thumb Print
_____ Address: _____			
Signature	Screening ___ Coherent ___ Consenting	Phone I Email	

Signing Location:	Observers:	Signing Service:	Fee:

Appointment Notes:

Record of Signed Documents: Loan Documents

Borrower's Affidavit	__ Ack __ Jurat 1 2 3 4	Disbursement of Proceeds	__ Ack __ Jurat 1 2 3 4
Compliance Agreement	__ Ack __ Jurat 1 2 3 4	Errors & Omissions Agreement	__ Ack __ Jurat 1 2 3 4
Correction Agreement	__ Ack __ Jurat 1 2 3 4	Financial Affidavit	__ Ack __ Jurat 1 2 3 4
Indemnity Debt/Lien Affidavit	__ Ack __ Jurat 1 2 3 4	Grant Deed	__ Ack __ Jurat 1 2 3 4
Deed of Trust	__ Ack __ Jurat 1 2 3 4	Marital Status Affidavit	__ Ack __ Jurat 1 2 3 4
Mortgage	__ Ack __ Jurat 1 2 3 4	Quit Claim Deed	__ Ack __ Jurat 1 2 3 4
Mortgagor's Affidavit	__ Ack __ Jurat 1 2 3 4	Signature/Name Affidavit	__ Ack __ Jurat 1 2 3 4
Occupancy Affidavit	__ Ack __ Jurat 1 2 3 4	Survey Affidavit	__ Ack __ Jurat 1 2 3 4
Owner's Affidavit	__ Ack __ Jurat 1 2 3 4	Warranty Deed	__ Ack __ Jurat 1 2 3 4
Payoff Affidavit	__ Ack __ Jurat 1 2 3 4	Other	__ Ack __ Jurat 1 2 3 4

Vehicle Docs:

Duplicate Title	__ Ack __ Jurat 1 2 3 4	Odometer/VIN Verification	__ Ack __ Jurat 1 2 3 4
Lien Release	__ Ack __ Jurat 1 2 3 4	Title Transfer	__ Ack __ Jurat 1 2 3 4

Wills/Trusts/ POA:

Living Trust	__ Ack __ Jurat 1 2 3 4	Power of Attorney	__ Ack __ Jurat 1 2 3 4
Last Will & Test	__ Ack __ Jurat 1 2 3 4	Trust Certification	__ Ack __ Jurat 1 2 3 4

Medical Docs:

Advance Healthcare Directive	__ Ack __ Jurat 1 2 3 4	HIPAA Release	__ Ack __ Jurat 1 2 3 4

Other Non-listed Docs:

Document Title: _____ Act Type 1 2 3 4		Document Title: _____ Act Type 1 2 3 4	
Document Title: _____ Act Type 1 2 3 4		Document Title: _____ Act Type 1 2 3 4	
Document Title: _____ Act Type 1 2 3 4		Document Title: _____ Act Type 1 2 3 4	
Document Title: _____ Act Type 1 2 3 4		Document Title: _____ Act Type 1 2 3 4	

Date		Time	AM	PM

1

Full Name ___ Signor ___ Witness	Verification Method DL PP Cred. Wit Other: _____ State: _____ Iss date: _____ Expiration: _____	Doc. Type ___ Paper ___ Electronic ___ Hybrid	Thumb Print
Address: _____			
Signature	Screening ___ Coherent ___ Consenting	Phone I Email	

2

Full Name ___ Signor ___ Witness	Verification Method DL PP Cred. Wit Other: _____ State: _____ Iss date: _____ Expiration: _____	Doc. Type ___ Paper ___ Electronic ___ Hybrid	Thumb Print
Address: _____			
Signature	Screening ___ Coherent ___ Consenting	Phone I Email	

3

Full Name ___ Signor ___ Witness	Verification Method DL PP Cred. Wit Other: _____ State: _____ Iss date: _____ Expiration: _____	Doc. Type ___ Paper ___ Electronic ___ Hybrid	Thumb Print
Address: _____			
Signature	Screening ___ Coherent ___ Consenting	Phone I Email	

4

Full Name ___ Signor ___ Witness	Verification Method DL PP Cred. Wit Other: _____ State: _____ Iss date: _____ Expiration: _____	Doc. Type ___ Paper ___ Electronic ___ Hybrid	Thumb Print
Address: _____			
Signature	Screening ___ Coherent ___ Consenting	Phone I Email	

Signing Location:	Observers:	Signing Service:	Fee:

Appointment Notes:

Record of Signed Documents: Loan Documents

Borrower's Affidavit	__ Ack __ Jurat 1 2 3 4	Disbursement of Proceeds	__ Ack __ Jurat 1 2 3 4
Compliance Agreement	__ Ack __ Jurat 1 2 3 4	Errors & Omissions Agreement	__ Ack __ Jurat 1 2 3 4
Correction Agreement	__ Ack __ Jurat 1 2 3 4	Financial Affidavit	__ Ack __ Jurat 1 2 3 4
Indemnity Debt/Lien Affidavit	__ Ack __ Jurat 1 2 3 4	Grant Deed	__ Ack __ Jurat 1 2 3 4
Deed of Trust	__ Ack __ Jurat 1 2 3 4	Marital Status Affidavit	__ Ack __ Jurat 1 2 3 4
Mortgage	__ Ack __ Jurat 1 2 3 4	Quit Claim Deed	__ Ack __ Jurat 1 2 3 4
Mortgagor's Affidavit	__ Ack __ Jurat 1 2 3 4	Signature/Name Affidavit	__ Ack __ Jurat 1 2 3 4
Occupancy Affidavit	__ Ack __ Jurat 1 2 3 4	Survey Affidavit	__ Ack __ Jurat 1 2 3 4
Owner's Affidavit	__ Ack __ Jurat 1 2 3 4	Warranty Deed	__ Ack __ Jurat 1 2 3 4
Payoff Affidavit	__ Ack __ Jurat 1 2 3 4	Other	__ Ack __ Jurat 1 2 3 4

Vehicle Docs:

Duplicate Title	__ Ack __ Jurat 1 2 3 4	Odometer/VIN Verification	__ Ack __ Jurat 1 2 3 4
Lien Release	__ Ack __ Jurat 1 2 3 4	Title Transfer	__ Ack __ Jurat 1 2 3 4

Wills/Trusts/ POA:

Living Trust	__ Ack __ Jurat 1 2 3 4	Power of Attorney	__ Ack __ Jurat 1 2 3 4
Last Will & Test	__ Ack __ Jurat 1 2 3 4	Trust Certification	__ Ack __ Jurat 1 2 3 4

Medical Docs:

Advance Healthcare Directive	__ Ack __ Jurat 1 2 3 4	HIPAA Release	__ Ack __ Jurat 1 2 3 4

Other Non-listed Docs:

Document Title: _____ Act Type 1 2 3 4		Document Title: _____ Act Type 1 2 3 4	
Document Title: _____ Act Type 1 2 3 4		Document Title: _____ Act Type 1 2 3 4	
Document Title: _____ Act Type 1 2 3 4		Document Title: _____ Act Type 1 2 3 4	
Document Title: _____ Act Type 1 2 3 4		Document Title: _____ Act Type 1 2 3 4	

Date		Time		AM	PM

1	Full Name ___ Signor ___ Witness _____ Address: _____	Verification Method DL PP Cred. Wit Other: _____ State: _____ Iss date: _____ Expiration: _____	Doc. Type ___ Paper ___ Electronic ___ Hybrid	Thumb Print
	Signature	Screening ___ Coherent ___ Consenting	Phone I Email	

2	Full Name ___ Signor ___ Witness _____ Address: _____	Verification Method DL PP Cred. Wit Other: _____ State: _____ Iss date: _____ Expiration: _____	Doc. Type ___ Paper ___ Electronic ___ Hybrid	Thumb Print
	Signature	Screening ___ Coherent ___ Consenting	Phone I Email	

3	Full Name ___ Signor ___ Witness _____ Address: _____	Verification Method DL PP Cred. Wit Other: _____ State: _____ Iss date: _____ Expiration: _____	Doc. Type ___ Paper ___ Electronic ___ Hybrid	Thumb Print
	Signature	Screening ___ Coherent ___ Consenting	Phone I Email	

4	Full Name ___ Signor ___ Witness _____ Address: _____	Verification Method DL PP Cred. Wit Other: _____ State: _____ Iss date: _____ Expiration: _____	Doc. Type ___ Paper ___ Electronic ___ Hybrid	Thumb Print
	Signature	Screening ___ Coherent ___ Consenting	Phone I Email	

Signing Location:	Observers:	Signing Service:	Fee:

Appointment Notes:

Record of Signed Documents: Loan Documents

Borrower's Affidavit	__ Ack __ Jurat 1 2 3 4	Disbursement of Proceeds	__ Ack __ Jurat 1 2 3 4
Compliance Agreement	__ Ack __ Jurat 1 2 3 4	Errors & Omissions Agreement	__ Ack __ Jurat 1 2 3 4
Correction Agreement	__ Ack __ Jurat 1 2 3 4	Financial Affidavit	__ Ack __ Jurat 1 2 3 4
Indemnity Debt/Lien Affidavit	__ Ack __ Jurat 1 2 3 4	Grant Deed	__ Ack __ Jurat 1 2 3 4
Deed of Trust	__ Ack __ Jurat 1 2 3 4	Marital Status Affidavit	__ Ack __ Jurat 1 2 3 4
Mortgage	__ Ack __ Jurat 1 2 3 4	Quit Claim Deed	__ Ack __ Jurat 1 2 3 4
Mortgagor's Affidavit	__ Ack __ Jurat 1 2 3 4	Signature/Name Affidavit	__ Ack __ Jurat 1 2 3 4
Occupancy Affidavit	__ Ack __ Jurat 1 2 3 4	Survey Affidavit	__ Ack __ Jurat 1 2 3 4
Owner's Affidavit	__ Ack __ Jurat 1 2 3 4	Warranty Deed	__ Ack __ Jurat 1 2 3 4
Payoff Affidavit	__ Ack __ Jurat 1 2 3 4	Other	__ Ack __ Jurat 1 2 3 4

Vehicle Docs:

Duplicate Title	__ Ack __ Jurat 1 2 3 4	Odometer/VIN Verification	__ Ack __ Jurat 1 2 3 4
Lien Release	__ Ack __ Jurat 1 2 3 4	Title Transfer	__ Ack __ Jurat 1 2 3 4

Wills/Trusts/ POA:

Living Trust	__ Ack __ Jurat 1 2 3 4	Power of Attorney	__ Ack __ Jurat 1 2 3 4
Last Will & Test	__ Ack __ Jurat 1 2 3 4	Trust Certification	__ Ack __ Jurat 1 2 3 4

Medical Docs:

Advance Healthcare Directive	__ Ack __ Jurat 1 2 3 4	HIPAA Release	__ Ack __ Jurat 1 2 3 4

Other Non-listed Docs:

Document Title: _____ Act Type 1 2 3 4		Document Title: _____ Act Type 1 2 3 4	
Document Title: _____ Act Type 1 2 3 4		Document Title: _____ Act Type 1 2 3 4	
Document Title: _____ Act Type 1 2 3 4		Document Title: _____ Act Type 1 2 3 4	
Document Title: _____ Act Type 1 2 3 4		Document Title: _____ Act Type 1 2 3 4	

Date			Time		AM	PM
1	Full Name ___ Signor ___ Witness _____ Address: _____		Verification Method DL PP Cred. Wit Other: _____ State: _____ Iss date: _____ Expiration: _____		Doc. Type ___ Paper ___ Electronic ___ Hybrid	Thumb Print
	Signature		Screening ___ Coherent ___ Consenting		Phone I Email	
2	Full Name ___ Signor ___ Witness _____ Address: _____		Verification Method DL PP Cred. Wit Other: _____ State: _____ Iss date: _____ Expiration: _____		Doc. Type ___ Paper ___ Electronic ___ Hybrid	Thumb Print
	Signature		Screening ___ Coherent ___ Consenting		Phone I Email	
3	Full Name ___ Signor ___ Witness _____ Address: _____		Verification Method DL PP Cred. Wit Other: _____ State: _____ Iss date: _____ Expiration: _____		Doc. Type ___ Paper ___ Electronic ___ Hybrid	Thumb Print
	Signature		Screening ___ Coherent ___ Consenting		Phone I Email	
4	Full Name ___ Signor ___ Witness _____ Address: _____		Verification Method DL PP Cred. Wit Other: _____ State: _____ Iss date: _____ Expiration: _____		Doc. Type ___ Paper ___ Electronic ___ Hybrid	Thumb Print
	Signature		Screening ___ Coherent ___ Consenting		Phone I Email	

Signing Location:	Observers:	Signing Service:	Fee:

Appointment Notes:

Record of Signed Documents: Loan Documents

Borrower's Affidavit	__ Ack __ Jurat 1 2 3 4	Disbursement of Proceeds	__ Ack __ Jurat 1 2 3 4
Compliance Agreement	__ Ack __ Jurat 1 2 3 4	Errors & Omissions Agreement	__ Ack __ Jurat 1 2 3 4
Correction Agreement	__ Ack __ Jurat 1 2 3 4	Financial Affidavit	__ Ack __ Jurat 1 2 3 4
Indemnity Debt/Lien Affidavit	__ Ack __ Jurat 1 2 3 4	Grant Deed	__ Ack __ Jurat 1 2 3 4
Deed of Trust	__ Ack __ Jurat 1 2 3 4	Marital Status Affidavit	__ Ack __ Jurat 1 2 3 4
Mortgage	__ Ack __ Jurat 1 2 3 4	Quit Claim Deed	__ Ack __ Jurat 1 2 3 4
Mortgagor's Affidavit	__ Ack __ Jurat 1 2 3 4	Signature/Name Affidavit	__ Ack __ Jurat 1 2 3 4
Occupancy Affidavit	__ Ack __ Jurat 1 2 3 4	Survey Affidavit	__ Ack __ Jurat 1 2 3 4
Owner's Affidavit	__ Ack __ Jurat 1 2 3 4	Warranty Deed	__ Ack __ Jurat 1 2 3 4
Payoff Affidavit	__ Ack __ Jurat 1 2 3 4	Other	__ Ack __ Jurat 1 2 3 4

Vehicle Docs:

Duplicate Title	__ Ack __ Jurat 1 2 3 4	Odometer/VIN Verification	__ Ack __ Jurat 1 2 3 4
Lien Release	__ Ack __ Jurat 1 2 3 4	Title Transfer	__ Ack __ Jurat 1 2 3 4

Wills/Trusts/ POA:

Living Trust	__ Ack __ Jurat 1 2 3 4	Power of Attorney	__ Ack __ Jurat 1 2 3 4
Last Will & Test	__ Ack __ Jurat 1 2 3 4	Trust Certification	__ Ack __ Jurat 1 2 3 4

Medical Docs:

Advance Healthcare Directive	__ Ack __ Jurat 1 2 3 4	HIPAA Release	__ Ack __ Jurat 1 2 3 4

Other Non-listed Docs:

Document Title: _____ Act Type 1 2 3 4	Document Title: _____ Act Type 1 2 3 4	
Document Title: _____ Act Type 1 2 3 4	Document Title: _____ Act Type 1 2 3 4	
Document Title: _____ Act Type 1 2 3 4	Document Title: _____ Act Type 1 2 3 4	
Document Title: _____ Act Type 1 2 3 4	Document Title: _____ Act Type 1 2 3 4	

Date		Time	AM	PM

1

Full Name ___ Signor ___ Witness	Verification Method DL PP Cred. Wit Other: _____ State: _____ Iss date: _____ Expiration: _____	Doc. Type ___ Paper ___ Electronic ___ Hybrid	Thumb Print
_____ Address: _____			
Signature	Screening ___ Coherent ___ Consenting	Phone I Email	

2

Full Name ___ Signor ___ Witness	Verification Method DL PP Cred. Wit Other: _____ State: _____ Iss date: _____ Expiration: _____	Doc. Type ___ Paper ___ Electronic ___ Hybrid	Thumb Print
_____ Address: _____			
Signature	Screening ___ Coherent ___ Consenting	Phone I Email	

3

Full Name ___ Signor ___ Witness	Verification Method DL PP Cred. Wit Other: _____ State: _____ Iss date: _____ Expiration: _____	Doc. Type ___ Paper ___ Electronic ___ Hybrid	Thumb Print
_____ Address: _____			
Signature	Screening ___ Coherent ___ Consenting	Phone I Email	

4

Full Name ___ Signor ___ Witness	Verification Method DL PP Cred. Wit Other: _____ State: _____ Iss date: _____ Expiration: _____	Doc. Type ___ Paper ___ Electronic ___ Hybrid	Thumb Print
_____ Address: _____			
Signature	Screening ___ Coherent ___ Consenting	Phone I Email	

Signing Location:	Observers:	Signing Service:	Fee:

Appointment Notes:

Record of Signed Documents: Loan Documents

Borrower's Affidavit	__ Ack __ Jurat 1 2 3 4	Disbursement of Proceeds	__ Ack __ Jurat 1 2 3 4
Compliance Agreement	__ Ack __ Jurat 1 2 3 4	Errors & Omissions Agreement	__ Ack __ Jurat 1 2 3 4
Correction Agreement	__ Ack __ Jurat 1 2 3 4	Financial Affidavit	__ Ack __ Jurat 1 2 3 4
Indemnity Debt/Lien Affidavit	__ Ack __ Jurat 1 2 3 4	Grant Deed	__ Ack __ Jurat 1 2 3 4
Deed of Trust	__ Ack __ Jurat 1 2 3 4	Marital Status Affidavit	__ Ack __ Jurat 1 2 3 4
Mortgage	__ Ack __ Jurat 1 2 3 4	Quit Claim Deed	__ Ack __ Jurat 1 2 3 4
Mortgagor's Affidavit	__ Ack __ Jurat 1 2 3 4	Signature/Name Affidavit	__ Ack __ Jurat 1 2 3 4
Occupancy Affidavit	__ Ack __ Jurat 1 2 3 4	Survey Affidavit	__ Ack __ Jurat 1 2 3 4
Owner's Affidavit	__ Ack __ Jurat 1 2 3 4	Warranty Deed	__ Ack __ Jurat 1 2 3 4
Payoff Affidavit	__ Ack __ Jurat 1 2 3 4	Other	__ Ack __ Jurat 1 2 3 4

Vehicle Docs:

Duplicate Title	__ Ack __ Jurat 1 2 3 4	Odometer/VIN Verification	__ Ack __ Jurat 1 2 3 4
Lien Release	__ Ack __ Jurat 1 2 3 4	Title Transfer	__ Ack __ Jurat 1 2 3 4

Wills/Trusts/ POA:

Living Trust	__ Ack __ Jurat 1 2 3 4	Power of Attorney	__ Ack __ Jurat 1 2 3 4
Last Will & Test	__ Ack __ Jurat 1 2 3 4	Trust Certification	__ Ack __ Jurat 1 2 3 4

Medical Docs:

Advance Healthcare Directive	__ Ack __ Jurat 1 2 3 4	HIPAA Release	__ Ack __ Jurat 1 2 3 4

Other Non-listed Docs:

Document Title: _____ Act Type 1 2 3 4		Document Title: _____ Act Type 1 2 3 4	
Document Title: _____ Act Type 1 2 3 4		Document Title: _____ Act Type 1 2 3 4	
Document Title: _____ Act Type 1 2 3 4		Document Title: _____ Act Type 1 2 3 4	
Document Title: _____ Act Type 1 2 3 4		Document Title: _____ Act Type 1 2 3 4	

Date		Time	AM	PM
1	Full Name ___ Signor ___ Witness _____ Address: _____	Verification Method DL PP Cred. Wit Other: _____ State: _____ Iss date: _____ Expiration: _____	Doc. Type ___ Paper ___ Electronic ___ Hybrid	Thumb Print
	Signature	Screening ___ Coherent ___ Consenting	Phone I Email	
2	Full Name ___ Signor ___ Witness _____ Address: _____	Verification Method DL PP Cred. Wit Other: _____ State: _____ Iss date: _____ Expiration: _____	Doc. Type ___ Paper ___ Electronic ___ Hybrid	Thumb Print
	Signature	Screening ___ Coherent ___ Consenting	Phone I Email	
3	Full Name ___ Signor ___ Witness _____ Address: _____	Verification Method DL PP Cred. Wit Other: _____ State: _____ Iss date: _____ Expiration: _____	Doc. Type ___ Paper ___ Electronic ___ Hybrid	Thumb Print
	Signature	Screening ___ Coherent ___ Consenting	Phone I Email	
4	Full Name ___ Signor ___ Witness _____ Address: _____	Verification Method DL PP Cred. Wit Other: _____ State: _____ Iss date: _____ Expiration: _____	Doc. Type ___ Paper ___ Electronic ___ Hybrid	Thumb Print
	Signature	Screening ___ Coherent ___ Consenting	Phone I Email	

Signing Location:	Observers:	Signing Service:	Fee:

Appointment Notes:

_____

_____

Record of Signed Documents: Loan Documents

Borrower's Affidavit	__ Ack __ Jurat 1 2 3 4	Disbursement of Proceeds	__ Ack __ Jurat 1 2 3 4
Compliance Agreement	__ Ack __ Jurat 1 2 3 4	Errors & Omissions Agreement	__ Ack __ Jurat 1 2 3 4
Correction Agreement	__ Ack __ Jurat 1 2 3 4	Financial Affidavit	__ Ack __ Jurat 1 2 3 4
Indemnity Debt/Lien Affidavit	__ Ack __ Jurat 1 2 3 4	Grant Deed	__ Ack __ Jurat 1 2 3 4
Deed of Trust	__ Ack __ Jurat 1 2 3 4	Marital Status Affidavit	__ Ack __ Jurat 1 2 3 4
Mortgage	__ Ack __ Jurat 1 2 3 4	Quit Claim Deed	__ Ack __ Jurat 1 2 3 4
Mortgagor's Affidavit	__ Ack __ Jurat 1 2 3 4	Signature/Name Affidavit	__ Ack __ Jurat 1 2 3 4
Occupancy Affidavit	__ Ack __ Jurat 1 2 3 4	Survey Affidavit	__ Ack __ Jurat 1 2 3 4
Owner's Affidavit	__ Ack __ Jurat 1 2 3 4	Warranty Deed	__ Ack __ Jurat 1 2 3 4
Payoff Affidavit	__ Ack __ Jurat 1 2 3 4	Other	__ Ack __ Jurat 1 2 3 4

Vehicle Docs:

Duplicate Title	__ Ack __ Jurat 1 2 3 4	Odometer/VIN Verification	__ Ack __ Jurat 1 2 3 4
Lien Release	__ Ack __ Jurat 1 2 3 4	Title Transfer	__ Ack __ Jurat 1 2 3 4

Wills/Trusts/ POA:

Living Trust	__ Ack __ Jurat 1 2 3 4	Power of Attorney	__ Ack __ Jurat 1 2 3 4
Last Will & Test	__ Ack __ Jurat 1 2 3 4	Trust Certification	__ Ack __ Jurat 1 2 3 4

Medical Docs:

Advance Healthcare Directive	__ Ack __ Jurat 1 2 3 4	HIPAA Release	__ Ack __ Jurat 1 2 3 4

Other Non-listed Docs:

Document Title: _____ Act Type 1 2 3 4		Document Title: _____ Act Type 1 2 3 4	
Document Title: _____ Act Type 1 2 3 4		Document Title: _____ Act Type 1 2 3 4	
Document Title: _____ Act Type 1 2 3 4		Document Title: _____ Act Type 1 2 3 4	
Document Title: _____ Act Type 1 2 3 4		Document Title: _____ Act Type 1 2 3 4	

Date			Time	AM	PM

1

Full Name ___ Signor ___ Witness	Verification Method DL PP Cred. Wit Other: _____ State: _____ Iss date: _____ Expiration: _____	Doc. Type ___ Paper ___ Electronic ___ Hybrid	Thumb Print
_____ Address: _____			
Signature	Screening ___ Coherent ___ Consenting	Phone I Email	

2

Full Name ___ Signor ___ Witness	Verification Method DL PP Cred. Wit Other: _____ State: _____ Iss date: _____ Expiration: _____	Doc. Type ___ Paper ___ Electronic ___ Hybrid	Thumb Print
_____ Address: _____			
Signature	Screening ___ Coherent ___ Consenting	Phone I Email	

3

Full Name ___ Signor ___ Witness	Verification Method DL PP Cred. Wit Other: _____ State: _____ Iss date: _____ Expiration: _____	Doc. Type ___ Paper ___ Electronic ___ Hybrid	Thumb Print
_____ Address: _____			
Signature	Screening ___ Coherent ___ Consenting	Phone I Email	

4

Full Name ___ Signor ___ Witness	Verification Method DL PP Cred. Wit Other: _____ State: _____ Iss date: _____ Expiration: _____	Doc. Type ___ Paper ___ Electronic ___ Hybrid	Thumb Print
_____ Address: _____			
Signature	Screening ___ Coherent ___ Consenting	Phone I Email	

Signing Location:	Observers:	Signing Service:	Fee:

Appointment Notes:

Record of Signed Documents: Loan Documents

Borrower's Affidavit	__ Ack __ Jurat 1 2 3 4	Disbursement of Proceeds	__ Ack __ Jurat 1 2 3 4
Compliance Agreement	__ Ack __ Jurat 1 2 3 4	Errors & Omissions Agreement	__ Ack __ Jurat 1 2 3 4
Correction Agreement	__ Ack __ Jurat 1 2 3 4	Financial Affidavit	__ Ack __ Jurat 1 2 3 4
Indemnity Debt/Lien Affidavit	__ Ack __ Jurat 1 2 3 4	Grant Deed	__ Ack __ Jurat 1 2 3 4
Deed of Trust	__ Ack __ Jurat 1 2 3 4	Marital Status Affidavit	__ Ack __ Jurat 1 2 3 4
Mortgage	__ Ack __ Jurat 1 2 3 4	Quit Claim Deed	__ Ack __ Jurat 1 2 3 4
Mortgagor's Affidavit	__ Ack __ Jurat 1 2 3 4	Signature/Name Affidavit	__ Ack __ Jurat 1 2 3 4
Occupancy Affidavit	__ Ack __ Jurat 1 2 3 4	Survey Affidavit	__ Ack __ Jurat 1 2 3 4
Owner's Affidavit	__ Ack __ Jurat 1 2 3 4	Warranty Deed	__ Ack __ Jurat 1 2 3 4
Payoff Affidavit	__ Ack __ Jurat 1 2 3 4	Other	__ Ack __ Jurat 1 2 3 4

Vehicle Docs:

Duplicate Title	__ Ack __ Jurat 1 2 3 4	Odometer/VIN Verification	__ Ack __ Jurat 1 2 3 4
Lien Release	__ Ack __ Jurat 1 2 3 4	Title Transfer	__ Ack __ Jurat 1 2 3 4

Wills/Trusts/ POA:

Living Trust	__ Ack __ Jurat 1 2 3 4	Power of Attorney	__ Ack __ Jurat 1 2 3 4
Last Will & Test	__ Ack __ Jurat 1 2 3 4	Trust Certification	__ Ack __ Jurat 1 2 3 4

Medical Docs:

Advance Healthcare Directive	__ Ack __ Jurat 1 2 3 4	HIPAA Release	__ Ack __ Jurat 1 2 3 4

Other Non-listed Docs:

Document Title: _____ Act Type 1 2 3 4		Document Title: _____ Act Type 1 2 3 4	
Document Title: _____ Act Type 1 2 3 4		Document Title: _____ Act Type 1 2 3 4	
Document Title: _____ Act Type 1 2 3 4		Document Title: _____ Act Type 1 2 3 4	
Document Title: _____ Act Type 1 2 3 4		Document Title: _____ Act Type 1 2 3 4	

Date		Time		AM	PM

1

Full Name ___ Signor ___ Witness	Verification Method DL PP Cred. Wit Other: _____ State: _____ Iss date: _____ Expiration: _____	Doc. Type ___ Paper ___ Electronic ___ Hybrid	Thumb Print
Address: _____			
Signature	Screening ___ Coherent ___ Consenting	Phone I Email	

2

Full Name ___ Signor ___ Witness	Verification Method DL PP Cred. Wit Other: _____ State: _____ Iss date: _____ Expiration: _____	Doc. Type ___ Paper ___ Electronic ___ Hybrid	Thumb Print
Address: _____			
Signature	Screening ___ Coherent ___ Consenting	Phone I Email	

3

Full Name ___ Signor ___ Witness	Verification Method DL PP Cred. Wit Other: _____ State: _____ Iss date: _____ Expiration: _____	Doc. Type ___ Paper ___ Electronic ___ Hybrid	Thumb Print
Address: _____			
Signature	Screening ___ Coherent ___ Consenting	Phone I Email	

4

Full Name ___ Signor ___ Witness	Verification Method DL PP Cred. Wit Other: _____ State: _____ Iss date: _____ Expiration: _____	Doc. Type ___ Paper ___ Electronic ___ Hybrid	Thumb Print
Address: _____			
Signature	Screening ___ Coherent ___ Consenting	Phone I Email	

Signing Location:	Observers:	Signing Service:	Fee:

Appointment Notes:

Record of Signed Documents: Loan Documents

Borrower's Affidavit	__ Ack __ Jurat 1 2 3 4	Disbursement of Proceeds	__ Ack __ Jurat 1 2 3 4
Compliance Agreement	__ Ack __ Jurat 1 2 3 4	Errors & Omissions Agreement	__ Ack __ Jurat 1 2 3 4
Correction Agreement	__ Ack __ Jurat 1 2 3 4	Financial Affidavit	__ Ack __ Jurat 1 2 3 4
Indemnity Debt/Lien Affidavit	__ Ack __ Jurat 1 2 3 4	Grant Deed	__ Ack __ Jurat 1 2 3 4
Deed of Trust	__ Ack __ Jurat 1 2 3 4	Marital Status Affidavit	__ Ack __ Jurat 1 2 3 4
Mortgage	__ Ack __ Jurat 1 2 3 4	Quit Claim Deed	__ Ack __ Jurat 1 2 3 4
Mortgagor's Affidavit	__ Ack __ Jurat 1 2 3 4	Signature/Name Affidavit	__ Ack __ Jurat 1 2 3 4
Occupancy Affidavit	__ Ack __ Jurat 1 2 3 4	Survey Affidavit	__ Ack __ Jurat 1 2 3 4
Owner's Affidavit	__ Ack __ Jurat 1 2 3 4	Warranty Deed	__ Ack __ Jurat 1 2 3 4
Payoff Affidavit	__ Ack __ Jurat 1 2 3 4	Other	__ Ack __ Jurat 1 2 3 4

Vehicle Docs:

Duplicate Title	__ Ack __ Jurat 1 2 3 4	Odometer/VIN Verification	__ Ack __ Jurat 1 2 3 4
Lien Release	__ Ack __ Jurat 1 2 3 4	Title Transfer	__ Ack __ Jurat 1 2 3 4

Wills/Trusts/ POA:

Living Trust	__ Ack __ Jurat 1 2 3 4	Power of Attorney	__ Ack __ Jurat 1 2 3 4
Last Will & Test	__ Ack __ Jurat 1 2 3 4	Trust Certification	__ Ack __ Jurat 1 2 3 4

Medical Docs:

Advance Healthcare Directive	__ Ack __ Jurat 1 2 3 4	HIPAA Release	__ Ack __ Jurat 1 2 3 4

Other Non-listed Docs:

Document Title: _____ Act Type 1 2 3 4		Document Title: _____ Act Type 1 2 3 4	
Document Title: _____ Act Type 1 2 3 4		Document Title: _____ Act Type 1 2 3 4	
Document Title: _____ Act Type 1 2 3 4		Document Title: _____ Act Type 1 2 3 4	
Document Title: _____ Act Type 1 2 3 4		Document Title: _____ Act Type 1 2 3 4	

Date		Time	AM	PM

1	Full Name ___ Signor ___ Witness _____ Address: _____	Verification Method DL PP Cred. Wit Other: _____ State: _____ Iss date: _____ Expiration: _____	Doc. Type ___ Paper ___ Electronic ___ Hybrid	Thumb Print
	Signature	Screening ___ Coherent ___ Consenting	Phone I Email	
2	Full Name ___ Signor ___ Witness _____ Address: _____	Verification Method DL PP Cred. Wit Other: _____ State: _____ Iss date: _____ Expiration: _____	Doc. Type ___ Paper ___ Electronic ___ Hybrid	Thumb Print
	Signature	Screening ___ Coherent ___ Consenting	Phone I Email	
3	Full Name ___ Signor ___ Witness _____ Address: _____	Verification Method DL PP Cred. Wit Other: _____ State: _____ Iss date: _____ Expiration: _____	Doc. Type ___ Paper ___ Electronic ___ Hybrid	Thumb Print
	Signature	Screening ___ Coherent ___ Consenting	Phone I Email	
4	Full Name ___ Signor ___ Witness _____ Address: _____	Verification Method DL PP Cred. Wit Other: _____ State: _____ Iss date: _____ Expiration: _____	Doc. Type ___ Paper ___ Electronic ___ Hybrid	Thumb Print
	Signature	Screening ___ Coherent ___ Consenting	Phone I Email	

Signing Location:	Observers:	Signing Service:	Fee:

Appointment Notes:

Record of Signed Documents: Loan Documents

Borrower's Affidavit	__ Ack __ Jurat 1 2 3 4	Disbursement of Proceeds __ Ack __ Jurat 1 2 3 4
Compliance Agreement	__ Ack __ Jurat 1 2 3 4	Errors & Omissions Agreement __ Ack __ Jurat 1 2 3 4
Correction Agreement	__ Ack __ Jurat 1 2 3 4	Financial Affidavit __ Ack __ Jurat 1 2 3 4
Indemnity Debt/Lien Affidavit	__ Ack __ Jurat 1 2 3 4	Grant Deed __ Ack __ Jurat 1 2 3 4
Deed of Trust	__ Ack __ Jurat 1 2 3 4	Marital Status Affidavit __ Ack __ Jurat 1 2 3 4
Mortgage	__ Ack __ Jurat 1 2 3 4	Quit Claim Deed __ Ack __ Jurat 1 2 3 4
Mortgagor's Affidavit	__ Ack __ Jurat 1 2 3 4	Signature/Name Affidavit __ Ack __ Jurat 1 2 3 4
Occupancy Affidavit	__ Ack __ Jurat 1 2 3 4	Survey Affidavit __ Ack __ Jurat 1 2 3 4
Owner's Affidavit	__ Ack __ Jurat 1 2 3 4	Warranty Deed __ Ack __ Jurat 1 2 3 4
Payoff Affidavit	__ Ack __ Jurat 1 2 3 4	Other __ Ack __ Jurat 1 2 3 4

Vehicle Docs:

Duplicate Title	__ Ack __ Jurat 1 2 3 4	Odometer/VIN Verification __ Ack __ Jurat 1 2 3 4
Lien Release	__ Ack __ Jurat 1 2 3 4	Title Transfer __ Ack __ Jurat 1 2 3 4

Wills/Trusts/ POA:

Living Trust	__ Ack __ Jurat 1 2 3 4	Power of Attorney __ Ack __ Jurat 1 2 3 4
Last Will & Test	__ Ack __ Jurat 1 2 3 4	Trust Certification __ Ack __ Jurat 1 2 3 4

Medical Docs:

Advance Healthcare Directive	__ Ack __ Jurat 1 2 3 4	HIPAA Release __ Ack __ Jurat 1 2 3 4

Other Non-listed Docs:

Document Title: _____ Act Type 1 2 3 4	Document Title: _____ Act Type 1 2 3 4
Document Title: _____ Act Type 1 2 3 4	Document Title: _____ Act Type 1 2 3 4
Document Title: _____ Act Type 1 2 3 4	Document Title: _____ Act Type 1 2 3 4
Document Title: _____ Act Type 1 2 3 4	Document Title: _____ Act Type 1 2 3 4

Date				Time		AM	PM

| 1 | Full Name ___ Signor ___ Witness

_____

Address: _____ | Verification Method
DL   PP   Cred. Wit
Other: _____
State: _____
Iss date: _____
Expiration: _____ | Doc. Type

___ Paper
___ Electronic
___ Hybrid | Thumb Print |
| | Signature | Screening
___ Coherent
___ Consenting | Phone I Email | |

| 2 | Full Name ___ Signor ___ Witness

_____

Address: _____ | Verification Method
DL   PP   Cred. Wit
Other: _____
State: _____
Iss date: _____
Expiration: _____ | Doc. Type

___ Paper
___ Electronic
___ Hybrid | Thumb Print |
| | Signature | Screening
___ Coherent
___ Consenting | Phone I Email | |

| 3 | Full Name ___ Signor ___ Witness

_____

Address: _____ | Verification Method
DL   PP   Cred. Wit
Other: _____
State: _____
Iss date: _____
Expiration: _____ | Doc. Type

___ Paper
___ Electronic
___ Hybrid | Thumb Print |
| | Signature | Screening
___ Coherent
___ Consenting | Phone I Email | |

| 4 | Full Name ___ Signor ___ Witness

_____

Address: _____ | Verification Method
DL   PP   Cred. Wit
Other: _____
State: _____
Iss date: _____
Expiration: _____ | Doc. Type

___ Paper
___ Electronic
___ Hybrid | Thumb Print |
| | Signature | Screening
___ Coherent
___ Consenting | Phone I Email | |

Signing Location:	Observers:	Signing Service:	Fee:

Appointment Notes:

Record of Signed Documents: Loan Documents

Borrower's Affidavit	__ Ack __ Jurat 1 2 3 4	Disbursement of Proceeds	__ Ack __ Jurat 1 2 3 4
Compliance Agreement	__ Ack __ Jurat 1 2 3 4	Errors & Omissions Agreement	__ Ack __ Jurat 1 2 3 4
Correction Agreement	__ Ack __ Jurat 1 2 3 4	Financial Affidavit	__ Ack __ Jurat 1 2 3 4
Indemnity Debt/Lien Affidavit	__ Ack __ Jurat 1 2 3 4	Grant Deed	__ Ack __ Jurat 1 2 3 4
Deed of Trust	__ Ack __ Jurat 1 2 3 4	Marital Status Affidavit	__ Ack __ Jurat 1 2 3 4
Mortgage	__ Ack __ Jurat 1 2 3 4	Quit Claim Deed	__ Ack __ Jurat 1 2 3 4
Mortgagor's Affidavit	__ Ack __ Jurat 1 2 3 4	Signature/Name Affidavit	__ Ack __ Jurat 1 2 3 4
Occupancy Affidavit	__ Ack __ Jurat 1 2 3 4	Survey Affidavit	__ Ack __ Jurat 1 2 3 4
Owner's Affidavit	__ Ack __ Jurat 1 2 3 4	Warranty Deed	__ Ack __ Jurat 1 2 3 4
Payoff Affidavit	__ Ack __ Jurat 1 2 3 4	Other	__ Ack __ Jurat 1 2 3 4

Vehicle Docs:

Duplicate Title	__ Ack __ Jurat 1 2 3 4	Odometer/VIN Verification	__ Ack __ Jurat 1 2 3 4
Lien Release	__ Ack __ Jurat 1 2 3 4	Title Transfer	__ Ack __ Jurat 1 2 3 4

Wills/Trusts/ POA:

Living Trust	__ Ack __ Jurat 1 2 3 4	Power of Attorney	__ Ack __ Jurat 1 2 3 4
Last Will & Test	__ Ack __ Jurat 1 2 3 4	Trust Certification	__ Ack __ Jurat 1 2 3 4

Medical Docs:

Advance Healthcare Directive	__ Ack __ Jurat 1 2 3 4	HIPAA Release	__ Ack __ Jurat 1 2 3 4

Other Non-listed Docs:

Document Title: _____ Act Type 1 2 3 4	Document Title: _____ Act Type 1 2 3 4
Document Title: _____ Act Type 1 2 3 4	Document Title: _____ Act Type 1 2 3 4
Document Title: _____ Act Type 1 2 3 4	Document Title: _____ Act Type 1 2 3 4
Document Title: _____ Act Type 1 2 3 4	Document Title: _____ Act Type 1 2 3 4

Date			Time		AM	PM

| 1 | Full Name ___ Signor ___ Witness _____ Address: _____ | | Verification Method DL PP Cred. Wit Other: _____ State: _____ Iss date: _____ Expiration: _____ | | Doc. Type ___ Paper ___ Electronic ___ Hybrid | Thumb Print |
| | Signature | | Screening ___ Coherent ___ Consenting | | Phone I Email | |

| 2 | Full Name ___ Signor ___ Witness _____ Address: _____ | | Verification Method DL PP Cred. Wit Other: _____ State: _____ Iss date: _____ Expiration: _____ | | Doc. Type ___ Paper ___ Electronic ___ Hybrid | Thumb Print |
| | Signature | | Screening ___ Coherent ___ Consenting | | Phone I Email | |

| 3 | Full Name ___ Signor ___ Witness _____ Address: _____ | | Verification Method DL PP Cred. Wit Other: _____ State: _____ Iss date: _____ Expiration: _____ | | Doc. Type ___ Paper ___ Electronic ___ Hybrid | Thumb Print |
| | Signature | | Screening ___ Coherent ___ Consenting | | Phone I Email | |

| 4 | Full Name ___ Signor ___ Witness _____ Address: _____ | | Verification Method DL PP Cred. Wit Other: _____ State: _____ Iss date: _____ Expiration: _____ | | Doc. Type ___ Paper ___ Electronic ___ Hybrid | Thumb Print |
| | Signature | | Screening ___ Coherent ___ Consenting | | Phone I Email | |

Signing Location:	Observers:	Signing Service:	Fee:

Appointment Notes:

Record of Signed Documents: Loan Documents

Document	Ack/Jurat	Document	Ack/Jurat
Borrower's Affidavit	__ Ack __ Jurat 1 2 3 4	Disbursement of Proceeds	__ Ack __ Jurat 1 2 3 4
Compliance Agreement	__ Ack __ Jurat 1 2 3 4	Errors & Omissions Agreement	__ Ack __ Jurat 1 2 3 4
Correction Agreement	__ Ack __ Jurat 1 2 3 4	Financial Affidavit	__ Ack __ Jurat 1 2 3 4
Indemnity Debt/Lien Affidavit	__ Ack __ Jurat 1 2 3 4	Grant Deed	__ Ack __ Jurat 1 2 3 4
Deed of Trust	__ Ack __ Jurat 1 2 3 4	Marital Status Affidavit	__ Ack __ Jurat 1 2 3 4
Mortgage	__ Ack __ Jurat 1 2 3 4	Quit Claim Deed	__ Ack __ Jurat 1 2 3 4
Mortgagor's Affidavit	__ Ack __ Jurat 1 2 3 4	Signature/Name Affidavit	__ Ack __ Jurat 1 2 3 4
Occupancy Affidavit	__ Ack __ Jurat 1 2 3 4	Survey Affidavit	__ Ack __ Jurat 1 2 3 4
Owner's Affidavit	__ Ack __ Jurat 1 2 3 4	Warranty Deed	__ Ack __ Jurat 1 2 3 4
Payoff Affidavit	__ Ack __ Jurat 1 2 3 4	Other	__ Ack __ Jurat 1 2 3 4

Vehicle Docs:

Document	Ack/Jurat	Document	Ack/Jurat
Duplicate Title	__ Ack __ Jurat 1 2 3 4	Odometer/VIN Verification	__ Ack __ Jurat 1 2 3 4
Lien Release	__ Ack __ Jurat 1 2 3 4	Title Transfer	__ Ack __ Jurat 1 2 3 4

Wills/Trusts/ POA:

Document	Ack/Jurat	Document	Ack/Jurat
Living Trust	__ Ack __ Jurat 1 2 3 4	Power of Attorney	__ Ack __ Jurat 1 2 3 4
Last Will & Test	__ Ack __ Jurat 1 2 3 4	Trust Certification	__ Ack __ Jurat 1 2 3 4

Medical Docs:

Document	Ack/Jurat	Document	Ack/Jurat
Advance Healthcare Directive	__ Ack __ Jurat 1 2 3 4	HIPAA Release	__ Ack __ Jurat 1 2 3 4

Other Non-listed Docs:

Document Title: _____ Act Type 1 2 3 4	Document Title: _____ Act Type 1 2 3 4
Document Title: _____ Act Type 1 2 3 4	Document Title: _____ Act Type 1 2 3 4
Document Title: _____ Act Type 1 2 3 4	Document Title: _____ Act Type 1 2 3 4
Document Title: _____ Act Type 1 2 3 4	Document Title: _____ Act Type 1 2 3 4

Date		Time	AM	PM

	Full Name ___ Signor ___ Witness	Verification Method DL PP Cred. Wit Other: _____ State: _____ Iss date: _____ Expiration: _____	Doc. Type ___ Paper ___ Electronic ___ Hybrid	Thumb Print
1	_____ Address: _____			
	Signature	Screening ___ Coherent ___ Consenting	Phone I Email	

	Full Name ___ Signor ___ Witness	Verification Method DL PP Cred. Wit Other: _____ State: _____ Iss date: _____ Expiration: _____	Doc. Type ___ Paper ___ Electronic ___ Hybrid	Thumb Print
2	_____ Address: _____			
	Signature	Screening ___ Coherent ___ Consenting	Phone I Email	

	Full Name ___ Signor ___ Witness	Verification Method DL PP Cred. Wit Other: _____ State: _____ Iss date: _____ Expiration: _____	Doc. Type ___ Paper ___ Electronic ___ Hybrid	Thumb Print
3	_____ Address: _____			
	Signature	Screening ___ Coherent ___ Consenting	Phone I Email	

	Full Name ___ Signor ___ Witness	Verification Method DL PP Cred. Wit Other: _____ State: _____ Iss date: _____ Expiration: _____	Doc. Type ___ Paper ___ Electronic ___ Hybrid	Thumb Print
4	_____ Address: _____			
	Signature	Screening ___ Coherent ___ Consenting	Phone I Email	

Signing Location:	Observers:	Signing Service:	Fee:

Appointment Notes:

Record of Signed Documents: Loan Documents

Borrower's Affidavit __ Ack __ Jurat 1 2 3 4	Disbursement of Proceeds __ Ack __ Jurat 1 2 3 4
Compliance Agreement __ Ack __ Jurat 1 2 3 4	Errors & Omissions Agreement __ Ack __ Jurat 1 2 3 4
Correction Agreement __ Ack __ Jurat 1 2 3 4	Financial Affidavit __ Ack __ Jurat 1 2 3 4
Indemnity Debt/Lien Affidavit __ Ack __ Jurat 1 2 3 4	Grant Deed __ Ack __ Jurat 1 2 3 4
Deed of Trust __ Ack __ Jurat 1 2 3 4	Marital Status Affidavit __ Ack __ Jurat 1 2 3 4
Mortgage __ Ack __ Jurat 1 2 3 4	Quit Claim Deed __ Ack __ Jurat 1 2 3 4
Mortgagor's Affidavit __ Ack __ Jurat 1 2 3 4	Signature/Name Affidavit __ Ack __ Jurat 1 2 3 4
Occupancy Affidavit __ Ack __ Jurat 1 2 3 4	Survey Affidavit __ Ack __ Jurat 1 2 3 4
Owner's Affidavit __ Ack __ Jurat 1 2 3 4	Warranty Deed __ Ack __ Jurat 1 2 3 4
Payoff Affidavit __ Ack __ Jurat 1 2 3 4	Other __ Ack __ Jurat 1 2 3 4

Vehicle Docs:

Duplicate Title __ Ack __ Jurat 1 2 3 4	Odometer/VIN Verification __ Ack __ Jurat 1 2 3 4
Lien Release __ Ack __ Jurat 1 2 3 4	Title Transfer __ Ack __ Jurat 1 2 3 4

Wills/Trusts/ POA:

Living Trust __ Ack __ Jurat 1 2 3 4	Power of Attorney __ Ack __ Jurat 1 2 3 4
Last Will & Test __ Ack __ Jurat 1 2 3 4	Trust Certification __ Ack __ Jurat 1 2 3 4

Medical Docs:

Advance Healthcare Directive __ Ack __ Jurat 1 2 3 4	HIPAA Release __ Ack __ Jurat 1 2 3 4

Other Non-listed Docs:

Document Title: _____ Act Type 1 2 3 4	Document Title: _____ Act Type 1 2 3 4
Document Title: _____ Act Type 1 2 3 4	Document Title: _____ Act Type 1 2 3 4
Document Title: _____ Act Type 1 2 3 4	Document Title: _____ Act Type 1 2 3 4
Document Title: _____ Act Type 1 2 3 4	Document Title: _____ Act Type 1 2 3 4

Date		Time		AM	PM

1	Full Name ___ Signor ___ Witness _____ Address: _____	Verification Method DL PP Cred. Wit Other: _____ State: _____ Iss date: _____ Expiration: _____	Doc. Type ___ Paper ___ Electronic ___ Hybrid	Thumb Print
	Signature	Screening ___ Coherent ___ Consenting	Phone I Email	

2	Full Name ___ Signor ___ Witness _____ Address: _____	Verification Method DL PP Cred. Wit Other: _____ State: _____ Iss date: _____ Expiration: _____	Doc. Type ___ Paper ___ Electronic ___ Hybrid	Thumb Print
	Signature	Screening ___ Coherent ___ Consenting	Phone I Email	

3	Full Name ___ Signor ___ Witness _____ Address: _____	Verification Method DL PP Cred. Wit Other: _____ State: _____ Iss date: _____ Expiration: _____	Doc. Type ___ Paper ___ Electronic ___ Hybrid	Thumb Print
	Signature	Screening ___ Coherent ___ Consenting	Phone I Email	

4	Full Name ___ Signor ___ Witness _____ Address: _____	Verification Method DL PP Cred. Wit Other: _____ State: _____ Iss date: _____ Expiration: _____	Doc. Type ___ Paper ___ Electronic ___ Hybrid	Thumb Print
	Signature	Screening ___ Coherent ___ Consenting	Phone I Email	

Signing Location:	Observers:	Signing Service:	Fee:

Appointment Notes:

Record of Signed Documents: Loan Documents

Borrower's Affidavit	__ Ack __ Jurat 1 2 3 4	Disbursement of Proceeds	__ Ack __ Jurat 1 2 3 4
Compliance Agreement	__ Ack __ Jurat 1 2 3 4	Errors & Omissions Agreement	__ Ack __ Jurat 1 2 3 4
Correction Agreement	__ Ack __ Jurat 1 2 3 4	Financial Affidavit	__ Ack __ Jurat 1 2 3 4
Indemnity Debt/Lien Affidavit	__ Ack __ Jurat 1 2 3 4	Grant Deed	__ Ack __ Jurat 1 2 3 4
Deed of Trust	__ Ack __ Jurat 1 2 3 4	Marital Status Affidavit	__ Ack __ Jurat 1 2 3 4
Mortgage	__ Ack __ Jurat 1 2 3 4	Quit Claim Deed	__ Ack __ Jurat 1 2 3 4
Mortgagor's Affidavit	__ Ack __ Jurat 1 2 3 4	Signature/Name Affidavit	__ Ack __ Jurat 1 2 3 4
Occupancy Affidavit	__ Ack __ Jurat 1 2 3 4	Survey Affidavit	__ Ack __ Jurat 1 2 3 4
Owner's Affidavit	__ Ack __ Jurat 1 2 3 4	Warranty Deed	__ Ack __ Jurat 1 2 3 4
Payoff Affidavit	__ Ack __ Jurat 1 2 3 4	Other	__ Ack __ Jurat 1 2 3 4

Vehicle Docs:

Duplicate Title	__ Ack __ Jurat 1 2 3 4	Odometer/VIN Verification	__ Ack __ Jurat 1 2 3 4
Lien Release	__ Ack __ Jurat 1 2 3 4	Title Transfer	__ Ack __ Jurat 1 2 3 4

Wills/Trusts/ POA:

Living Trust	__ Ack __ Jurat 1 2 3 4	Power of Attorney	__ Ack __ Jurat 1 2 3 4
Last Will & Test	__ Ack __ Jurat 1 2 3 4	Trust Certification	__ Ack __ Jurat 1 2 3 4

Medical Docs:

Advance Healthcare Directive	__ Ack __ Jurat 1 2 3 4	HIPAA Release	__ Ack __ Jurat 1 2 3 4

Other Non-listed Docs:

Document Title: _____ Act Type 1 2 3 4	Document Title: _____ Act Type 1 2 3 4
Document Title: _____ Act Type 1 2 3 4	Document Title: _____ Act Type 1 2 3 4
Document Title: _____ Act Type 1 2 3 4	Document Title: _____ Act Type 1 2 3 4
Document Title: _____ Act Type 1 2 3 4	Document Title: _____ Act Type 1 2 3 4

Date		Time	AM	PM

1	Full Name ___ Signor ___ Witness _____ Address: _____	Verification Method DL PP Cred. Wit Other: _____ State: _____ Iss date: _____ Expiration: _____	Doc. Type ___ Paper ___ Electronic ___ Hybrid	Thumb Print
	Signature	Screening ___ Coherent ___ Consenting	Phone I Email	
2	Full Name ___ Signor ___ Witness _____ Address: _____	Verification Method DL PP Cred. Wit Other: _____ State: _____ Iss date: _____ Expiration: _____	Doc. Type ___ Paper ___ Electronic ___ Hybrid	Thumb Print
	Signature	Screening ___ Coherent ___ Consenting	Phone I Email	
3	Full Name ___ Signor ___ Witness _____ Address: _____	Verification Method DL PP Cred. Wit Other: _____ State: _____ Iss date: _____ Expiration: _____	Doc. Type ___ Paper ___ Electronic ___ Hybrid	Thumb Print
	Signature	Screening ___ Coherent ___ Consenting	Phone I Email	
4	Full Name ___ Signor ___ Witness _____ Address: _____	Verification Method DL PP Cred. Wit Other: _____ State: _____ Iss date: _____ Expiration: _____	Doc. Type ___ Paper ___ Electronic ___ Hybrid	Thumb Print
	Signature	Screening ___ Coherent ___ Consenting	Phone I Email	

Signing Location:	Observers:	Signing Service:	Fee:

Appointment Notes:

Record of Signed Documents: Loan Documents

Borrower's Affidavit	__ Ack __ Jurat 1 2 3 4	Disbursement of Proceeds	__ Ack __ Jurat 1 2 3 4
Compliance Agreement	__ Ack __ Jurat 1 2 3 4	Errors & Omissions Agreement	__ Ack __ Jurat 1 2 3 4
Correction Agreement	__ Ack __ Jurat 1 2 3 4	Financial Affidavit	__ Ack __ Jurat 1 2 3 4
Indemnity Debt/Lien Affidavit	__ Ack __ Jurat 1 2 3 4	Grant Deed	__ Ack __ Jurat 1 2 3 4
Deed of Trust	__ Ack __ Jurat 1 2 3 4	Marital Status Affidavit	__ Ack __ Jurat 1 2 3 4
Mortgage	__ Ack __ Jurat 1 2 3 4	Quit Claim Deed	__ Ack __ Jurat 1 2 3 4
Mortgagor's Affidavit	__ Ack __ Jurat 1 2 3 4	Signature/Name Affidavit	__ Ack __ Jurat 1 2 3 4
Occupancy Affidavit	__ Ack __ Jurat 1 2 3 4	Survey Affidavit	__ Ack __ Jurat 1 2 3 4
Owner's Affidavit	__ Ack __ Jurat 1 2 3 4	Warranty Deed	__ Ack __ Jurat 1 2 3 4
Payoff Affidavit	__ Ack __ Jurat 1 2 3 4	Other	__ Ack __ Jurat 1 2 3 4

Vehicle Docs:

Duplicate Title	__ Ack __ Jurat 1 2 3 4	Odometer/VIN Verification	__ Ack __ Jurat 1 2 3 4
Lien Release	__ Ack __ Jurat 1 2 3 4	Title Transfer	__ Ack __ Jurat 1 2 3 4

Wills/Trusts/ POA:

Living Trust	__ Ack __ Jurat 1 2 3 4	Power of Attorney	__ Ack __ Jurat 1 2 3 4
Last Will & Test	__ Ack __ Jurat 1 2 3 4	Trust Certification	__ Ack __ Jurat 1 2 3 4

Medical Docs:

Advance Healthcare Directive	__ Ack __ Jurat 1 2 3 4	HIPAA Release	__ Ack __ Jurat 1 2 3 4

Other Non-listed Docs:

Document Title: _____ Act Type 1 2 3 4	Document Title: _____ Act Type 1 2 3 4
Document Title: _____ Act Type 1 2 3 4	Document Title: _____ Act Type 1 2 3 4
Document Title: _____ Act Type 1 2 3 4	Document Title: _____ Act Type 1 2 3 4
Document Title: _____ Act Type 1 2 3 4	Document Title: _____ Act Type 1 2 3 4

Date			Time		AM	PM
1	Full Name ___ Signor ___ Witness _____ Address: _____		Verification Method DL PP Cred. Wit Other: _____ State: _____ Iss date: _____ Expiration: _____		Doc. Type ___ Paper ___ Electronic ___ Hybrid	Thumb Print
	Signature		Screening ___ Coherent ___ Consenting		Phone I Email	
2	Full Name ___ Signor ___ Witness _____ Address: _____		Verification Method DL PP Cred. Wit Other: _____ State: _____ Iss date: _____ Expiration: _____		Doc. Type ___ Paper ___ Electronic ___ Hybrid	Thumb Print
	Signature		Screening ___ Coherent ___ Consenting		Phone I Email	
3	Full Name ___ Signor ___ Witness _____ Address: _____		Verification Method DL PP Cred. Wit Other: _____ State: _____ Iss date: _____ Expiration: _____		Doc. Type ___ Paper ___ Electronic ___ Hybrid	Thumb Print
	Signature		Screening ___ Coherent ___ Consenting		Phone I Email	
4	Full Name ___ Signor ___ Witness _____ Address: _____		Verification Method DL PP Cred. Wit Other: _____ State: _____ Iss date: _____ Expiration: _____		Doc. Type ___ Paper ___ Electronic ___ Hybrid	Thumb Print
	Signature		Screening ___ Coherent ___ Consenting		Phone I Email	

Signing Location:	Observers:	Signing Service:	Fee:

Appointment Notes:

Record of Signed Documents: Loan Documents

Borrower's Affidavit	__ Ack __ Jurat 1 2 3 4	Disbursement of Proceeds	__ Ack __ Jurat 1 2 3 4
Compliance Agreement	__ Ack __ Jurat 1 2 3 4	Errors & Omissions Agreement	__ Ack __ Jurat 1 2 3 4
Correction Agreement	__ Ack __ Jurat 1 2 3 4	Financial Affidavit	__ Ack __ Jurat 1 2 3 4
Indemnity Debt/Lien Affidavit	__ Ack __ Jurat 1 2 3 4	Grant Deed	__ Ack __ Jurat 1 2 3 4
Deed of Trust	__ Ack __ Jurat 1 2 3 4	Marital Status Affidavit	__ Ack __ Jurat 1 2 3 4
Mortgage	__ Ack __ Jurat 1 2 3 4	Quit Claim Deed	__ Ack __ Jurat 1 2 3 4
Mortgagor's Affidavit	__ Ack __ Jurat 1 2 3 4	Signature/Name Affidavit	__ Ack __ Jurat 1 2 3 4
Occupancy Affidavit	__ Ack __ Jurat 1 2 3 4	Survey Affidavit	__ Ack __ Jurat 1 2 3 4
Owner's Affidavit	__ Ack __ Jurat 1 2 3 4	Warranty Deed	__ Ack __ Jurat 1 2 3 4
Payoff Affidavit	__ Ack __ Jurat 1 2 3 4	Other	__ Ack __ Jurat 1 2 3 4

Vehicle Docs:

Duplicate Title	__ Ack __ Jurat 1 2 3 4	Odometer/VIN Verification	__ Ack __ Jurat 1 2 3 4
Lien Release	__ Ack __ Jurat 1 2 3 4	Title Transfer	__ Ack __ Jurat 1 2 3 4

Wills/Trusts/ POA:

Living Trust	__ Ack __ Jurat 1 2 3 4	Power of Attorney	__ Ack __ Jurat 1 2 3 4
Last Will & Test	__ Ack __ Jurat 1 2 3 4	Trust Certification	__ Ack __ Jurat 1 2 3 4

Medical Docs:

Advance Healthcare Directive	__ Ack __ Jurat 1 2 3 4	HIPAA Release	__ Ack __ Jurat 1 2 3 4

Other Non-listed Docs:

Document Title: _____ Act Type 1 2 3 4		Document Title: _____ Act Type 1 2 3 4	
Document Title: _____ Act Type 1 2 3 4		Document Title: _____ Act Type 1 2 3 4	
Document Title: _____ Act Type 1 2 3 4		Document Title: _____ Act Type 1 2 3 4	
Document Title: _____ Act Type 1 2 3 4		Document Title: _____ Act Type 1 2 3 4	

Date		Time	AM	PM

1

Full Name ___ Signor ___ Witness	Verification Method DL PP Cred. Wit Other: _____ State: _____ Iss date: _____ Expiration: _____	Doc. Type ___ Paper ___ Electronic ___ Hybrid	Thumb Print

_____
Address: _____

Signature	Screening ___ Coherent ___ Consenting	Phone I Email

2

Full Name ___ Signor ___ Witness	Verification Method DL PP Cred. Wit Other: _____ State: _____ Iss date: _____ Expiration: _____	Doc. Type ___ Paper ___ Electronic ___ Hybrid	Thumb Print

_____
Address: _____

Signature	Screening ___ Coherent ___ Consenting	Phone I Email

3

Full Name ___ Signor ___ Witness	Verification Method DL PP Cred. Wit Other: _____ State: _____ Iss date: _____ Expiration: _____	Doc. Type ___ Paper ___ Electronic ___ Hybrid	Thumb Print

_____
Address: _____

Signature	Screening ___ Coherent ___ Consenting	Phone I Email

4

Full Name ___ Signor ___ Witness	Verification Method DL PP Cred. Wit Other: _____ State: _____ Iss date: _____ Expiration: _____	Doc. Type ___ Paper ___ Electronic ___ Hybrid	Thumb Print

_____
Address: _____

Signature	Screening ___ Coherent ___ Consenting	Phone I Email

Signing Location:	Observers:	Signing Service:	Fee:

Appointment Notes:

Record of Signed Documents: Loan Documents

Borrower's Affidavit	__ Ack __ Jurat 1 2 3 4	Disbursement of Proceeds	__ Ack __ Jurat 1 2 3 4
Compliance Agreement	__ Ack __ Jurat 1 2 3 4	Errors & Omissions Agreement	__ Ack __ Jurat 1 2 3 4
Correction Agreement	__ Ack __ Jurat 1 2 3 4	Financial Affidavit	__ Ack __ Jurat 1 2 3 4
Indemnity Debt/Lien Affidavit	__ Ack __ Jurat 1 2 3 4	Grant Deed	__ Ack __ Jurat 1 2 3 4
Deed of Trust	__ Ack __ Jurat 1 2 3 4	Marital Status Affidavit	__ Ack __ Jurat 1 2 3 4
Mortgage	__ Ack __ Jurat 1 2 3 4	Quit Claim Deed	__ Ack __ Jurat 1 2 3 4
Mortgagor's Affidavit	__ Ack __ Jurat 1 2 3 4	Signature/Name Affidavit	__ Ack __ Jurat 1 2 3 4
Occupancy Affidavit	__ Ack __ Jurat 1 2 3 4	Survey Affidavit	__ Ack __ Jurat 1 2 3 4
Owner's Affidavit	__ Ack __ Jurat 1 2 3 4	Warranty Deed	__ Ack __ Jurat 1 2 3 4
Payoff Affidavit	__ Ack __ Jurat 1 2 3 4	Other	__ Ack __ Jurat 1 2 3 4

Vehicle Docs:

Duplicate Title	__ Ack __ Jurat 1 2 3 4	Odometer/VIN Verification	__ Ack __ Jurat 1 2 3 4
Lien Release	__ Ack __ Jurat 1 2 3 4	Title Transfer	__ Ack __ Jurat 1 2 3 4

Wills/Trusts/ POA:

Living Trust	__ Ack __ Jurat 1 2 3 4	Power of Attorney	__ Ack __ Jurat 1 2 3 4
Last Will & Test	__ Ack __ Jurat 1 2 3 4	Trust Certification	__ Ack __ Jurat 1 2 3 4

Medical Docs:

Advance Healthcare Directive	__ Ack __ Jurat 1 2 3 4	HIPAA Release	__ Ack __ Jurat 1 2 3 4

Other Non-listed Docs:

Document Title: _____ Act Type 1 2 3 4	Document Title: _____ Act Type 1 2 3 4
Document Title: _____ Act Type 1 2 3 4	Document Title: _____ Act Type 1 2 3 4
Document Title: _____ Act Type 1 2 3 4	Document Title: _____ Act Type 1 2 3 4
Document Title: _____ Act Type 1 2 3 4	Document Title: _____ Act Type 1 2 3 4

Date			Time		AM	PM

1

Full Name ___ Signor ___ Witness	Verification Method	Doc. Type	Thumb Print
_____	DL PP Cred. Wit		
	Other: _____	___ Paper	
Address: _____	State: _____	___ Electronic	
	Iss date: _____	___ Hybrid	
	Expiration: _____		
Signature	Screening ___ Coherent ___ Consenting	Phone I Email	

2

Full Name ___ Signor ___ Witness	Verification Method	Doc. Type	Thumb Print
_____	DL PP Cred. Wit		
	Other: _____	___ Paper	
Address: _____	State: _____	___ Electronic	
	Iss date: _____	___ Hybrid	
	Expiration: _____		
Signature	Screening ___ Coherent ___ Consenting	Phone I Email	

3

Full Name ___ Signor ___ Witness	Verification Method	Doc. Type	Thumb Print
_____	DL PP Cred. Wit		
	Other: _____	___ Paper	
Address: _____	State: _____	___ Electronic	
	Iss date: _____	___ Hybrid	
	Expiration: _____		
Signature	Screening ___ Coherent ___ Consenting	Phone I Email	

4

Full Name ___ Signor ___ Witness	Verification Method	Doc. Type	Thumb Print
_____	DL PP Cred. Wit		
	Other: _____	___ Paper	
Address: _____	State: _____	___ Electronic	
	Iss date: _____	___ Hybrid	
	Expiration: _____		
Signature	Screening ___ Coherent ___ Consenting	Phone I Email	

Signing Location:	Observers:	Signing Service:	Fee:

Appointment Notes:

Record of Signed Documents: Loan Documents

Borrower's Affidavit __ Ack __ Jurat 1 2 3 4	Disbursement of Proceeds __ Ack __ Jurat 1 2 3 4
Compliance Agreement __ Ack __ Jurat 1 2 3 4	Errors & Omissions Agreement __ Ack __ Jurat 1 2 3 4
Correction Agreement __ Ack __ Jurat 1 2 3 4	Financial Affidavit __ Ack __ Jurat 1 2 3 4
Indemnity Debt/Lien Affidavit __ Ack __ Jurat 1 2 3 4	Grant Deed __ Ack __ Jurat 1 2 3 4
Deed of Trust __ Ack __ Jurat 1 2 3 4	Marital Status Affidavit __ Ack __ Jurat 1 2 3 4
Mortgage __ Ack __ Jurat 1 2 3 4	Quit Claim Deed __ Ack __ Jurat 1 2 3 4
Mortgagor's Affidavit __ Ack __ Jurat 1 2 3 4	Signature/Name Affidavit __ Ack __ Jurat 1 2 3 4
Occupancy Affidavit __ Ack __ Jurat 1 2 3 4	Survey Affidavit __ Ack __ Jurat 1 2 3 4
Owner's Affidavit __ Ack __ Jurat 1 2 3 4	Warranty Deed __ Ack __ Jurat 1 2 3 4
Payoff Affidavit __ Ack __ Jurat 1 2 3 4	Other __ Ack __ Jurat 1 2 3 4

Vehicle Docs:

Duplicate Title __ Ack __ Jurat 1 2 3 4	Odometer/VIN Verification __ Ack __ Jurat 1 2 3 4
Lien Release __ Ack __ Jurat 1 2 3 4	Title Transfer __ Ack __ Jurat 1 2 3 4

Wills/Trusts/ POA:

Living Trust __ Ack __ Jurat 1 2 3 4	Power of Attorney __ Ack __ Jurat 1 2 3 4
Last Will & Test __ Ack __ Jurat 1 2 3 4	Trust Certification __ Ack __ Jurat 1 2 3 4

Medical Docs:

Advance Healthcare Directive __ Ack __ Jurat 1 2 3 4	HIPAA Release __ Ack __ Jurat 1 2 3 4

Other Non-listed Docs:

Document Title: _____ Act Type 1 2 3 4	Document Title: _____ Act Type 1 2 3 4
Document Title: _____ Act Type 1 2 3 4	Document Title: _____ Act Type 1 2 3 4
Document Title: _____ Act Type 1 2 3 4	Document Title: _____ Act Type 1 2 3 4
Document Title: _____ Act Type 1 2 3 4	Document Title: _____ Act Type 1 2 3 4

Date			Time		AM	PM
1	Full Name ___ Signor ___ Witness _____ Address: _____		Verification Method DL PP Cred. Wit Other: _____ State: _____ Iss date: _____ Expiration: _____		Doc. Type ___ Paper ___ Electronic ___ Hybrid	Thumb Print
	Signature		Screening ___ Coherent ___ Consenting		Phone I Email	
2	Full Name ___ Signor ___ Witness _____ Address: _____		Verification Method DL PP Cred. Wit Other: _____ State: _____ Iss date: _____ Expiration: _____		Doc. Type ___ Paper ___ Electronic ___ Hybrid	Thumb Print
	Signature		Screening ___ Coherent ___ Consenting		Phone I Email	
3	Full Name ___ Signor ___ Witness _____ Address: _____		Verification Method DL PP Cred. Wit Other: _____ State: _____ Iss date: _____ Expiration: _____		Doc. Type ___ Paper ___ Electronic ___ Hybrid	Thumb Print
	Signature		Screening ___ Coherent ___ Consenting		Phone I Email	
4	Full Name ___ Signor ___ Witness _____ Address: _____		Verification Method DL PP Cred. Wit Other: _____ State: _____ Iss date: _____ Expiration: _____		Doc. Type ___ Paper ___ Electronic ___ Hybrid	Thumb Print
	Signature		Screening ___ Coherent ___ Consenting		Phone I Email	

Signing Location:	Observers:	Signing Service:	Fee:

Appointment Notes:

Record of Signed Documents: Loan Documents

Borrower's Affidavit	__ Ack __ Jurat 1 2 3 4	Disbursement of Proceeds	__ Ack __ Jurat 1 2 3 4
Compliance Agreement	__ Ack __ Jurat 1 2 3 4	Errors & Omissions Agreement	__ Ack __ Jurat 1 2 3 4
Correction Agreement	__ Ack __ Jurat 1 2 3 4	Financial Affidavit	__ Ack __ Jurat 1 2 3 4
Indemnity Debt/Lien Affidavit	__ Ack __ Jurat 1 2 3 4	Grant Deed	__ Ack __ Jurat 1 2 3 4
Deed of Trust	__ Ack __ Jurat 1 2 3 4	Marital Status Affidavit	__ Ack __ Jurat 1 2 3 4
Mortgage	__ Ack __ Jurat 1 2 3 4	Quit Claim Deed	__ Ack __ Jurat 1 2 3 4
Mortgagor's Affidavit	__ Ack __ Jurat 1 2 3 4	Signature/Name Affidavit	__ Ack __ Jurat 1 2 3 4
Occupancy Affidavit	__ Ack __ Jurat 1 2 3 4	Survey Affidavit	__ Ack __ Jurat 1 2 3 4
Owner's Affidavit	__ Ack __ Jurat 1 2 3 4	Warranty Deed	__ Ack __ Jurat 1 2 3 4
Payoff Affidavit	__ Ack __ Jurat 1 2 3 4	Other	__ Ack __ Jurat 1 2 3 4

Vehicle Docs:

Duplicate Title	__ Ack __ Jurat 1 2 3 4	Odometer/VIN Verification	__ Ack __ Jurat 1 2 3 4
Lien Release	__ Ack __ Jurat 1 2 3 4	Title Transfer	__ Ack __ Jurat 1 2 3 4

Wills/Trusts/ POA:

Living Trust	__ Ack __ Jurat 1 2 3 4	Power of Attorney	__ Ack __ Jurat 1 2 3 4
Last Will & Test	__ Ack __ Jurat 1 2 3 4	Trust Certification	__ Ack __ Jurat 1 2 3 4

Medical Docs:

Advance Healthcare Directive	__ Ack __ Jurat 1 2 3 4	HIPAA Release	__ Ack __ Jurat 1 2 3 4

Other Non-listed Docs:

Document Title: _____ Act Type 1 2 3 4		Document Title: _____ Act Type 1 2 3 4	
Document Title: _____ Act Type 1 2 3 4		Document Title: _____ Act Type 1 2 3 4	
Document Title: _____ Act Type 1 2 3 4		Document Title: _____ Act Type 1 2 3 4	
Document Title: _____ Act Type 1 2 3 4		Document Title: _____ Act Type 1 2 3 4	

Date			Time		AM	PM

1	Full Name ___ Signor ___ Witness	Verification Method DL PP Cred. Wit Other: _____ State: _____ Iss date: _____ Expiration: _____	Doc. Type ___ Paper ___ Electronic ___ Hybrid	Thumb Print
	Address: _____			
	Signature	Screening ___ Coherent ___ Consenting	Phone l Email	

2	Full Name ___ Signor ___ Witness	Verification Method DL PP Cred. Wit Other: _____ State: _____ Iss date: _____ Expiration: _____	Doc. Type ___ Paper ___ Electronic ___ Hybrid	Thumb Print
	Address: _____			
	Signature	Screening ___ Coherent ___ Consenting	Phone l Email	

3	Full Name ___ Signor ___ Witness	Verification Method DL PP Cred. Wit Other: _____ State: _____ Iss date: _____ Expiration: _____	Doc. Type ___ Paper ___ Electronic ___ Hybrid	Thumb Print
	Address: _____			
	Signature	Screening ___ Coherent ___ Consenting	Phone l Email	

4	Full Name ___ Signor ___ Witness	Verification Method DL PP Cred. Wit Other: _____ State: _____ Iss date: _____ Expiration: _____	Doc. Type ___ Paper ___ Electronic ___ Hybrid	Thumb Print
	Address: _____			
	Signature	Screening ___ Coherent ___ Consenting	Phone l Email	

Signing Location:	Observers:	Signing Service:	Fee:

Appointment Notes:

Record of Signed Documents: Loan Documents

Borrower's Affidavit	__ Ack __ Jurat 1 2 3 4	Disbursement of Proceeds	__ Ack __ Jurat 1 2 3 4
Compliance Agreement	__ Ack __ Jurat 1 2 3 4	Errors & Omissions Agreement	__ Ack __ Jurat 1 2 3 4
Correction Agreement	__ Ack __ Jurat 1 2 3 4	Financial Affidavit	__ Ack __ Jurat 1 2 3 4
Indemnity Debt/Lien Affidavit	__ Ack __ Jurat 1 2 3 4	Grant Deed	__ Ack __ Jurat 1 2 3 4
Deed of Trust	__ Ack __ Jurat 1 2 3 4	Marital Status Affidavit	__ Ack __ Jurat 1 2 3 4
Mortgage	__ Ack __ Jurat 1 2 3 4	Quit Claim Deed	__ Ack __ Jurat 1 2 3 4
Mortgagor's Affidavit	__ Ack __ Jurat 1 2 3 4	Signature/Name Affidavit	__ Ack __ Jurat 1 2 3 4
Occupancy Affidavit	__ Ack __ Jurat 1 2 3 4	Survey Affidavit	__ Ack __ Jurat 1 2 3 4
Owner's Affidavit	__ Ack __ Jurat 1 2 3 4	Warranty Deed	__ Ack __ Jurat 1 2 3 4
Payoff Affidavit	__ Ack __ Jurat 1 2 3 4	Other	__ Ack __ Jurat 1 2 3 4

Vehicle Docs:

Duplicate Title	__ Ack __ Jurat 1 2 3 4	Odometer/VIN Verification	__ Ack __ Jurat 1 2 3 4
Lien Release	__ Ack __ Jurat 1 2 3 4	Title Transfer	__ Ack __ Jurat 1 2 3 4

Wills/Trusts/ POA:

Living Trust	__ Ack __ Jurat 1 2 3 4	Power of Attorney	__ Ack __ Jurat 1 2 3 4
Last Will & Test	__ Ack __ Jurat 1 2 3 4	Trust Certification	__ Ack __ Jurat 1 2 3 4

Medical Docs:

Advance Healthcare Directive	__ Ack __ Jurat 1 2 3 4	HIPAA Release	__ Ack __ Jurat 1 2 3 4

Other Non-listed Docs:

Document Title: _____ Act Type 1 2 3 4	Document Title: _____ Act Type 1 2 3 4
Document Title: _____ Act Type 1 2 3 4	Document Title: _____ Act Type 1 2 3 4
Document Title: _____ Act Type 1 2 3 4	Document Title: _____ Act Type 1 2 3 4
Document Title: _____ Act Type 1 2 3 4	Document Title: _____ Act Type 1 2 3 4

Date		Time		AM	PM

1	**Full Name** ___ Signor ___ Witness _____ Address: _____	**Verification Method** DL PP Cred. Wit Other: _____ State: _____ Iss date: _____ Expiration: _____	**Doc. Type** ___ Paper ___ Electronic ___ Hybrid	Thumb Print
	Signature	**Screening** ___ Coherent ___ Consenting	Phone I Email	

2	**Full Name** ___ Signor ___ Witness _____ Address: _____	**Verification Method** DL PP Cred. Wit Other: _____ State: _____ Iss date: _____ Expiration: _____	**Doc. Type** ___ Paper ___ Electronic ___ Hybrid	Thumb Print
	Signature	**Screening** ___ Coherent ___ Consenting	Phone I Email	

3	**Full Name** ___ Signor ___ Witness _____ Address: _____	**Verification Method** DL PP Cred. Wit Other: _____ State: _____ Iss date: _____ Expiration: _____	**Doc. Type** ___ Paper ___ Electronic ___ Hybrid	Thumb Print
	Signature	**Screening** ___ Coherent ___ Consenting	Phone I Email	

4	**Full Name** ___ Signor ___ Witness _____ Address: _____	**Verification Method** DL PP Cred. Wit Other: _____ State: _____ Iss date: _____ Expiration: _____	**Doc. Type** ___ Paper ___ Electronic ___ Hybrid	Thumb Print
	Signature	**Screening** ___ Coherent ___ Consenting	Phone I Email	

Signing Location:	Observers:	Signing Service:	Fee:

Appointment Notes:

Record of Signed Documents: Loan Documents

Borrower's Affidavit	__ Ack __ Jurat 1 2 3 4	Disbursement of Proceeds	__ Ack __ Jurat 1 2 3 4
Compliance Agreement	__ Ack __ Jurat 1 2 3 4	Errors & Omissions Agreement	__ Ack __ Jurat 1 2 3 4
Correction Agreement	__ Ack __ Jurat 1 2 3 4	Financial Affidavit	__ Ack __ Jurat 1 2 3 4
Indemnity Debt/Lien Affidavit	__ Ack __ Jurat 1 2 3 4	Grant Deed	__ Ack __ Jurat 1 2 3 4
Deed of Trust	__ Ack __ Jurat 1 2 3 4	Marital Status Affidavit	__ Ack __ Jurat 1 2 3 4
Mortgage	__ Ack __ Jurat 1 2 3 4	Quit Claim Deed	__ Ack __ Jurat 1 2 3 4
Mortgagor's Affidavit	__ Ack __ Jurat 1 2 3 4	Signature/Name Affidavit	__ Ack __ Jurat 1 2 3 4
Occupancy Affidavit	__ Ack __ Jurat 1 2 3 4	Survey Affidavit	__ Ack __ Jurat 1 2 3 4
Owner's Affidavit	__ Ack __ Jurat 1 2 3 4	Warranty Deed	__ Ack __ Jurat 1 2 3 4
Payoff Affidavit	__ Ack __ Jurat 1 2 3 4	Other	__ Ack __ Jurat 1 2 3 4

Vehicle Docs:

Duplicate Title	__ Ack __ Jurat 1 2 3 4	Odometer/VIN Verification	__ Ack __ Jurat 1 2 3 4
Lien Release	__ Ack __ Jurat 1 2 3 4	Title Transfer	__ Ack __ Jurat 1 2 3 4

Wills/Trusts/ POA:

Living Trust	__ Ack __ Jurat 1 2 3 4	Power of Attorney	__ Ack __ Jurat 1 2 3 4
Last Will & Test	__ Ack __ Jurat 1 2 3 4	Trust Certification	__ Ack __ Jurat 1 2 3 4

Medical Docs:

Advance Healthcare Directive	__ Ack __ Jurat 1 2 3 4	HIPAA Release	__ Ack __ Jurat 1 2 3 4

Other Non-listed Docs:

Document Title: _____ Act Type 1 2 3 4	Document Title: _____ Act Type 1 2 3 4
Document Title: _____ Act Type 1 2 3 4	Document Title: _____ Act Type 1 2 3 4
Document Title: _____ Act Type 1 2 3 4	Document Title: _____ Act Type 1 2 3 4
Document Title: _____ Act Type 1 2 3 4	Document Title: _____ Act Type 1 2 3 4

Date		Time	AM	PM

1	Full Name ___ Signor ___ Witness	Verification Method	Doc. Type	Thumb Print
	_____	DL PP Cred. Wit		
		Other: _____	___ Paper	
	Address: _____	State: _____	___ Electronic	
		Iss date: _____	___ Hybrid	
		Expiration: _____		
	Signature	Screening	Phone I Email	
		___ Coherent		
		___ Consenting		

2	Full Name ___ Signor ___ Witness	Verification Method	Doc. Type	Thumb Print
	_____	DL PP Cred. Wit		
		Other: _____	___ Paper	
	Address: _____	State: _____	___ Electronic	
		Iss date: _____	___ Hybrid	
		Expiration: _____		
	Signature	Screening	Phone I Email	
		___ Coherent		
		___ Consenting		

3	Full Name ___ Signor ___ Witness	Verification Method	Doc. Type	Thumb Print
	_____	DL PP Cred. Wit		
		Other: _____	___ Paper	
	Address: _____	State: _____	___ Electronic	
		Iss date: _____	___ Hybrid	
		Expiration: _____		
	Signature	Screening	Phone I Email	
		___ Coherent		
		___ Consenting		

4	Full Name ___ Signor ___ Witness	Verification Method	Doc. Type	Thumb Print
	_____	DL PP Cred. Wit		
		Other: _____	___ Paper	
	Address: _____	State: _____	___ Electronic	
		Iss date: _____	___ Hybrid	
		Expiration: _____		
	Signature	Screening	Phone I Email	
		___ Coherent		
		___ Consenting		

Signing Location:	Observers:	Signing Service:	Fee:

Appointment Notes:

Record of Signed Documents: Loan Documents

Borrower's Affidavit	__ Ack __ Jurat 1 2 3 4	Disbursement of Proceeds	__ Ack __ Jurat 1 2 3 4
Compliance Agreement	__ Ack __ Jurat 1 2 3 4	Errors & Omissions Agreement	__ Ack __ Jurat 1 2 3 4
Correction Agreement	__ Ack __ Jurat 1 2 3 4	Financial Affidavit	__ Ack __ Jurat 1 2 3 4
Indemnity Debt/Lien Affidavit	__ Ack __ Jurat 1 2 3 4	Grant Deed	__ Ack __ Jurat 1 2 3 4
Deed of Trust	__ Ack __ Jurat 1 2 3 4	Marital Status Affidavit	__ Ack __ Jurat 1 2 3 4
Mortgage	__ Ack __ Jurat 1 2 3 4	Quit Claim Deed	__ Ack __ Jurat 1 2 3 4
Mortgagor's Affidavit	__ Ack __ Jurat 1 2 3 4	Signature/Name Affidavit	__ Ack __ Jurat 1 2 3 4
Occupancy Affidavit	__ Ack __ Jurat 1 2 3 4	Survey Affidavit	__ Ack __ Jurat 1 2 3 4
Owner's Affidavit	__ Ack __ Jurat 1 2 3 4	Warranty Deed	__ Ack __ Jurat 1 2 3 4
Payoff Affidavit	__ Ack __ Jurat 1 2 3 4	Other	__ Ack __ Jurat 1 2 3 4

Vehicle Docs:

Duplicate Title	__ Ack __ Jurat 1 2 3 4	Odometer/VIN Verification	__ Ack __ Jurat 1 2 3 4
Lien Release	__ Ack __ Jurat 1 2 3 4	Title Transfer	__ Ack __ Jurat 1 2 3 4

Wills/Trusts/ POA:

Living Trust	__ Ack __ Jurat 1 2 3 4	Power of Attorney	__ Ack __ Jurat 1 2 3 4
Last Will & Test	__ Ack __ Jurat 1 2 3 4	Trust Certification	__ Ack __ Jurat 1 2 3 4

Medical Docs:

Advance Healthcare Directive	__ Ack __ Jurat 1 2 3 4	HIPAA Release	__ Ack __ Jurat 1 2 3 4

Other Non-listed Docs:

Document Title: _____ Act Type 1 2 3 4		Document Title: _____ Act Type 1 2 3 4	
Document Title: _____ Act Type 1 2 3 4		Document Title: _____ Act Type 1 2 3 4	
Document Title: _____ Act Type 1 2 3 4		Document Title: _____ Act Type 1 2 3 4	
Document Title: _____ Act Type 1 2 3 4		Document Title: _____ Act Type 1 2 3 4	

Date			Time	AM	PM
1	Full Name ___ Signor ___ Witness		Verification Method DL PP Cred. Wit Other: _____ State: _____ Iss date: _____ Expiration: _____	Doc. Type ___ Paper ___ Electronic ___ Hybrid	Thumb Print
	Signature		Screening ___ Coherent ___ Consenting	Phone I Email	
2	Full Name ___ Signor ___ Witness		Verification Method DL PP Cred. Wit Other: _____ State: _____ Iss date: _____ Expiration: _____	Doc. Type ___ Paper ___ Electronic ___ Hybrid	Thumb Print
	Signature		Screening ___ Coherent ___ Consenting	Phone I Email	
3	Full Name ___ Signor ___ Witness		Verification Method DL PP Cred. Wit Other: _____ State: _____ Iss date: _____ Expiration: _____	Doc. Type ___ Paper ___ Electronic ___ Hybrid	Thumb Print
	Signature		Screening ___ Coherent ___ Consenting	Phone I Email	
4	Full Name ___ Signor ___ Witness		Verification Method DL PP Cred. Wit Other: _____ State: _____ Iss date: _____ Expiration: _____	Doc. Type ___ Paper ___ Electronic ___ Hybrid	Thumb Print
	Signature		Screening ___ Coherent ___ Consenting	Phone I Email	

Signing Location:	Observers:	Signing Service:	Fee:

Appointment Notes:

Record of Signed Documents: Loan Documents

Borrower's Affidavit	__ Ack __ Jurat 1 2 3 4	Disbursement of Proceeds	__ Ack __ Jurat 1 2 3 4
Compliance Agreement	__ Ack __ Jurat 1 2 3 4	Errors & Omissions Agreement	__ Ack __ Jurat 1 2 3 4
Correction Agreement	__ Ack __ Jurat 1 2 3 4	Financial Affidavit	__ Ack __ Jurat 1 2 3 4
Indemnity Debt/Lien Affidavit	__ Ack __ Jurat 1 2 3 4	Grant Deed	__ Ack __ Jurat 1 2 3 4
Deed of Trust	__ Ack __ Jurat 1 2 3 4	Marital Status Affidavit	__ Ack __ Jurat 1 2 3 4
Mortgage	__ Ack __ Jurat 1 2 3 4	Quit Claim Deed	__ Ack __ Jurat 1 2 3 4
Mortgagor's Affidavit	__ Ack __ Jurat 1 2 3 4	Signature/Name Affidavit	__ Ack __ Jurat 1 2 3 4
Occupancy Affidavit	__ Ack __ Jurat 1 2 3 4	Survey Affidavit	__ Ack __ Jurat 1 2 3 4
Owner's Affidavit	__ Ack __ Jurat 1 2 3 4	Warranty Deed	__ Ack __ Jurat 1 2 3 4
Payoff Affidavit	__ Ack __ Jurat 1 2 3 4	Other	__ Ack __ Jurat 1 2 3 4

Vehicle Docs:

Duplicate Title	__ Ack __ Jurat 1 2 3 4	Odometer/VIN Verification	__ Ack __ Jurat 1 2 3 4
Lien Release	__ Ack __ Jurat 1 2 3 4	Title Transfer	__ Ack __ Jurat 1 2 3 4

Wills/Trusts/ POA:

Living Trust	__ Ack __ Jurat 1 2 3 4	Power of Attorney	__ Ack __ Jurat 1 2 3 4
Last Will & Test	__ Ack __ Jurat 1 2 3 4	Trust Certification	__ Ack __ Jurat 1 2 3 4

Medical Docs:

Advance Healthcare Directive	__ Ack __ Jurat 1 2 3 4	HIPAA Release	__ Ack __ Jurat 1 2 3 4

Other Non-listed Docs:

Document Title: _____ Act Type 1 2 3 4	Document Title: _____ Act Type 1 2 3 4
Document Title: _____ Act Type 1 2 3 4	Document Title: _____ Act Type 1 2 3 4
Document Title: _____ Act Type 1 2 3 4	Document Title: _____ Act Type 1 2 3 4
Document Title: _____ Act Type 1 2 3 4	Document Title: _____ Act Type 1 2 3 4

Date			Time	AM	PM

1	Full Name ___ Signor ___ Witness _____ Address: _____		Verification Method DL PP Cred. Wit Other: _____ State: _____ Iss date: _____ Expiration: _____	Doc. Type ___ Paper ___ Electronic ___ Hybrid	Thumb Print
	Signature		Screening ___ Coherent ___ Consenting	Phone I Email	
2	Full Name ___ Signor ___ Witness _____ Address: _____		Verification Method DL PP Cred. Wit Other: _____ State: _____ Iss date: _____ Expiration: _____	Doc. Type ___ Paper ___ Electronic ___ Hybrid	Thumb Print
	Signature		Screening ___ Coherent ___ Consenting	Phone I Email	
3	Full Name ___ Signor ___ Witness _____ Address: _____		Verification Method DL PP Cred. Wit Other: _____ State: _____ Iss date: _____ Expiration: _____	Doc. Type ___ Paper ___ Electronic ___ Hybrid	Thumb Print
	Signature		Screening ___ Coherent ___ Consenting	Phone I Email	
4	Full Name ___ Signor ___ Witness _____ Address: _____		Verification Method DL PP Cred. Wit Other: _____ State: _____ Iss date: _____ Expiration: _____	Doc. Type ___ Paper ___ Electronic ___ Hybrid	Thumb Print
	Signature		Screening ___ Coherent ___ Consenting	Phone I Email	

Signing Location:	Observers:	Signing Service:	Fee:

Appointment Notes:

Record of Signed Documents: Loan Documents

Borrower's Affidavit	__ Ack __ Jurat 1 2 3 4	Disbursement of Proceeds	__ Ack __ Jurat 1 2 3 4
Compliance Agreement	__ Ack __ Jurat 1 2 3 4	Errors & Omissions Agreement	__ Ack __ Jurat 1 2 3 4
Correction Agreement	__ Ack __ Jurat 1 2 3 4	Financial Affidavit	__ Ack __ Jurat 1 2 3 4
Indemnity Debt/Lien Affidavit	__ Ack __ Jurat 1 2 3 4	Grant Deed	__ Ack __ Jurat 1 2 3 4
Deed of Trust	__ Ack __ Jurat 1 2 3 4	Marital Status Affidavit	__ Ack __ Jurat 1 2 3 4
Mortgage	__ Ack __ Jurat 1 2 3 4	Quit Claim Deed	__ Ack __ Jurat 1 2 3 4
Mortgagor's Affidavit	__ Ack __ Jurat 1 2 3 4	Signature/Name Affidavit	__ Ack __ Jurat 1 2 3 4
Occupancy Affidavit	__ Ack __ Jurat 1 2 3 4	Survey Affidavit	__ Ack __ Jurat 1 2 3 4
Owner's Affidavit	__ Ack __ Jurat 1 2 3 4	Warranty Deed	__ Ack __ Jurat 1 2 3 4
Payoff Affidavit	__ Ack __ Jurat 1 2 3 4	Other	__ Ack __ Jurat 1 2 3 4

Vehicle Docs:

Duplicate Title	__ Ack __ Jurat 1 2 3 4	Odometer/VIN Verification	__ Ack __ Jurat 1 2 3 4
Lien Release	__ Ack __ Jurat 1 2 3 4	Title Transfer	__ Ack __ Jurat 1 2 3 4

Wills/Trusts/ POA:

Living Trust	__ Ack __ Jurat 1 2 3 4	Power of Attorney	__ Ack __ Jurat 1 2 3 4
Last Will & Test	__ Ack __ Jurat 1 2 3 4	Trust Certification	__ Ack __ Jurat 1 2 3 4

Medical Docs:

Advance Healthcare Directive	__ Ack __ Jurat 1 2 3 4	HIPAA Release	__ Ack __ Jurat 1 2 3 4

Other Non-listed Docs:

Document Title: _____ Act Type 1 2 3 4	Document Title: _____ Act Type 1 2 3 4
Document Title: _____ Act Type 1 2 3 4	Document Title: _____ Act Type 1 2 3 4
Document Title: _____ Act Type 1 2 3 4	Document Title: _____ Act Type 1 2 3 4
Document Title: _____ Act Type 1 2 3 4	Document Title: _____ Act Type 1 2 3 4

Date		Time	AM	PM

1	Full Name ___ Signor ___ Witness _____ Address: _____	Verification Method DL PP Cred. Wit Other: _____ State: _____ Iss date: _____ Expiration: _____	Doc. Type ___ Paper ___ Electronic ___ Hybrid	Thumb Print
	Signature	Screening ___ Coherent ___ Consenting	Phone | Email	
2	Full Name ___ Signor ___ Witness _____ Address: _____	Verification Method DL PP Cred. Wit Other: _____ State: _____ Iss date: _____ Expiration: _____	Doc. Type ___ Paper ___ Electronic ___ Hybrid	Thumb Print
	Signature	Screening ___ Coherent ___ Consenting	Phone | Email	
3	Full Name ___ Signor ___ Witness _____ Address: _____	Verification Method DL PP Cred. Wit Other: _____ State: _____ Iss date: _____ Expiration: _____	Doc. Type ___ Paper ___ Electronic ___ Hybrid	Thumb Print
	Signature	Screening ___ Coherent ___ Consenting	Phone | Email	
4	Full Name ___ Signor ___ Witness _____ Address: _____	Verification Method DL PP Cred. Wit Other: _____ State: _____ Iss date: _____ Expiration: _____	Doc. Type ___ Paper ___ Electronic ___ Hybrid	Thumb Print
	Signature	Screening ___ Coherent ___ Consenting	Phone | Email	

Signing Location:	Observers:	Signing Service:	Fee:

Appointment Notes:

_____

_____

_____

Record of Signed Documents: Loan Documents

Borrower's Affidavit	__ Ack __ Jurat 1 2 3 4	Disbursement of Proceeds	__ Ack __ Jurat 1 2 3 4
Compliance Agreement	__ Ack __ Jurat 1 2 3 4	Errors & Omissions Agreement	__ Ack __ Jurat 1 2 3 4
Correction Agreement	__ Ack __ Jurat 1 2 3 4	Financial Affidavit	__ Ack __ Jurat 1 2 3 4
Indemnity Debt/Lien Affidavit	__ Ack __ Jurat 1 2 3 4	Grant Deed	__ Ack __ Jurat 1 2 3 4
Deed of Trust	__ Ack __ Jurat 1 2 3 4	Marital Status Affidavit	__ Ack __ Jurat 1 2 3 4
Mortgage	__ Ack __ Jurat 1 2 3 4	Quit Claim Deed	__ Ack __ Jurat 1 2 3 4
Mortgagor's Affidavit	__ Ack __ Jurat 1 2 3 4	Signature/Name Affidavit	__ Ack __ Jurat 1 2 3 4
Occupancy Affidavit	__ Ack __ Jurat 1 2 3 4	Survey Affidavit	__ Ack __ Jurat 1 2 3 4
Owner's Affidavit	__ Ack __ Jurat 1 2 3 4	Warranty Deed	__ Ack __ Jurat 1 2 3 4
Payoff Affidavit	__ Ack __ Jurat 1 2 3 4	Other	__ Ack __ Jurat 1 2 3 4

Vehicle Docs:

Duplicate Title	__ Ack __ Jurat 1 2 3 4	Odometer/VIN Verification	__ Ack __ Jurat 1 2 3 4
Lien Release	__ Ack __ Jurat 1 2 3 4	Title Transfer	__ Ack __ Jurat 1 2 3 4

Wills/Trusts/ POA:

Living Trust	__ Ack __ Jurat 1 2 3 4	Power of Attorney	__ Ack __ Jurat 1 2 3 4
Last Will & Test	__ Ack __ Jurat 1 2 3 4	Trust Certification	__ Ack __ Jurat 1 2 3 4

Medical Docs:

Advance Healthcare Directive	__ Ack __ Jurat 1 2 3 4	HIPAA Release	__ Ack __ Jurat 1 2 3 4

Other Non-listed Docs:

Document Title: _____ Act Type 1 2 3 4		Document Title: _____ Act Type 1 2 3 4	
Document Title: _____ Act Type 1 2 3 4		Document Title: _____ Act Type 1 2 3 4	
Document Title: _____ Act Type 1 2 3 4		Document Title: _____ Act Type 1 2 3 4	
Document Title: _____ Act Type 1 2 3 4		Document Title: _____ Act Type 1 2 3 4	

Date		Time	AM	PM
1	Full Name ___ Signor ___ Witness ————————————————————— Address: —————————————————	Verification Method DL PP Cred. Wit Other: _____ State: _____ Iss date: _____ Expiration: _____	Doc. Type ___ Paper ___ Electronic ___ Hybrid	Thumb Print
	Signature	Screening ___ Coherent ___ Consenting	Phone I Email	
2	Full Name ___ Signor ___ Witness ————————————————————— Address: —————————————————	Verification Method DL PP Cred. Wit Other: _____ State: _____ Iss date: _____ Expiration: _____	Doc. Type ___ Paper ___ Electronic ___ Hybrid	Thumb Print
	Signature	Screening ___ Coherent ___ Consenting	Phone I Email	
3	Full Name ___ Signor ___ Witness ————————————————————— Address: —————————————————	Verification Method DL PP Cred. Wit Other: _____ State: _____ Iss date: _____ Expiration: _____	Doc. Type ___ Paper ___ Electronic ___ Hybrid	Thumb Print
	Signature	Screening ___ Coherent ___ Consenting	Phone I Email	
4	Full Name ___ Signor ___ Witness ————————————————————— Address: —————————————————	Verification Method DL PP Cred. Wit Other: _____ State: _____ Iss date: _____ Expiration: _____	Doc. Type ___ Paper ___ Electronic ___ Hybrid	Thumb Print
	Signature	Screening ___ Coherent ___ Consenting	Phone I Email	

Signing Location:	Observers:	Signing Service:	Fee:

Appointment Notes:

Record of Signed Documents: Loan Documents

Borrower's Affidavit	__ Ack __ Jurat 1 2 3 4	Disbursement of Proceeds	__ Ack __ Jurat 1 2 3 4
Compliance Agreement	__ Ack __ Jurat 1 2 3 4	Errors & Omissions Agreement	__ Ack __ Jurat 1 2 3 4
Correction Agreement	__ Ack __ Jurat 1 2 3 4	Financial Affidavit	__ Ack __ Jurat 1 2 3 4
Indemnity Debt/Lien Affidavit	__ Ack __ Jurat 1 2 3 4	Grant Deed	__ Ack __ Jurat 1 2 3 4
Deed of Trust	__ Ack __ Jurat 1 2 3 4	Marital Status Affidavit	__ Ack __ Jurat 1 2 3 4
Mortgage	__ Ack __ Jurat 1 2 3 4	Quit Claim Deed	__ Ack __ Jurat 1 2 3 4
Mortgagor's Affidavit	__ Ack __ Jurat 1 2 3 4	Signature/Name Affidavit	__ Ack __ Jurat 1 2 3 4
Occupancy Affidavit	__ Ack __ Jurat 1 2 3 4	Survey Affidavit	__ Ack __ Jurat 1 2 3 4
Owner's Affidavit	__ Ack __ Jurat 1 2 3 4	Warranty Deed	__ Ack __ Jurat 1 2 3 4
Payoff Affidavit	__ Ack __ Jurat 1 2 3 4	Other	__ Ack __ Jurat 1 2 3 4

Vehicle Docs:

Duplicate Title	__ Ack __ Jurat 1 2 3 4	Odometer/VIN Verification	__ Ack __ Jurat 1 2 3 4
Lien Release	__ Ack __ Jurat 1 2 3 4	Title Transfer	__ Ack __ Jurat 1 2 3 4

Wills/Trusts/ POA:

Living Trust	__ Ack __ Jurat 1 2 3 4	Power of Attorney	__ Ack __ Jurat 1 2 3 4
Last Will & Test	__ Ack __ Jurat 1 2 3 4	Trust Certification	__ Ack __ Jurat 1 2 3 4

Medical Docs:

Advance Healthcare Directive	__ Ack __ Jurat 1 2 3 4	HIPAA Release	__ Ack __ Jurat 1 2 3 4

Other Non-listed Docs:

Document Title: _____ Act Type 1 2 3 4		Document Title: _____ Act Type 1 2 3 4	
Document Title: _____ Act Type 1 2 3 4		Document Title: _____ Act Type 1 2 3 4	
Document Title: _____ Act Type 1 2 3 4		Document Title: _____ Act Type 1 2 3 4	
Document Title: _____ Act Type 1 2 3 4		Document Title: _____ Act Type 1 2 3 4	

Date		Time	AM	PM

1

Full Name ___ Signor ___ Witness	Verification Method DL PP Cred. Wit Other: _____ State: _____ Iss date: _____ Expiration: _____	Doc. Type ___ Paper ___ Electronic ___ Hybrid	Thumb Print
_____ Address: _____			
Signature	Screening ___ Coherent ___ Consenting	Phone l Email	

2

Full Name ___ Signor ___ Witness	Verification Method DL PP Cred. Wit Other: _____ State: _____ Iss date: _____ Expiration: _____	Doc. Type ___ Paper ___ Electronic ___ Hybrid	Thumb Print
_____ Address: _____			
Signature	Screening ___ Coherent ___ Consenting	Phone l Email	

3

Full Name ___ Signor ___ Witness	Verification Method DL PP Cred. Wit Other: _____ State: _____ Iss date: _____ Expiration: _____	Doc. Type ___ Paper ___ Electronic ___ Hybrid	Thumb Print
_____ Address: _____			
Signature	Screening ___ Coherent ___ Consenting	Phone l Email	

4

Full Name ___ Signor ___ Witness	Verification Method DL PP Cred. Wit Other: _____ State: _____ Iss date: _____ Expiration: _____	Doc. Type ___ Paper ___ Electronic ___ Hybrid	Thumb Print
_____ Address: _____			
Signature	Screening ___ Coherent ___ Consenting	Phone l Email	

Signing Location:	Observers:	Signing Service:	Fee:

Appointment Notes:

Record of Signed Documents: Loan Documents

Borrower's Affidavit	__ Ack __ Jurat 1 2 3 4	Disbursement of Proceeds	__ Ack __ Jurat 1 2 3 4
Compliance Agreement	__ Ack __ Jurat 1 2 3 4	Errors & Omissions Agreement	__ Ack __ Jurat 1 2 3 4
Correction Agreement	__ Ack __ Jurat 1 2 3 4	Financial Affidavit	__ Ack __ Jurat 1 2 3 4
Indemnity Debt/Lien Affidavit	__ Ack __ Jurat 1 2 3 4	Grant Deed	__ Ack __ Jurat 1 2 3 4
Deed of Trust	__ Ack __ Jurat 1 2 3 4	Marital Status Affidavit	__ Ack __ Jurat 1 2 3 4
Mortgage	__ Ack __ Jurat 1 2 3 4	Quit Claim Deed	__ Ack __ Jurat 1 2 3 4
Mortgagor's Affidavit	__ Ack __ Jurat 1 2 3 4	Signature/Name Affidavit	__ Ack __ Jurat 1 2 3 4
Occupancy Affidavit	__ Ack __ Jurat 1 2 3 4	Survey Affidavit	__ Ack __ Jurat 1 2 3 4
Owner's Affidavit	__ Ack __ Jurat 1 2 3 4	Warranty Deed	__ Ack __ Jurat 1 2 3 4
Payoff Affidavit	__ Ack __ Jurat 1 2 3 4	Other	__ Ack __ Jurat 1 2 3 4

Vehicle Docs:

Duplicate Title	__ Ack __ Jurat 1 2 3 4	Odometer/VIN Verification	__ Ack __ Jurat 1 2 3 4
Lien Release	__ Ack __ Jurat 1 2 3 4	Title Transfer	__ Ack __ Jurat 1 2 3 4

Wills/Trusts/ POA:

Living Trust	__ Ack __ Jurat 1 2 3 4	Power of Attorney	__ Ack __ Jurat 1 2 3 4
Last Will & Test	__ Ack __ Jurat 1 2 3 4	Trust Certification	__ Ack __ Jurat 1 2 3 4

Medical Docs:

Advance Healthcare Directive	__ Ack __ Jurat 1 2 3 4	HIPAA Release	__ Ack __ Jurat 1 2 3 4

Other Non-listed Docs:

Document Title: _____ Act Type 1 2 3 4		Document Title: _____ Act Type 1 2 3 4	
Document Title: _____ Act Type 1 2 3 4		Document Title: _____ Act Type 1 2 3 4	
Document Title: _____ Act Type 1 2 3 4		Document Title: _____ Act Type 1 2 3 4	
Document Title: _____ Act Type 1 2 3 4		Document Title: _____ Act Type 1 2 3 4	

Date			Time		AM	PM

	Full Name ___ Signor ___ Witness	Verification Method DL PP Cred. Wit Other: _____ State: _____ Iss date: _____ Expiration: _____	Doc. Type ___ Paper ___ Electronic ___ Hybrid	Thumb Print
1	_____ Address: _____			
	Signature	Screening ___ Coherent ___ Consenting	Phone I Email	

	Full Name ___ Signor ___ Witness	Verification Method DL PP Cred. Wit Other: _____ State: _____ Iss date: _____ Expiration: _____	Doc. Type ___ Paper ___ Electronic ___ Hybrid	Thumb Print
2	_____ Address: _____			
	Signature	Screening ___ Coherent ___ Consenting	Phone I Email	

	Full Name ___ Signor ___ Witness	Verification Method DL PP Cred. Wit Other: _____ State: _____ Iss date: _____ Expiration: _____	Doc. Type ___ Paper ___ Electronic ___ Hybrid	Thumb Print
3	_____ Address: _____			
	Signature	Screening ___ Coherent ___ Consenting	Phone I Email	

	Full Name ___ Signor ___ Witness	Verification Method DL PP Cred. Wit Other: _____ State: _____ Iss date: _____ Expiration: _____	Doc. Type ___ Paper ___ Electronic ___ Hybrid	Thumb Print
4	_____ Address: _____			
	Signature	Screening ___ Coherent ___ Consenting	Phone I Email	

Signing Location:	Observers:	Signing Service:	Fee:

Appointment Notes:

Record of Signed Documents: Loan Documents

Borrower's Affidavit __ Ack __ Jurat 1 2 3 4	Disbursement of Proceeds __ Ack __ Jurat 1 2 3 4
Compliance Agreement __ Ack __ Jurat 1 2 3 4	Errors & Omissions Agreement __ Ack __ Jurat 1 2 3 4
Correction Agreement __ Ack __ Jurat 1 2 3 4	Financial Affidavit __ Ack __ Jurat 1 2 3 4
Indemnity Debt/Lien Affidavit __ Ack __ Jurat 1 2 3 4	Grant Deed __ Ack __ Jurat 1 2 3 4
Deed of Trust __ Ack __ Jurat 1 2 3 4	Marital Status Affidavit __ Ack __ Jurat 1 2 3 4
Mortgage __ Ack __ Jurat 1 2 3 4	Quit Claim Deed __ Ack __ Jurat 1 2 3 4
Mortgagor's Affidavit __ Ack __ Jurat 1 2 3 4	Signature/Name Affidavit __ Ack __ Jurat 1 2 3 4
Occupancy Affidavit __ Ack __ Jurat 1 2 3 4	Survey Affidavit __ Ack __ Jurat 1 2 3 4
Owner's Affidavit __ Ack __ Jurat 1 2 3 4	Warranty Deed __ Ack __ Jurat 1 2 3 4
Payoff Affidavit __ Ack __ Jurat 1 2 3 4	Other __ Ack __ Jurat 1 2 3 4

Vehicle Docs:

Duplicate Title __ Ack __ Jurat 1 2 3 4	Odometer/VIN Verification __ Ack __ Jurat 1 2 3 4
Lien Release __ Ack __ Jurat 1 2 3 4	Title Transfer __ Ack __ Jurat 1 2 3 4

Wills/Trusts/ POA:

Living Trust __ Ack __ Jurat 1 2 3 4	Power of Attorney __ Ack __ Jurat 1 2 3 4
Last Will & Test __ Ack __ Jurat 1 2 3 4	Trust Certification __ Ack __ Jurat 1 2 3 4

Medical Docs:

Advance Healthcare Directive __ Ack __ Jurat 1 2 3 4	HIPAA Release __ Ack __ Jurat 1 2 3 4

Other Non-listed Docs:

Document Title: _____ Act Type 1 2 3 4	Document Title: _____ Act Type 1 2 3 4
Document Title: _____ Act Type 1 2 3 4	Document Title: _____ Act Type 1 2 3 4
Document Title: _____ Act Type 1 2 3 4	Document Title: _____ Act Type 1 2 3 4
Document Title: _____ Act Type 1 2 3 4	Document Title: _____ Act Type 1 2 3 4

Date		Time	AM	PM
1	**Full Name** ___ Signor ___ Witness _____ Address: _____	**Verification Method** DL PP Cred. Wit Other: _____ State: _____ Iss date: _____ Expiration: _____	**Doc. Type** ___ Paper ___ Electronic ___ Hybrid	**Thumb Print**
1	**Signature**	**Screening** ___ Coherent ___ Consenting	**Phone | Email**	
2	**Full Name** ___ Signor ___ Witness _____ Address: _____	**Verification Method** DL PP Cred. Wit Other: _____ State: _____ Iss date: _____ Expiration: _____	**Doc. Type** ___ Paper ___ Electronic ___ Hybrid	**Thumb Print**
2	**Signature**	**Screening** ___ Coherent ___ Consenting	**Phone | Email**	
3	**Full Name** ___ Signor ___ Witness _____ Address: _____	**Verification Method** DL PP Cred. Wit Other: _____ State: _____ Iss date: _____ Expiration: _____	**Doc. Type** ___ Paper ___ Electronic ___ Hybrid	**Thumb Print**
3	**Signature**	**Screening** ___ Coherent ___ Consenting	**Phone | Email**	
4	**Full Name** ___ Signor ___ Witness _____ Address: _____	**Verification Method** DL PP Cred. Wit Other: _____ State: _____ Iss date: _____ Expiration: _____	**Doc. Type** ___ Paper ___ Electronic ___ Hybrid	**Thumb Print**
4	**Signature**	**Screening** ___ Coherent ___ Consenting	**Phone | Email**	

Signing Location:	Observers:	Signing Service:	Fee:

Appointment Notes:

Record of Signed Documents: Loan Documents

Borrower's Affidavit	__ Ack __ Jurat 1 2 3 4	Disbursement of Proceeds	__ Ack __ Jurat 1 2 3 4
Compliance Agreement	__ Ack __ Jurat 1 2 3 4	Errors & Omissions Agreement	__ Ack __ Jurat 1 2 3 4
Correction Agreement	__ Ack __ Jurat 1 2 3 4	Financial Affidavit	__ Ack __ Jurat 1 2 3 4
Indemnity Debt/Lien Affidavit	__ Ack __ Jurat 1 2 3 4	Grant Deed	__ Ack __ Jurat 1 2 3 4
Deed of Trust	__ Ack __ Jurat 1 2 3 4	Marital Status Affidavit	__ Ack __ Jurat 1 2 3 4
Mortgage	__ Ack __ Jurat 1 2 3 4	Quit Claim Deed	__ Ack __ Jurat 1 2 3 4
Mortgagor's Affidavit	__ Ack __ Jurat 1 2 3 4	Signature/Name Affidavit	__ Ack __ Jurat 1 2 3 4
Occupancy Affidavit	__ Ack __ Jurat 1 2 3 4	Survey Affidavit	__ Ack __ Jurat 1 2 3 4
Owner's Affidavit	__ Ack __ Jurat 1 2 3 4	Warranty Deed	__ Ack __ Jurat 1 2 3 4
Payoff Affidavit	__ Ack __ Jurat 1 2 3 4	Other	__ Ack __ Jurat 1 2 3 4

Vehicle Docs:

Duplicate Title	__ Ack __ Jurat 1 2 3 4	Odometer/VIN Verification	__ Ack __ Jurat 1 2 3 4
Lien Release	__ Ack __ Jurat 1 2 3 4	Title Transfer	__ Ack __ Jurat 1 2 3 4

Wills/Trusts/ POA:

Living Trust	__ Ack __ Jurat 1 2 3 4	Power of Attorney	__ Ack __ Jurat 1 2 3 4
Last Will & Test	__ Ack __ Jurat 1 2 3 4	Trust Certification	__ Ack __ Jurat 1 2 3 4

Medical Docs:

Advance Healthcare Directive	__ Ack __ Jurat 1 2 3 4	HIPAA Release	__ Ack __ Jurat 1 2 3 4

Other Non-listed Docs:

Document Title: _____ Act Type 1 2 3 4		Document Title: _____ Act Type 1 2 3 4	
Document Title: _____ Act Type 1 2 3 4		Document Title: _____ Act Type 1 2 3 4	
Document Title: _____ Act Type 1 2 3 4		Document Title: _____ Act Type 1 2 3 4	
Document Title: _____ Act Type 1 2 3 4		Document Title: _____ Act Type 1 2 3 4	

Date			Time		AM	PM
1	Full Name ___ Signor ___ Witness _____ Address: _____		Verification Method DL PP Cred. Wit Other: _____ State: _____ Iss date: _____ Expiration: _____		Doc. Type ___ Paper ___ Electronic ___ Hybrid	Thumb Print
	Signature		Screening ___ Coherent ___ Consenting		Phone I Email	
2	Full Name ___ Signor ___ Witness _____ Address: _____		Verification Method DL PP Cred. Wit Other: _____ State: _____ Iss date: _____ Expiration: _____		Doc. Type ___ Paper ___ Electronic ___ Hybrid	Thumb Print
	Signature		Screening ___ Coherent ___ Consenting		Phone I Email	
3	Full Name ___ Signor ___ Witness _____ Address: _____		Verification Method DL PP Cred. Wit Other: _____ State: _____ Iss date: _____ Expiration: _____		Doc. Type ___ Paper ___ Electronic ___ Hybrid	Thumb Print
	Signature		Screening ___ Coherent ___ Consenting		Phone I Email	
4	Full Name ___ Signor ___ Witness _____ Address: _____		Verification Method DL PP Cred. Wit Other: _____ State: _____ Iss date: _____ Expiration: _____		Doc. Type ___ Paper ___ Electronic ___ Hybrid	Thumb Print
	Signature		Screening ___ Coherent ___ Consenting		Phone I Email	

Signing Location:	Observers:	Signing Service:	Fee:

Appointment Notes:

Record of Signed Documents: Loan Documents

Borrower's Affidavit	__ Ack __ Jurat 1 2 3 4	Disbursement of Proceeds	__ Ack __ Jurat 1 2 3 4
Compliance Agreement	__ Ack __ Jurat 1 2 3 4	Errors & Omissions Agreement	__ Ack __ Jurat 1 2 3 4
Correction Agreement	__ Ack __ Jurat 1 2 3 4	Financial Affidavit	__ Ack __ Jurat 1 2 3 4
Indemnity Debt/Lien Affidavit	__ Ack __ Jurat 1 2 3 4	Grant Deed	__ Ack __ Jurat 1 2 3 4
Deed of Trust	__ Ack __ Jurat 1 2 3 4	Marital Status Affidavit	__ Ack __ Jurat 1 2 3 4
Mortgage	__ Ack __ Jurat 1 2 3 4	Quit Claim Deed	__ Ack __ Jurat 1 2 3 4
Mortgagor's Affidavit	__ Ack __ Jurat 1 2 3 4	Signature/Name Affidavit	__ Ack __ Jurat 1 2 3 4
Occupancy Affidavit	__ Ack __ Jurat 1 2 3 4	Survey Affidavit	__ Ack __ Jurat 1 2 3 4
Owner's Affidavit	__ Ack __ Jurat 1 2 3 4	Warranty Deed	__ Ack __ Jurat 1 2 3 4
Payoff Affidavit	__ Ack __ Jurat 1 2 3 4	Other	__ Ack __ Jurat 1 2 3 4

Vehicle Docs:

Duplicate Title	__ Ack __ Jurat 1 2 3 4	Odometer/VIN Verification	__ Ack __ Jurat 1 2 3 4
Lien Release	__ Ack __ Jurat 1 2 3 4	Title Transfer	__ Ack __ Jurat 1 2 3 4

Wills/Trusts/ POA:

Living Trust	__ Ack __ Jurat 1 2 3 4	Power of Attorney	__ Ack __ Jurat 1 2 3 4
Last Will & Test	__ Ack __ Jurat 1 2 3 4	Trust Certification	__ Ack __ Jurat 1 2 3 4

Medical Docs:

Advance Healthcare Directive	__ Ack __ Jurat 1 2 3 4	HIPAA Release	__ Ack __ Jurat 1 2 3 4

Other Non-listed Docs:

Document Title: _____ Act Type 1 2 3 4	Document Title: _____ Act Type 1 2 3 4
Document Title: _____ Act Type 1 2 3 4	Document Title: _____ Act Type 1 2 3 4
Document Title: _____ Act Type 1 2 3 4	Document Title: _____ Act Type 1 2 3 4
Document Title: _____ Act Type 1 2 3 4	Document Title: _____ Act Type 1 2 3 4

Date		Time	AM	PM

1	Full Name ___ Signor ___ Witness _____ Address: _____	Verification Method DL PP Cred. Wit Other: _____ State: _____ Iss date: _____ Expiration: _____	Doc. Type ___ Paper ___ Electronic ___ Hybrid	Thumb Print
	Signature	Screening ___ Coherent ___ Consenting	Phone I Email	
2	Full Name ___ Signor ___ Witness _____ Address: _____	Verification Method DL PP Cred. Wit Other: _____ State: _____ Iss date: _____ Expiration: _____	Doc. Type ___ Paper ___ Electronic ___ Hybrid	Thumb Print
	Signature	Screening ___ Coherent ___ Consenting	Phone I Email	
3	Full Name ___ Signor ___ Witness _____ Address: _____	Verification Method DL PP Cred. Wit Other: _____ State: _____ Iss date: _____ Expiration: _____	Doc. Type ___ Paper ___ Electronic ___ Hybrid	Thumb Print
	Signature	Screening ___ Coherent ___ Consenting	Phone I Email	
4	Full Name ___ Signor ___ Witness _____ Address: _____	Verification Method DL PP Cred. Wit Other: _____ State: _____ Iss date: _____ Expiration: _____	Doc. Type ___ Paper ___ Electronic ___ Hybrid	Thumb Print
	Signature	Screening ___ Coherent ___ Consenting	Phone I Email	

Signing Location:	Observers:	Signing Service:	Fee:

Appointment Notes:

Record of Signed Documents: Loan Documents

Borrower's Affidavit	__ Ack __ Jurat 1 2 3 4	
Compliance Agreement	__ Ack __ Jurat 1 2 3 4	
Correction Agreement	__ Ack __ Jurat 1 2 3 4	
Indemnity Debt/Lien Affidavit	__ Ack __ Jurat 1 2 3 4	
Deed of Trust	__ Ack __ Jurat 1 2 3 4	
Mortgage	__ Ack __ Jurat 1 2 3 4	
Mortgagor's Affidavit	__ Ack __ Jurat 1 2 3 4	
Occupancy Affidavit	__ Ack __ Jurat 1 2 3 4	
Owner's Affidavit	__ Ack __ Jurat 1 2 3 4	
Payoff Affidavit	__ Ack __ Jurat 1 2 3 4	
Disbursement of Proceeds	__ Ack __ Jurat 1 2 3 4	
Errors & Omissions Agreement	__ Ack __ Jurat 1 2 3 4	
Financial Affidavit	__ Ack __ Jurat 1 2 3 4	
Grant Deed	__ Ack __ Jurat 1 2 3 4	
Marital Status Affidavit	__ Ack __ Jurat 1 2 3 4	
Quit Claim Deed	__ Ack __ Jurat 1 2 3 4	
Signature/Name Affidavit	__ Ack __ Jurat 1 2 3 4	
Survey Affidavit	__ Ack __ Jurat 1 2 3 4	
Warranty Deed	__ Ack __ Jurat 1 2 3 4	
Other	__ Ack __ Jurat 1 2 3 4	

Vehicle Docs:

Duplicate Title __ Ack __ Jurat 1 2 3 4	Odometer/VIN Verification __ Ack __ Jurat 1 2 3 4
Lien Release __ Ack __ Jurat 1 2 3 4	Title Transfer __ Ack __ Jurat 1 2 3 4

Wills/Trusts/ POA:

Living Trust __ Ack __ Jurat 1 2 3 4	Power of Attorney __ Ack __ Jurat 1 2 3 4
Last Will & Test __ Ack __ Jurat 1 2 3 4	Trust Certification __ Ack __ Jurat 1 2 3 4

Medical Docs:

Advance Healthcare Directive __ Ack __ Jurat 1 2 3 4	HIPAA Release __ Ack __ Jurat 1 2 3 4

Other Non-listed Docs:

Document Title: _____ Act Type 1 2 3 4	Document Title: _____ Act Type 1 2 3 4
Document Title: _____ Act Type 1 2 3 4	Document Title: _____ Act Type 1 2 3 4
Document Title: _____ Act Type 1 2 3 4	Document Title: _____ Act Type 1 2 3 4
Document Title: _____ Act Type 1 2 3 4	Document Title: _____ Act Type 1 2 3 4

Date		Time		AM	PM

| 1 | Full Name ___ Signor ___ Witness

_____

Address: _____ | Verification Method
DL   PP   Cred. Wit
Other: _____
State: _____
Iss date: _____
Expiration: _____ | Doc. Type

___ Paper
___ Electronic
___ Hybrid | Thumb Print |
| | Signature | Screening
___ Coherent
___ Consenting | Phone I Email | |

| 2 | Full Name ___ Signor ___ Witness

_____

Address: _____ | Verification Method
DL   PP   Cred. Wit
Other: _____
State: _____
Iss date: _____
Expiration: _____ | Doc. Type

___ Paper
___ Electronic
___ Hybrid | Thumb Print |
| | Signature | Screening
___ Coherent
___ Consenting | Phone I Email | |

| 3 | Full Name ___ Signor ___ Witness

_____

Address: _____ | Verification Method
DL   PP   Cred. Wit
Other: _____
State: _____
Iss date: _____
Expiration: _____ | Doc. Type

___ Paper
___ Electronic
___ Hybrid | Thumb Print |
| | Signature | Screening
___ Coherent
___ Consenting | Phone I Email | |

| 4 | Full Name ___ Signor ___ Witness

_____

Address: _____ | Verification Method
DL   PP   Cred. Wit
Other: _____
State: _____
Iss date: _____
Expiration: _____ | Doc. Type

___ Paper
___ Electronic
___ Hybrid | Thumb Print |
| | Signature | Screening
___ Coherent
___ Consenting | Phone I Email | |

Signing Location:	Observers:	Signing Service:	Fee:

Appointment Notes:

_____

_____

_____

Record of Signed Documents: Loan Documents

Borrower's Affidavit	__ Ack __ Jurat 1 2 3 4	Disbursement of Proceeds	__ Ack __ Jurat 1 2 3 4
Compliance Agreement	__ Ack __ Jurat 1 2 3 4	Errors & Omissions Agreement	__ Ack __ Jurat 1 2 3 4
Correction Agreement	__ Ack __ Jurat 1 2 3 4	Financial Affidavit	__ Ack __ Jurat 1 2 3 4
Indemnity Debt/Lien Affidavit	__ Ack __ Jurat 1 2 3 4	Grant Deed	__ Ack __ Jurat 1 2 3 4
Deed of Trust	__ Ack __ Jurat 1 2 3 4	Marital Status Affidavit	__ Ack __ Jurat 1 2 3 4
Mortgage	__ Ack __ Jurat 1 2 3 4	Quit Claim Deed	__ Ack __ Jurat 1 2 3 4
Mortgagor's Affidavit	__ Ack __ Jurat 1 2 3 4	Signature/Name Affidavit	__ Ack __ Jurat 1 2 3 4
Occupancy Affidavit	__ Ack __ Jurat 1 2 3 4	Survey Affidavit	__ Ack __ Jurat 1 2 3 4
Owner's Affidavit	__ Ack __ Jurat 1 2 3 4	Warranty Deed	__ Ack __ Jurat 1 2 3 4
Payoff Affidavit	__ Ack __ Jurat 1 2 3 4	Other	__ Ack __ Jurat 1 2 3 4

Vehicle Docs:

Duplicate Title	__ Ack __ Jurat 1 2 3 4	Odometer/VIN Verification	__ Ack __ Jurat 1 2 3 4
Lien Release	__ Ack __ Jurat 1 2 3 4	Title Transfer	__ Ack __ Jurat 1 2 3 4

Wills/Trusts/ POA:

Living Trust	__ Ack __ Jurat 1 2 3 4	Power of Attorney	__ Ack __ Jurat 1 2 3 4
Last Will & Test	__ Ack __ Jurat 1 2 3 4	Trust Certification	__ Ack __ Jurat 1 2 3 4

Medical Docs:

Advance Healthcare Directive	__ Ack __ Jurat 1 2 3 4	HIPAA Release	__ Ack __ Jurat 1 2 3 4

Other Non-listed Docs:

Document Title: _____ Act Type 1 2 3 4		Document Title: _____ Act Type 1 2 3 4	
Document Title: _____ Act Type 1 2 3 4		Document Title: _____ Act Type 1 2 3 4	
Document Title: _____ Act Type 1 2 3 4		Document Title: _____ Act Type 1 2 3 4	
Document Title: _____ Act Type 1 2 3 4		Document Title: _____ Act Type 1 2 3 4	

Date		Time		AM	PM

1

Full Name ___ Signor ___ Witness	Verification Method DL PP Cred. Wit Other: _____ State: _____ Iss date: _____ Expiration: _____	Doc. Type ___ Paper ___ Electronic ___ Hybrid	Thumb Print
_____ Address: _____			
Signature	Screening ___ Coherent ___ Consenting	Phone I Email	

2

Full Name ___ Signor ___ Witness	Verification Method DL PP Cred. Wit Other: _____ State: _____ Iss date: _____ Expiration: _____	Doc. Type ___ Paper ___ Electronic ___ Hybrid	Thumb Print
_____ Address: _____			
Signature	Screening ___ Coherent ___ Consenting	Phone I Email	

3

Full Name ___ Signor ___ Witness	Verification Method DL PP Cred. Wit Other: _____ State: _____ Iss date: _____ Expiration: _____	Doc. Type ___ Paper ___ Electronic ___ Hybrid	Thumb Print
_____ Address: _____			
Signature	Screening ___ Coherent ___ Consenting	Phone I Email	

4

Full Name ___ Signor ___ Witness	Verification Method DL PP Cred. Wit Other: _____ State: _____ Iss date: _____ Expiration: _____	Doc. Type ___ Paper ___ Electronic ___ Hybrid	Thumb Print
_____ Address: _____			
Signature	Screening ___ Coherent ___ Consenting	Phone I Email	

Signing Location:	Observers:	Signing Service:	Fee:

Appointment Notes:

Record of Signed Documents: Loan Documents

Borrower's Affidavit	__ Ack __ Jurat 1 2 3 4	Disbursement of Proceeds	__ Ack __ Jurat 1 2 3 4
Compliance Agreement	__ Ack __ Jurat 1 2 3 4	Errors & Omissions Agreement	__ Ack __ Jurat 1 2 3 4
Correction Agreement	__ Ack __ Jurat 1 2 3 4	Financial Affidavit	__ Ack __ Jurat 1 2 3 4
Indemnity Debt/Lien Affidavit	__ Ack __ Jurat 1 2 3 4	Grant Deed	__ Ack __ Jurat 1 2 3 4
Deed of Trust	__ Ack __ Jurat 1 2 3 4	Marital Status Affidavit	__ Ack __ Jurat 1 2 3 4
Mortgage	__ Ack __ Jurat 1 2 3 4	Quit Claim Deed	__ Ack __ Jurat 1 2 3 4
Mortgagor's Affidavit	__ Ack __ Jurat 1 2 3 4	Signature/Name Affidavit	__ Ack __ Jurat 1 2 3 4
Occupancy Affidavit	__ Ack __ Jurat 1 2 3 4	Survey Affidavit	__ Ack __ Jurat 1 2 3 4
Owner's Affidavit	__ Ack __ Jurat 1 2 3 4	Warranty Deed	__ Ack __ Jurat 1 2 3 4
Payoff Affidavit	__ Ack __ Jurat 1 2 3 4	Other	__ Ack __ Jurat 1 2 3 4

Vehicle Docs:

Duplicate Title	__ Ack __ Jurat 1 2 3 4	Odometer/VIN Verification	__ Ack __ Jurat 1 2 3 4
Lien Release	__ Ack __ Jurat 1 2 3 4	Title Transfer	__ Ack __ Jurat 1 2 3 4

Wills/Trusts/ POA:

Living Trust	__ Ack __ Jurat 1 2 3 4	Power of Attorney	__ Ack __ Jurat 1 2 3 4
Last Will & Test	__ Ack __ Jurat 1 2 3 4	Trust Certification	__ Ack __ Jurat 1 2 3 4

Medical Docs:

Advance Healthcare Directive	__ Ack __ Jurat 1 2 3 4	HIPAA Release	__ Ack __ Jurat 1 2 3 4

Other Non-listed Docs:

Document Title: _____ Act Type 1 2 3 4	Document Title: _____ Act Type 1 2 3 4
Document Title: _____ Act Type 1 2 3 4	Document Title: _____ Act Type 1 2 3 4
Document Title: _____ Act Type 1 2 3 4	Document Title: _____ Act Type 1 2 3 4
Document Title: _____ Act Type 1 2 3 4	Document Title: _____ Act Type 1 2 3 4

Date		Time	AM	PM
1	**Full Name** ___ Signor ___ Witness _____ Address: _____	Verification Method DL PP Cred. Wit Other: _____ State: _____ Iss date: _____ Expiration: _____	Doc. Type ___ Paper ___ Electronic ___ Hybrid	Thumb Print
	Signature	Screening ___ Coherent ___ Consenting	Phone I Email	
2	**Full Name** ___ Signor ___ Witness _____ Address: _____	Verification Method DL PP Cred. Wit Other: _____ State: _____ Iss date: _____ Expiration: _____	Doc. Type ___ Paper ___ Electronic ___ Hybrid	Thumb Print
	Signature	Screening ___ Coherent ___ Consenting	Phone I Email	
3	**Full Name** ___ Signor ___ Witness _____ Address: _____	Verification Method DL PP Cred. Wit Other: _____ State: _____ Iss date: _____ Expiration: _____	Doc. Type ___ Paper ___ Electronic ___ Hybrid	Thumb Print
	Signature	Screening ___ Coherent ___ Consenting	Phone I Email	
4	**Full Name** ___ Signor ___ Witness _____ Address: _____	Verification Method DL PP Cred. Wit Other: _____ State: _____ Iss date: _____ Expiration: _____	Doc. Type ___ Paper ___ Electronic ___ Hybrid	Thumb Print
	Signature	Screening ___ Coherent ___ Consenting	Phone I Email	

Signing Location:	Observers:	Signing Service:	Fee:

Appointment Notes:

Record of Signed Documents: Loan Documents

Borrower's Affidavit	__ Ack __ Jurat 1 2 3 4	Disbursement of Proceeds	__ Ack __ Jurat 1 2 3 4
Compliance Agreement	__ Ack __ Jurat 1 2 3 4	Errors & Omissions Agreement	__ Ack __ Jurat 1 2 3 4
Correction Agreement	__ Ack __ Jurat 1 2 3 4	Financial Affidavit	__ Ack __ Jurat 1 2 3 4
Indemnity Debt/Lien Affidavit	__ Ack __ Jurat 1 2 3 4	Grant Deed	__ Ack __ Jurat 1 2 3 4
Deed of Trust	__ Ack __ Jurat 1 2 3 4	Marital Status Affidavit	__ Ack __ Jurat 1 2 3 4
Mortgage	__ Ack __ Jurat 1 2 3 4	Quit Claim Deed	__ Ack __ Jurat 1 2 3 4
Mortgagor's Affidavit	__ Ack __ Jurat 1 2 3 4	Signature/Name Affidavit	__ Ack __ Jurat 1 2 3 4
Occupancy Affidavit	__ Ack __ Jurat 1 2 3 4	Survey Affidavit	__ Ack __ Jurat 1 2 3 4
Owner's Affidavit	__ Ack __ Jurat 1 2 3 4	Warranty Deed	__ Ack __ Jurat 1 2 3 4
Payoff Affidavit	__ Ack __ Jurat 1 2 3 4	Other	__ Ack __ Jurat 1 2 3 4

Vehicle Docs:

Duplicate Title	__ Ack __ Jurat 1 2 3 4	Odometer/VIN Verification	__ Ack __ Jurat 1 2 3 4
Lien Release	__ Ack __ Jurat 1 2 3 4	Title Transfer	__ Ack __ Jurat 1 2 3 4

Wills/Trusts/ POA:

Living Trust	__ Ack __ Jurat 1 2 3 4	Power of Attorney	__ Ack __ Jurat 1 2 3 4
Last Will & Test	__ Ack __ Jurat 1 2 3 4	Trust Certification	__ Ack __ Jurat 1 2 3 4

Medical Docs:

Advance Healthcare Directive	__ Ack __ Jurat 1 2 3 4	HIPAA Release	__ Ack __ Jurat 1 2 3 4

Other Non-listed Docs:

Document Title: _____ Act Type 1 2 3 4		Document Title: _____ Act Type 1 2 3 4	
Document Title: _____ Act Type 1 2 3 4		Document Title: _____ Act Type 1 2 3 4	
Document Title: _____ Act Type 1 2 3 4		Document Title: _____ Act Type 1 2 3 4	
Document Title: _____ Act Type 1 2 3 4		Document Title: _____ Act Type 1 2 3 4	

Date			Time		AM	PM
1	Full Name ___ Signor ___ Witness		Verification Method DL PP Cred. Wit Other: _____ State: _____ Iss date: _____ Expiration: _____		Doc. Type ___ Paper ___ Electronic ___ Hybrid	Thumb Print
	_____					
	Address: _____					
	Signature		Screening ___ Coherent ___ Consenting		Phone I Email	
2	Full Name ___ Signor ___ Witness		Verification Method DL PP Cred. Wit Other: _____ State: _____ Iss date: _____ Expiration: _____		Doc. Type ___ Paper ___ Electronic ___ Hybrid	Thumb Print
	_____					
	Address: _____					
	Signature		Screening ___ Coherent ___ Consenting		Phone I Email	
3	Full Name ___ Signor ___ Witness		Verification Method DL PP Cred. Wit Other: _____ State: _____ Iss date: _____ Expiration: _____		Doc. Type ___ Paper ___ Electronic ___ Hybrid	Thumb Print
	_____					
	Address: _____					
	Signature		Screening ___ Coherent ___ Consenting		Phone I Email	
4	Full Name ___ Signor ___ Witness		Verification Method DL PP Cred. Wit Other: _____ State: _____ Iss date: _____ Expiration: _____		Doc. Type ___ Paper ___ Electronic ___ Hybrid	Thumb Print
	_____					
	Address: _____					
	Signature		Screening ___ Coherent ___ Consenting		Phone I Email	

Signing Location:	Observers:	Signing Service:	Fee:

Appointment Notes:

Record of Signed Documents: Loan Documents

Borrower's Affidavit	__ Ack __ Jurat 1 2 3 4	Disbursement of Proceeds	__ Ack __ Jurat 1 2 3 4
Compliance Agreement	__ Ack __ Jurat 1 2 3 4	Errors & Omissions Agreement	__ Ack __ Jurat 1 2 3 4
Correction Agreement	__ Ack __ Jurat 1 2 3 4	Financial Affidavit	__ Ack __ Jurat 1 2 3 4
Indemnity Debt/Lien Affidavit	__ Ack __ Jurat 1 2 3 4	Grant Deed	__ Ack __ Jurat 1 2 3 4
Deed of Trust	__ Ack __ Jurat 1 2 3 4	Marital Status Affidavit	__ Ack __ Jurat 1 2 3 4
Mortgage	__ Ack __ Jurat 1 2 3 4	Quit Claim Deed	__ Ack __ Jurat 1 2 3 4
Mortgagor's Affidavit	__ Ack __ Jurat 1 2 3 4	Signature/Name Affidavit	__ Ack __ Jurat 1 2 3 4
Occupancy Affidavit	__ Ack __ Jurat 1 2 3 4	Survey Affidavit	__ Ack __ Jurat 1 2 3 4
Owner's Affidavit	__ Ack __ Jurat 1 2 3 4	Warranty Deed	__ Ack __ Jurat 1 2 3 4
Payoff Affidavit	__ Ack __ Jurat 1 2 3 4	Other	__ Ack __ Jurat 1 2 3 4

Vehicle Docs:

Duplicate Title	__ Ack __ Jurat 1 2 3 4	Odometer/VIN Verification	__ Ack __ Jurat 1 2 3 4
Lien Release	__ Ack __ Jurat 1 2 3 4	Title Transfer	__ Ack __ Jurat 1 2 3 4

Wills/Trusts/ POA:

Living Trust	__ Ack __ Jurat 1 2 3 4	Power of Attorney	__ Ack __ Jurat 1 2 3 4
Last Will & Test	__ Ack __ Jurat 1 2 3 4	Trust Certification	__ Ack __ Jurat 1 2 3 4

Medical Docs:

Advance Healthcare Directive	__ Ack __ Jurat 1 2 3 4	HIPAA Release	__ Ack __ Jurat 1 2 3 4

Other Non-listed Docs:

Document Title: _____ Act Type 1 2 3 4		Document Title: _____ Act Type 1 2 3 4	
Document Title: _____ Act Type 1 2 3 4		Document Title: _____ Act Type 1 2 3 4	
Document Title: _____ Act Type 1 2 3 4		Document Title: _____ Act Type 1 2 3 4	
Document Title: _____ Act Type 1 2 3 4		Document Title: _____ Act Type 1 2 3 4	

Date			Time		AM	PM
1	Full Name ___ Signor ___ Witness _____ Address: _____		Verification Method DL PP Cred. Wit Other: _____ State: _____ Iss date: _____ Expiration: _____		Doc. Type ___ Paper ___ Electronic ___ Hybrid	Thumb Print
	Signature		Screening ___ Coherent ___ Consenting		Phone I Email	
2	Full Name ___ Signor ___ Witness _____ Address: _____		Verification Method DL PP Cred. Wit Other: _____ State: _____ Iss date: _____ Expiration: _____		Doc. Type ___ Paper ___ Electronic ___ Hybrid	Thumb Print
	Signature		Screening ___ Coherent ___ Consenting		Phone I Email	
3	Full Name ___ Signor ___ Witness _____ Address: _____		Verification Method DL PP Cred. Wit Other: _____ State: _____ Iss date: _____ Expiration: _____		Doc. Type ___ Paper ___ Electronic ___ Hybrid	Thumb Print
	Signature		Screening ___ Coherent ___ Consenting		Phone I Email	
4	Full Name ___ Signor ___ Witness _____ Address: _____		Verification Method DL PP Cred. Wit Other: _____ State: _____ Iss date: _____ Expiration: _____		Doc. Type ___ Paper ___ Electronic ___ Hybrid	Thumb Print
	Signature		Screening ___ Coherent ___ Consenting		Phone I Email	

Signing Location:	Observers:	Signing Service:	Fee:

Appointment Notes:

Record of Signed Documents: Loan Documents

Borrower's Affidavit	__ Ack __ Jurat 1 2 3 4	Disbursement of Proceeds	__ Ack __ Jurat 1 2 3 4
Compliance Agreement	__ Ack __ Jurat 1 2 3 4	Errors & Omissions Agreement	__ Ack __ Jurat 1 2 3 4
Correction Agreement	__ Ack __ Jurat 1 2 3 4	Financial Affidavit	__ Ack __ Jurat 1 2 3 4
Indemnity Debt/Lien Affidavit	__ Ack __ Jurat 1 2 3 4	Grant Deed	__ Ack __ Jurat 1 2 3 4
Deed of Trust	__ Ack __ Jurat 1 2 3 4	Marital Status Affidavit	__ Ack __ Jurat 1 2 3 4
Mortgage	__ Ack __ Jurat 1 2 3 4	Quit Claim Deed	__ Ack __ Jurat 1 2 3 4
Mortgagor's Affidavit	__ Ack __ Jurat 1 2 3 4	Signature/Name Affidavit	__ Ack __ Jurat 1 2 3 4
Occupancy Affidavit	__ Ack __ Jurat 1 2 3 4	Survey Affidavit	__ Ack __ Jurat 1 2 3 4
Owner's Affidavit	__ Ack __ Jurat 1 2 3 4	Warranty Deed	__ Ack __ Jurat 1 2 3 4
Payoff Affidavit	__ Ack __ Jurat 1 2 3 4	Other	__ Ack __ Jurat 1 2 3 4

Vehicle Docs:

Duplicate Title	__ Ack __ Jurat 1 2 3 4	Odometer/VIN Verification	__ Ack __ Jurat 1 2 3 4
Lien Release	__ Ack __ Jurat 1 2 3 4	Title Transfer	__ Ack __ Jurat 1 2 3 4

Wills/Trusts/ POA:

Living Trust	__ Ack __ Jurat 1 2 3 4	Power of Attorney	__ Ack __ Jurat 1 2 3 4
Last Will & Test	__ Ack __ Jurat 1 2 3 4	Trust Certification	__ Ack __ Jurat 1 2 3 4

Medical Docs:

Advance Healthcare Directive	__ Ack __ Jurat 1 2 3 4	HIPAA Release	__ Ack __ Jurat 1 2 3 4

Other Non-listed Docs:

Document Title: _____ Act Type 1 2 3 4	Document Title: _____ Act Type 1 2 3 4
Document Title: _____ Act Type 1 2 3 4	Document Title: _____ Act Type 1 2 3 4
Document Title: _____ Act Type 1 2 3 4	Document Title: _____ Act Type 1 2 3 4
Document Title: _____ Act Type 1 2 3 4	Document Title: _____ Act Type 1 2 3 4

Date				Time		AM	PM

Entry 1

Full Name ___ Signor ___ Witness	Verification Method	Doc. Type	Thumb Print
_____	DL PP Cred. Wit		
	Other: _____	___ Paper	
Address: _____	State: _____	___ Electronic	
	Iss date: _____	___ Hybrid	
	Expiration: _____		
Signature	Screening	Phone I Email	
	___ Coherent		
	___ Consenting		

Entry 2

Full Name ___ Signor ___ Witness	Verification Method	Doc. Type	Thumb Print
_____	DL PP Cred. Wit		
	Other: _____	___ Paper	
Address: _____	State: _____	___ Electronic	
	Iss date: _____	___ Hybrid	
	Expiration: _____		
Signature	Screening	Phone I Email	
	___ Coherent		
	___ Consenting		

Entry 3

Full Name ___ Signor ___ Witness	Verification Method	Doc. Type	Thumb Print
_____	DL PP Cred. Wit		
	Other: _____	___ Paper	
Address: _____	State: _____	___ Electronic	
	Iss date: _____	___ Hybrid	
	Expiration: _____		
Signature	Screening	Phone I Email	
	___ Coherent		
	___ Consenting		

Entry 4

Full Name ___ Signor ___ Witness	Verification Method	Doc. Type	Thumb Print
_____	DL PP Cred. Wit		
	Other: _____	___ Paper	
Address: _____	State: _____	___ Electronic	
	Iss date: _____	___ Hybrid	
	Expiration: _____		
Signature	Screening	Phone I Email	
	___ Coherent		
	___ Consenting		

Signing Location:	Observers:	Signing Service:	Fee:

Appointment Notes:

Record of Signed Documents: Loan Documents

Borrower's Affidavit	__ Ack __ Jurat 1 2 3 4	Disbursement of Proceeds	__ Ack __ Jurat 1 2 3 4
Compliance Agreement	__ Ack __ Jurat 1 2 3 4	Errors & Omissions Agreement	__ Ack __ Jurat 1 2 3 4
Correction Agreement	__ Ack __ Jurat 1 2 3 4	Financial Affidavit	__ Ack __ Jurat 1 2 3 4
Indemnity Debt/Lien Affidavit	__ Ack __ Jurat 1 2 3 4	Grant Deed	__ Ack __ Jurat 1 2 3 4
Deed of Trust	__ Ack __ Jurat 1 2 3 4	Marital Status Affidavit	__ Ack __ Jurat 1 2 3 4
Mortgage	__ Ack __ Jurat 1 2 3 4	Quit Claim Deed	__ Ack __ Jurat 1 2 3 4
Mortgagor's Affidavit	__ Ack __ Jurat 1 2 3 4	Signature/Name Affidavit	__ Ack __ Jurat 1 2 3 4
Occupancy Affidavit	__ Ack __ Jurat 1 2 3 4	Survey Affidavit	__ Ack __ Jurat 1 2 3 4
Owner's Affidavit	__ Ack __ Jurat 1 2 3 4	Warranty Deed	__ Ack __ Jurat 1 2 3 4
Payoff Affidavit	__ Ack __ Jurat 1 2 3 4	Other	__ Ack __ Jurat 1 2 3 4

Vehicle Docs:

Duplicate Title	__ Ack __ Jurat 1 2 3 4	Odometer/VIN Verification	__ Ack __ Jurat 1 2 3 4
Lien Release	__ Ack __ Jurat 1 2 3 4	Title Transfer	__ Ack __ Jurat 1 2 3 4

Wills/Trusts/ POA:

Living Trust	__ Ack __ Jurat 1 2 3 4	Power of Attorney	__ Ack __ Jurat 1 2 3 4
Last Will & Test	__ Ack __ Jurat 1 2 3 4	Trust Certification	__ Ack __ Jurat 1 2 3 4

Medical Docs:

Advance Healthcare Directive	__ Ack __ Jurat 1 2 3 4	HIPAA Release	__ Ack __ Jurat 1 2 3 4

Other Non-listed Docs:

Document Title: _____ Act Type 1 2 3 4	Document Title: _____ Act Type 1 2 3 4
Document Title: _____ Act Type 1 2 3 4	Document Title: _____ Act Type 1 2 3 4
Document Title: _____ Act Type 1 2 3 4	Document Title: _____ Act Type 1 2 3 4
Document Title: _____ Act Type 1 2 3 4	Document Title: _____ Act Type 1 2 3 4

Date				Time		AM	PM

1

Full Name ___ Signor ___ Witness	Verification Method	Doc. Type	Thumb Print
	DL PP Cred. Wit		
_____	Other: _____	___ Paper	
	State: _____	___ Electronic	
Address: _____	Iss date: _____	___ Hybrid	
	Expiration: _____		
Signature	Screening	Phone I Email	
	___ Coherent		
	___ Consenting		

2

Full Name ___ Signor ___ Witness	Verification Method	Doc. Type	Thumb Print
	DL PP Cred. Wit		
_____	Other: _____	___ Paper	
	State: _____	___ Electronic	
Address: _____	Iss date: _____	___ Hybrid	
	Expiration: _____		
Signature	Screening	Phone I Email	
	___ Coherent		
	___ Consenting		

3

Full Name ___ Signor ___ Witness	Verification Method	Doc. Type	Thumb Print
	DL PP Cred. Wit		
_____	Other: _____	___ Paper	
	State: _____	___ Electronic	
Address: _____	Iss date: _____	___ Hybrid	
	Expiration: _____		
Signature	Screening	Phone I Email	
	___ Coherent		
	___ Consenting		

4

Full Name ___ Signor ___ Witness	Verification Method	Doc. Type	Thumb Print
	DL PP Cred. Wit		
_____	Other: _____	___ Paper	
	State: _____	___ Electronic	
Address: _____	Iss date: _____	___ Hybrid	
	Expiration: _____		
Signature	Screening	Phone I Email	
	___ Coherent		
	___ Consenting		

Signing Location:	Observers:	Signing Service:	Fee:

Appointment Notes:

Record of Signed Documents: Loan Documents

Borrower's Affidavit	__ Ack __ Jurat 1 2 3 4	Disbursement of Proceeds	__ Ack __ Jurat 1 2 3 4
Compliance Agreement	__ Ack __ Jurat 1 2 3 4	Errors & Omissions Agreement	__ Ack __ Jurat 1 2 3 4
Correction Agreement	__ Ack __ Jurat 1 2 3 4	Financial Affidavit	__ Ack __ Jurat 1 2 3 4
Indemnity Debt/Lien Affidavit	__ Ack __ Jurat 1 2 3 4	Grant Deed	__ Ack __ Jurat 1 2 3 4
Deed of Trust	__ Ack __ Jurat 1 2 3 4	Marital Status Affidavit	__ Ack __ Jurat 1 2 3 4
Mortgage	__ Ack __ Jurat 1 2 3 4	Quit Claim Deed	__ Ack __ Jurat 1 2 3 4
Mortgagor's Affidavit	__ Ack __ Jurat 1 2 3 4	Signature/Name Affidavit	__ Ack __ Jurat 1 2 3 4
Occupancy Affidavit	__ Ack __ Jurat 1 2 3 4	Survey Affidavit	__ Ack __ Jurat 1 2 3 4
Owner's Affidavit	__ Ack __ Jurat 1 2 3 4	Warranty Deed	__ Ack __ Jurat 1 2 3 4
Payoff Affidavit	__ Ack __ Jurat 1 2 3 4	Other	__ Ack __ Jurat 1 2 3 4

Vehicle Docs:

Duplicate Title	__ Ack __ Jurat 1 2 3 4	Odometer/VIN Verification	__ Ack __ Jurat 1 2 3 4
Lien Release	__ Ack __ Jurat 1 2 3 4	Title Transfer	__ Ack __ Jurat 1 2 3 4

Wills/Trusts/ POA:

Living Trust	__ Ack __ Jurat 1 2 3 4	Power of Attorney	__ Ack __ Jurat 1 2 3 4
Last Will & Test	__ Ack __ Jurat 1 2 3 4	Trust Certification	__ Ack __ Jurat 1 2 3 4

Medical Docs:

Advance Healthcare Directive	__ Ack __ Jurat 1 2 3 4	HIPAA Release	__ Ack __ Jurat 1 2 3 4

Other Non-listed Docs:

Document Title: _____ Act Type 1 2 3 4	Document Title: _____ Act Type 1 2 3 4
Document Title: _____ Act Type 1 2 3 4	Document Title: _____ Act Type 1 2 3 4
Document Title: _____ Act Type 1 2 3 4	Document Title: _____ Act Type 1 2 3 4
Document Title: _____ Act Type 1 2 3 4	Document Title: _____ Act Type 1 2 3 4

Date			Time		AM	PM

1

Full Name ___ Signor ___ Witness	Verification Method DL PP Cred. Wit Other: _____ State: _____ Iss date: _____ Expiration: _____	Doc. Type ___ Paper ___ Electronic ___ Hybrid	Thumb Print
_____ Address: _____			
Signature	Screening ___ Coherent ___ Consenting	Phone I Email	

2

Full Name ___ Signor ___ Witness	Verification Method DL PP Cred. Wit Other: _____ State: _____ Iss date: _____ Expiration: _____	Doc. Type ___ Paper ___ Electronic ___ Hybrid	Thumb Print
_____ Address: _____			
Signature	Screening ___ Coherent ___ Consenting	Phone I Email	

3

Full Name ___ Signor ___ Witness	Verification Method DL PP Cred. Wit Other: _____ State: _____ Iss date: _____ Expiration: _____	Doc. Type ___ Paper ___ Electronic ___ Hybrid	Thumb Print
_____ Address: _____			
Signature	Screening ___ Coherent ___ Consenting	Phone I Email	

4

Full Name ___ Signor ___ Witness	Verification Method DL PP Cred. Wit Other: _____ State: _____ Iss date: _____ Expiration: _____	Doc. Type ___ Paper ___ Electronic ___ Hybrid	Thumb Print
_____ Address: _____			
Signature	Screening ___ Coherent ___ Consenting	Phone I Email	

Signing Location:	Observers:	Signing Service:	Fee:

Appointment Notes:

Record of Signed Documents: Loan Documents

Document	Act	Disbursement	Act
Borrower's Affidavit	__ Ack __ Jurat 1 2 3 4	Disbursement of Proceeds	__ Ack __ Jurat 1 2 3 4
Compliance Agreement	__ Ack __ Jurat 1 2 3 4	Errors & Omissions Agreement	__ Ack __ Jurat 1 2 3 4
Correction Agreement	__ Ack __ Jurat 1 2 3 4	Financial Affidavit	__ Ack __ Jurat 1 2 3 4
Indemnity Debt/Lien Affidavit	__ Ack __ Jurat 1 2 3 4	Grant Deed	__ Ack __ Jurat 1 2 3 4
Deed of Trust	__ Ack __ Jurat 1 2 3 4	Marital Status Affidavit	__ Ack __ Jurat 1 2 3 4
Mortgage	__ Ack __ Jurat 1 2 3 4	Quit Claim Deed	__ Ack __ Jurat 1 2 3 4
Mortgagor's Affidavit	__ Ack __ Jurat 1 2 3 4	Signature/Name Affidavit	__ Ack __ Jurat 1 2 3 4
Occupancy Affidavit	__ Ack __ Jurat 1 2 3 4	Survey Affidavit	__ Ack __ Jurat 1 2 3 4
Owner's Affidavit	__ Ack __ Jurat 1 2 3 4	Warranty Deed	__ Ack __ Jurat 1 2 3 4
Payoff Affidavit	__ Ack __ Jurat 1 2 3 4	Other	__ Ack __ Jurat 1 2 3 4

Vehicle Docs:

Document	Act	Document	Act
Duplicate Title	__ Ack __ Jurat 1 2 3 4	Odometer/VIN Verification	__ Ack __ Jurat 1 2 3 4
Lien Release	__ Ack __ Jurat 1 2 3 4	Title Transfer	__ Ack __ Jurat 1 2 3 4

Wills/Trusts/ POA:

Document	Act	Document	Act
Living Trust	__ Ack __ Jurat 1 2 3 4	Power of Attorney	__ Ack __ Jurat 1 2 3 4
Last Will & Test	__ Ack __ Jurat 1 2 3 4	Trust Certification	__ Ack __ Jurat 1 2 3 4

Medical Docs:

Document	Act	Document	Act
Advance Healthcare Directive	__ Ack __ Jurat 1 2 3 4	HIPAA Release	__ Ack __ Jurat 1 2 3 4

Other Non-listed Docs:

Document Title:	Act Type	Document Title:	Act Type
Document Title: _____ 1 2 3 4	Act Type	Document Title: _____ 1 2 3 4	Act Type
Document Title: _____ 1 2 3 4	Act Type	Document Title: _____ 1 2 3 4	Act Type
Document Title: _____ 1 2 3 4	Act Type	Document Title: _____ 1 2 3 4	Act Type
Document Title: _____ 1 2 3 4	Act Type	Document Title: _____ 1 2 3 4	Act Type

Date		Time	AM	PM
1	**Full Name** ___ Signor ___ Witness _____ Address: _____	**Verification Method** DL PP Cred. Wit Other: _____ State: _____ Iss date: _____ Expiration: _____	**Doc. Type** ___ Paper ___ Electronic ___ Hybrid	Thumb Print
	Signature	Screening ___ Coherent ___ Consenting	Phone I Email	
2	**Full Name** ___ Signor ___ Witness _____ Address: _____	**Verification Method** DL PP Cred. Wit Other: _____ State: _____ Iss date: _____ Expiration: _____	**Doc. Type** ___ Paper ___ Electronic ___ Hybrid	Thumb Print
	Signature	Screening ___ Coherent ___ Consenting	Phone I Email	
3	**Full Name** ___ Signor ___ Witness _____ Address: _____	**Verification Method** DL PP Cred. Wit Other: _____ State: _____ Iss date: _____ Expiration: _____	**Doc. Type** ___ Paper ___ Electronic ___ Hybrid	Thumb Print
	Signature	Screening ___ Coherent ___ Consenting	Phone I Email	
4	**Full Name** ___ Signor ___ Witness _____ Address: _____	**Verification Method** DL PP Cred. Wit Other: _____ State: _____ Iss date: _____ Expiration: _____	**Doc. Type** ___ Paper ___ Electronic ___ Hybrid	Thumb Print
	Signature	Screening ___ Coherent ___ Consenting	Phone I Email	

Signing Location:	Observers:	Signing Service:	Fee:

Appointment Notes:

Record of Signed Documents: Loan Documents

Borrower's Affidavit	__ Ack __ Jurat 1 2 3 4	Disbursement of Proceeds	__ Ack __ Jurat 1 2 3 4
Compliance Agreement	__ Ack __ Jurat 1 2 3 4	Errors & Omissions Agreement	__ Ack __ Jurat 1 2 3 4
Correction Agreement	__ Ack __ Jurat 1 2 3 4	Financial Affidavit	__ Ack __ Jurat 1 2 3 4
Indemnity Debt/Lien Affidavit	__ Ack __ Jurat 1 2 3 4	Grant Deed	__ Ack __ Jurat 1 2 3 4
Deed of Trust	__ Ack __ Jurat 1 2 3 4	Marital Status Affidavit	__ Ack __ Jurat 1 2 3 4
Mortgage	__ Ack __ Jurat 1 2 3 4	Quit Claim Deed	__ Ack __ Jurat 1 2 3 4
Mortgagor's Affidavit	__ Ack __ Jurat 1 2 3 4	Signature/Name Affidavit	__ Ack __ Jurat 1 2 3 4
Occupancy Affidavit	__ Ack __ Jurat 1 2 3 4	Survey Affidavit	__ Ack __ Jurat 1 2 3 4
Owner's Affidavit	__ Ack __ Jurat 1 2 3 4	Warranty Deed	__ Ack __ Jurat 1 2 3 4
Payoff Affidavit	__ Ack __ Jurat 1 2 3 4	Other	__ Ack __ Jurat 1 2 3 4

Vehicle Docs:

Duplicate Title	__ Ack __ Jurat 1 2 3 4	Odometer/VIN Verification	__ Ack __ Jurat 1 2 3 4
Lien Release	__ Ack __ Jurat 1 2 3 4	Title Transfer	__ Ack __ Jurat 1 2 3 4

Wills/Trusts/ POA:

Living Trust	__ Ack __ Jurat 1 2 3 4	Power of Attorney	__ Ack __ Jurat 1 2 3 4
Last Will & Test	__ Ack __ Jurat 1 2 3 4	Trust Certification	__ Ack __ Jurat 1 2 3 4

Medical Docs:

Advance Healthcare Directive	__ Ack __ Jurat 1 2 3 4	HIPAA Release	__ Ack __ Jurat 1 2 3 4

Other Non-listed Docs:

Document Title: _____ Act Type 1 2 3 4	Document Title: _____ Act Type 1 2 3 4
Document Title: _____ Act Type 1 2 3 4	Document Title: _____ Act Type 1 2 3 4
Document Title: _____ Act Type 1 2 3 4	Document Title: _____ Act Type 1 2 3 4
Document Title: _____ Act Type 1 2 3 4	Document Title: _____ Act Type 1 2 3 4

Date			Time		AM	PM

| 1 | **Full Name** ___ Signor ___ Witness

_____

Address: _____ | | **Verification Method**
DL   PP   Cred. Wit
Other: _____
State: _____
Iss date: _____
Expiration: _____ | | **Doc. Type**

___ Paper
___ Electronic
___ Hybrid | **Thumb Print** |
| | **Signature** | | **Screening**
___ Coherent
___ Consenting | | **Phone I Email** | |

| 2 | **Full Name** ___ Signor ___ Witness

_____

Address: _____ | | **Verification Method**
DL   PP   Cred. Wit
Other: _____
State: _____
Iss date: _____
Expiration: _____ | | **Doc. Type**

___ Paper
___ Electronic
___ Hybrid | **Thumb Print** |
| | **Signature** | | **Screening**
___ Coherent
___ Consenting | | **Phone I Email** | |

| 3 | **Full Name** ___ Signor ___ Witness

_____

Address: _____ | | **Verification Method**
DL   PP   Cred. Wit
Other: _____
State: _____
Iss date: _____
Expiration: _____ | | **Doc. Type**

___ Paper
___ Electronic
___ Hybrid | **Thumb Print** |
| | **Signature** | | **Screening**
___ Coherent
___ Consenting | | **Phone I Email** | |

| 4 | **Full Name** ___ Signor ___ Witness

_____

Address: _____ | | **Verification Method**
DL   PP   Cred. Wit
Other: _____
State: _____
Iss date: _____
Expiration: _____ | | **Doc. Type**

___ Paper
___ Electronic
___ Hybrid | **Thumb Print** |
| | **Signature** | | **Screening**
___ Coherent
___ Consenting | | **Phone I Email** | |

Signing Location:	Observers:	Signing Service:	Fee:

Appointment Notes:

Record of Signed Documents: Loan Documents

Borrower's Affidavit	__ Ack __ Jurat 1 2 3 4	Disbursement of Proceeds	__ Ack __ Jurat 1 2 3 4
Compliance Agreement	__ Ack __ Jurat 1 2 3 4	Errors & Omissions Agreement	__ Ack __ Jurat 1 2 3 4
Correction Agreement	__ Ack __ Jurat 1 2 3 4	Financial Affidavit	__ Ack __ Jurat 1 2 3 4
Indemnity Debt/Lien Affidavit	__ Ack __ Jurat 1 2 3 4	Grant Deed	__ Ack __ Jurat 1 2 3 4
Deed of Trust	__ Ack __ Jurat 1 2 3 4	Marital Status Affidavit	__ Ack __ Jurat 1 2 3 4
Mortgage	__ Ack __ Jurat 1 2 3 4	Quit Claim Deed	__ Ack __ Jurat 1 2 3 4
Mortgagor's Affidavit	__ Ack __ Jurat 1 2 3 4	Signature/Name Affidavit	__ Ack __ Jurat 1 2 3 4
Occupancy Affidavit	__ Ack __ Jurat 1 2 3 4	Survey Affidavit	__ Ack __ Jurat 1 2 3 4
Owner's Affidavit	__ Ack __ Jurat 1 2 3 4	Warranty Deed	__ Ack __ Jurat 1 2 3 4
Payoff Affidavit	__ Ack __ Jurat 1 2 3 4	Other	__ Ack __ Jurat 1 2 3 4

Vehicle Docs:

Duplicate Title	__ Ack __ Jurat 1 2 3 4	Odometer/VIN Verification	__ Ack __ Jurat 1 2 3 4
Lien Release	__ Ack __ Jurat 1 2 3 4	Title Transfer	__ Ack __ Jurat 1 2 3 4

Wills/Trusts/ POA:

Living Trust	__ Ack __ Jurat 1 2 3 4	Power of Attorney	__ Ack __ Jurat 1 2 3 4
Last Will & Test	__ Ack __ Jurat 1 2 3 4	Trust Certification	__ Ack __ Jurat 1 2 3 4

Medical Docs:

Advance Healthcare Directive	__ Ack __ Jurat 1 2 3 4	HIPAA Release	__ Ack __ Jurat 1 2 3 4

Other Non-listed Docs:

Document Title: _____ Act Type 1 2 3 4		Document Title: _____ Act Type 1 2 3 4	
Document Title: _____ Act Type 1 2 3 4		Document Title: _____ Act Type 1 2 3 4	
Document Title: _____ Act Type 1 2 3 4		Document Title: _____ Act Type 1 2 3 4	
Document Title: _____ Act Type 1 2 3 4		Document Title: _____ Act Type 1 2 3 4	

Date		Time	AM	PM
1	**Full Name** ___ Signor ___ Witness _____ Address: _____	Verification Method DL PP Cred. Wit Other: _____ State: _____ Iss date: _____ Expiration: _____	Doc. Type ___ Paper ___ Electronic ___ Hybrid	Thumb Print
	Signature	Screening ___ Coherent ___ Consenting	Phone I Email	
2	**Full Name** ___ Signor ___ Witness _____ Address: _____	Verification Method DL PP Cred. Wit Other: _____ State: _____ Iss date: _____ Expiration: _____	Doc. Type ___ Paper ___ Electronic ___ Hybrid	Thumb Print
	Signature	Screening ___ Coherent ___ Consenting	Phone I Email	
3	**Full Name** ___ Signor ___ Witness _____ Address: _____	Verification Method DL PP Cred. Wit Other: _____ State: _____ Iss date: _____ Expiration: _____	Doc. Type ___ Paper ___ Electronic ___ Hybrid	Thumb Print
	Signature	Screening ___ Coherent ___ Consenting	Phone I Email	
4	**Full Name** ___ Signor ___ Witness _____ Address: _____	Verification Method DL PP Cred. Wit Other: _____ State: _____ Iss date: _____ Expiration: _____	Doc. Type ___ Paper ___ Electronic ___ Hybrid	Thumb Print
	Signature	Screening ___ Coherent ___ Consenting	Phone I Email	

Signing Location:	Observers:	Signing Service:	Fee:

Appointment Notes:

Record of Signed Documents: Loan Documents

Borrower's Affidavit	__ Ack __ Jurat 1 2 3 4	Disbursement of Proceeds	__ Ack __ Jurat 1 2 3 4
Compliance Agreement	__ Ack __ Jurat 1 2 3 4	Errors & Omissions Agreement	__ Ack __ Jurat 1 2 3 4
Correction Agreement	__ Ack __ Jurat 1 2 3 4	Financial Affidavit	__ Ack __ Jurat 1 2 3 4
Indemnity Debt/Lien Affidavit	__ Ack __ Jurat 1 2 3 4	Grant Deed	__ Ack __ Jurat 1 2 3 4
Deed of Trust	__ Ack __ Jurat 1 2 3 4	Marital Status Affidavit	__ Ack __ Jurat 1 2 3 4
Mortgage	__ Ack __ Jurat 1 2 3 4	Quit Claim Deed	__ Ack __ Jurat 1 2 3 4
Mortgagor's Affidavit	__ Ack __ Jurat 1 2 3 4	Signature/Name Affidavit	__ Ack __ Jurat 1 2 3 4
Occupancy Affidavit	__ Ack __ Jurat 1 2 3 4	Survey Affidavit	__ Ack __ Jurat 1 2 3 4
Owner's Affidavit	__ Ack __ Jurat 1 2 3 4	Warranty Deed	__ Ack __ Jurat 1 2 3 4
Payoff Affidavit	__ Ack __ Jurat 1 2 3 4	Other	__ Ack __ Jurat 1 2 3 4

Vehicle Docs:

Duplicate Title	__ Ack __ Jurat 1 2 3 4	Odometer/VIN Verification	__ Ack __ Jurat 1 2 3 4
Lien Release	__ Ack __ Jurat 1 2 3 4	Title Transfer	__ Ack __ Jurat 1 2 3 4

Wills/Trusts/ POA:

Living Trust	__ Ack __ Jurat 1 2 3 4	Power of Attorney	__ Ack __ Jurat 1 2 3 4
Last Will & Test	__ Ack __ Jurat 1 2 3 4	Trust Certification	__ Ack __ Jurat 1 2 3 4

Medical Docs:

Advance Healthcare Directive	__ Ack __ Jurat 1 2 3 4	HIPAA Release	__ Ack __ Jurat 1 2 3 4

Other Non-listed Docs:

Document Title: _____ Act Type 1 2 3 4	Document Title: _____ Act Type 1 2 3 4
Document Title: _____ Act Type 1 2 3 4	Document Title: _____ Act Type 1 2 3 4
Document Title: _____ Act Type 1 2 3 4	Document Title: _____ Act Type 1 2 3 4
Document Title: _____ Act Type 1 2 3 4	Document Title: _____ Act Type 1 2 3 4

Date		Time		AM	PM

	Full Name ___ Signor ___ Witness	Verification Method DL PP Cred. Wit	Doc. Type	Thumb Print
1	_____ Address: _____	Other: _____ State: _____ Iss date: _____ Expiration: _____	___ Paper ___ Electronic ___ Hybrid	
	Signature	Screening ___ Coherent ___ Consenting	Phone I Email	

	Full Name ___ Signor ___ Witness	Verification Method DL PP Cred. Wit	Doc. Type	Thumb Print
2	_____ Address: _____	Other: _____ State: _____ Iss date: _____ Expiration: _____	___ Paper ___ Electronic ___ Hybrid	
	Signature	Screening ___ Coherent ___ Consenting	Phone I Email	

	Full Name ___ Signor ___ Witness	Verification Method DL PP Cred. Wit	Doc. Type	Thumb Print
3	_____ Address: _____	Other: _____ State: _____ Iss date: _____ Expiration: _____	___ Paper ___ Electronic ___ Hybrid	
	Signature	Screening ___ Coherent ___ Consenting	Phone I Email	

	Full Name ___ Signor ___ Witness	Verification Method DL PP Cred. Wit	Doc. Type	Thumb Print
4	_____ Address: _____	Other: _____ State: _____ Iss date: _____ Expiration: _____	___ Paper ___ Electronic ___ Hybrid	
	Signature	Screening ___ Coherent ___ Consenting	Phone I Email	

Signing Location:	Observers:	Signing Service:	Fee:

Appointment Notes:

Record of Signed Documents: Loan Documents

Borrower's Affidavit	__ Ack __ Jurat 1 2 3 4	Disbursement of Proceeds	__ Ack __ Jurat 1 2 3 4
Compliance Agreement	__ Ack __ Jurat 1 2 3 4	Errors & Omissions Agreement	__ Ack __ Jurat 1 2 3 4
Correction Agreement	__ Ack __ Jurat 1 2 3 4	Financial Affidavit	__ Ack __ Jurat 1 2 3 4
Indemnity Debt/Lien Affidavit	__ Ack __ Jurat 1 2 3 4	Grant Deed	__ Ack __ Jurat 1 2 3 4
Deed of Trust	__ Ack __ Jurat 1 2 3 4	Marital Status Affidavit	__ Ack __ Jurat 1 2 3 4
Mortgage	__ Ack __ Jurat 1 2 3 4	Quit Claim Deed	__ Ack __ Jurat 1 2 3 4
Mortgagor's Affidavit	__ Ack __ Jurat 1 2 3 4	Signature/Name Affidavit	__ Ack __ Jurat 1 2 3 4
Occupancy Affidavit	__ Ack __ Jurat 1 2 3 4	Survey Affidavit	__ Ack __ Jurat 1 2 3 4
Owner's Affidavit	__ Ack __ Jurat 1 2 3 4	Warranty Deed	__ Ack __ Jurat 1 2 3 4
Payoff Affidavit	__ Ack __ Jurat 1 2 3 4	Other	__ Ack __ Jurat 1 2 3 4

Vehicle Docs:

Duplicate Title	__ Ack __ Jurat 1 2 3 4	Odometer/VIN Verification	__ Ack __ Jurat 1 2 3 4
Lien Release	__ Ack __ Jurat 1 2 3 4	Title Transfer	__ Ack __ Jurat 1 2 3 4

Wills/Trusts/ POA:

Living Trust	__ Ack __ Jurat 1 2 3 4	Power of Attorney	__ Ack __ Jurat 1 2 3 4
Last Will & Test	__ Ack __ Jurat 1 2 3 4	Trust Certification	__ Ack __ Jurat 1 2 3 4

Medical Docs:

Advance Healthcare Directive	__ Ack __ Jurat 1 2 3 4	HIPAA Release	__ Ack __ Jurat 1 2 3 4

Other Non-listed Docs:

Document Title: _____ Act Type 1 2 3 4	Document Title: _____ Act Type 1 2 3 4
Document Title: _____ Act Type 1 2 3 4	Document Title: _____ Act Type 1 2 3 4
Document Title: _____ Act Type 1 2 3 4	Document Title: _____ Act Type 1 2 3 4
Document Title: _____ Act Type 1 2 3 4	Document Title: _____ Act Type 1 2 3 4

Date			Time	AM	PM

1	Full Name ___ Signor ___ Witness _____ Address: _____		Verification Method DL PP Cred. Wit Other: _____ State: _____ Iss date: _____ Expiration: _____	Doc. Type ___ Paper ___ Electronic ___ Hybrid	Thumb Print
	Signature		Screening ___ Coherent ___ Consenting	Phone I Email	
2	Full Name ___ Signor ___ Witness _____ Address: _____		Verification Method DL PP Cred. Wit Other: _____ State: _____ Iss date: _____ Expiration: _____	Doc. Type ___ Paper ___ Electronic ___ Hybrid	Thumb Print
	Signature		Screening ___ Coherent ___ Consenting	Phone I Email	
3	Full Name ___ Signor ___ Witness _____ Address: _____		Verification Method DL PP Cred. Wit Other: _____ State: _____ Iss date: _____ Expiration: _____	Doc. Type ___ Paper ___ Electronic ___ Hybrid	Thumb Print
	Signature		Screening ___ Coherent ___ Consenting	Phone I Email	
4	Full Name ___ Signor ___ Witness _____ Address: _____		Verification Method DL PP Cred. Wit Other: _____ State: _____ Iss date: _____ Expiration: _____	Doc. Type ___ Paper ___ Electronic ___ Hybrid	Thumb Print
	Signature		Screening ___ Coherent ___ Consenting	Phone I Email	

Signing Location:	Observers:	Signing Service:	Fee:

Appointment Notes:

Record of Signed Documents: Loan Documents

Borrower's Affidavit	__ Ack __ Jurat 1 2 3 4	Disbursement of Proceeds	__ Ack __ Jurat 1 2 3 4
Compliance Agreement	__ Ack __ Jurat 1 2 3 4	Errors & Omissions Agreement	__ Ack __ Jurat 1 2 3 4
Correction Agreement	__ Ack __ Jurat 1 2 3 4	Financial Affidavit	__ Ack __ Jurat 1 2 3 4
Indemnity Debt/Lien Affidavit	__ Ack __ Jurat 1 2 3 4	Grant Deed	__ Ack __ Jurat 1 2 3 4
Deed of Trust	__ Ack __ Jurat 1 2 3 4	Marital Status Affidavit	__ Ack __ Jurat 1 2 3 4
Mortgage	__ Ack __ Jurat 1 2 3 4	Quit Claim Deed	__ Ack __ Jurat 1 2 3 4
Mortgagor's Affidavit	__ Ack __ Jurat 1 2 3 4	Signature/Name Affidavit	__ Ack __ Jurat 1 2 3 4
Occupancy Affidavit	__ Ack __ Jurat 1 2 3 4	Survey Affidavit	__ Ack __ Jurat 1 2 3 4
Owner's Affidavit	__ Ack __ Jurat 1 2 3 4	Warranty Deed	__ Ack __ Jurat 1 2 3 4
Payoff Affidavit	__ Ack __ Jurat 1 2 3 4	Other	__ Ack __ Jurat 1 2 3 4

Vehicle Docs:

Duplicate Title	__ Ack __ Jurat 1 2 3 4	Odometer/VIN Verification	__ Ack __ Jurat 1 2 3 4
Lien Release	__ Ack __ Jurat 1 2 3 4	Title Transfer	__ Ack __ Jurat 1 2 3 4

Wills/Trusts/ POA:

Living Trust	__ Ack __ Jurat 1 2 3 4	Power of Attorney	__ Ack __ Jurat 1 2 3 4
Last Will & Test	__ Ack __ Jurat 1 2 3 4	Trust Certification	__ Ack __ Jurat 1 2 3 4

Medical Docs:

Advance Healthcare Directive	__ Ack __ Jurat 1 2 3 4	HIPAA Release	__ Ack __ Jurat 1 2 3 4

Other Non-listed Docs:

Document Title: _____ Act Type 1 2 3 4	Document Title: _____ Act Type 1 2 3 4
Document Title: _____ Act Type 1 2 3 4	Document Title: _____ Act Type 1 2 3 4
Document Title: _____ Act Type 1 2 3 4	Document Title: _____ Act Type 1 2 3 4
Document Title: _____ Act Type 1 2 3 4	Document Title: _____ Act Type 1 2 3 4

Date		Time		AM	PM

| 1 | Full Name ___ Signor ___ Witness

_____

Address: _____ | Verification Method
DL   PP   Cred. Wit
Other: _____
State: _____
Iss date: _____
Expiration: _____ | Doc. Type

___ Paper
___ Electronic
___ Hybrid | Thumb Print |
| | Signature | Screening
___ Coherent
___ Consenting | Phone I Email | |

| 2 | Full Name ___ Signor ___ Witness

_____

Address: _____ | Verification Method
DL   PP   Cred. Wit
Other: _____
State: _____
Iss date: _____
Expiration: _____ | Doc. Type

___ Paper
___ Electronic
___ Hybrid | Thumb Print |
| | Signature | Screening
___ Coherent
___ Consenting | Phone I Email | |

| 3 | Full Name ___ Signor ___ Witness

_____

Address: _____ | Verification Method
DL   PP   Cred. Wit
Other: _____
State: _____
Iss date: _____
Expiration: _____ | Doc. Type

___ Paper
___ Electronic
___ Hybrid | Thumb Print |
| | Signature | Screening
___ Coherent
___ Consenting | Phone I Email | |

| 4 | Full Name ___ Signor ___ Witness

_____

Address: _____ | Verification Method
DL   PP   Cred. Wit
Other: _____
State: _____
Iss date: _____
Expiration: _____ | Doc. Type

___ Paper
___ Electronic
___ Hybrid | Thumb Print |
| | Signature | Screening
___ Coherent
___ Consenting | Phone I Email | |

Signing Location:	Observers:	Signing Service:	Fee:

Appointment Notes:

Record of Signed Documents: Loan Documents

Borrower's Affidavit	__ Ack __ Jurat 1 2 3 4	Disbursement of Proceeds	__ Ack __ Jurat 1 2 3 4
Compliance Agreement	__ Ack __ Jurat 1 2 3 4	Errors & Omissions Agreement	__ Ack __ Jurat 1 2 3 4
Correction Agreement	__ Ack __ Jurat 1 2 3 4	Financial Affidavit	__ Ack __ Jurat 1 2 3 4
Indemnity Debt/Lien Affidavit	__ Ack __ Jurat 1 2 3 4	Grant Deed	__ Ack __ Jurat 1 2 3 4
Deed of Trust	__ Ack __ Jurat 1 2 3 4	Marital Status Affidavit	__ Ack __ Jurat 1 2 3 4
Mortgage	__ Ack __ Jurat 1 2 3 4	Quit Claim Deed	__ Ack __ Jurat 1 2 3 4
Mortgagor's Affidavit	__ Ack __ Jurat 1 2 3 4	Signature/Name Affidavit	__ Ack __ Jurat 1 2 3 4
Occupancy Affidavit	__ Ack __ Jurat 1 2 3 4	Survey Affidavit	__ Ack __ Jurat 1 2 3 4
Owner's Affidavit	__ Ack __ Jurat 1 2 3 4	Warranty Deed	__ Ack __ Jurat 1 2 3 4
Payoff Affidavit	__ Ack __ Jurat 1 2 3 4	Other	__ Ack __ Jurat 1 2 3 4

Vehicle Docs:

Duplicate Title	__ Ack __ Jurat 1 2 3 4	Odometer/VIN Verification	__ Ack __ Jurat 1 2 3 4
Lien Release	__ Ack __ Jurat 1 2 3 4	Title Transfer	__ Ack __ Jurat 1 2 3 4

Wills/Trusts/ POA:

Living Trust	__ Ack __ Jurat 1 2 3 4	Power of Attorney	__ Ack __ Jurat 1 2 3 4
Last Will & Test	__ Ack __ Jurat 1 2 3 4	Trust Certification	__ Ack __ Jurat 1 2 3 4

Medical Docs:

Advance Healthcare Directive	__ Ack __ Jurat 1 2 3 4	HIPAA Release	__ Ack __ Jurat 1 2 3 4

Other Non-listed Docs:

Document Title: _____ Act Type 1 2 3 4	Document Title: _____ Act Type 1 2 3 4
Document Title: _____ Act Type 1 2 3 4	Document Title: _____ Act Type 1 2 3 4
Document Title: _____ Act Type 1 2 3 4	Document Title: _____ Act Type 1 2 3 4
Document Title: _____ Act Type 1 2 3 4	Document Title: _____ Act Type 1 2 3 4

Date		Time	AM	PM

| 1 | Full Name ___ Signor ___ Witness

_____

Address: _____ | Verification Method
DL   PP   Cred. Wit
Other: _____
State: _____
Iss date: _____
Expiration: _____ | Doc. Type

___ Paper
___ Electronic
___ Hybrid | Thumb Print |
| | Signature | Screening
___ Coherent
___ Consenting | Phone I Email | |

| 2 | Full Name ___ Signor ___ Witness

_____

Address: _____ | Verification Method
DL   PP   Cred. Wit
Other: _____
State: _____
Iss date: _____
Expiration: _____ | Doc. Type

___ Paper
___ Electronic
___ Hybrid | Thumb Print |
| | Signature | Screening
___ Coherent
___ Consenting | Phone I Email | |

| 3 | Full Name ___ Signor ___ Witness

_____

Address: _____ | Verification Method
DL   PP   Cred. Wit
Other: _____
State: _____
Iss date: _____
Expiration: _____ | Doc. Type

___ Paper
___ Electronic
___ Hybrid | Thumb Print |
| | Signature | Screening
___ Coherent
___ Consenting | Phone I Email | |

| 4 | Full Name ___ Signor ___ Witness

_____

Address: _____ | Verification Method
DL   PP   Cred. Wit
Other: _____
State: _____
Iss date: _____
Expiration: _____ | Doc. Type

___ Paper
___ Electronic
___ Hybrid | Thumb Print |
| | Signature | Screening
___ Coherent
___ Consenting | Phone I Email | |

Signing Location:	Observers:	Signing Service:	Fee:

Appointment Notes:

Record of Signed Documents: Loan Documents

Borrower's Affidavit	__ Ack __ Jurat 1 2 3 4	Disbursement of Proceeds	__ Ack __ Jurat 1 2 3 4
Compliance Agreement	__ Ack __ Jurat 1 2 3 4	Errors & Omissions Agreement	__ Ack __ Jurat 1 2 3 4
Correction Agreement	__ Ack __ Jurat 1 2 3 4	Financial Affidavit	__ Ack __ Jurat 1 2 3 4
Indemnity Debt/Lien Affidavit	__ Ack __ Jurat 1 2 3 4	Grant Deed	__ Ack __ Jurat 1 2 3 4
Deed of Trust	__ Ack __ Jurat 1 2 3 4	Marital Status Affidavit	__ Ack __ Jurat 1 2 3 4
Mortgage	__ Ack __ Jurat 1 2 3 4	Quit Claim Deed	__ Ack __ Jurat 1 2 3 4
Mortgagor's Affidavit	__ Ack __ Jurat 1 2 3 4	Signature/Name Affidavit	__ Ack __ Jurat 1 2 3 4
Occupancy Affidavit	__ Ack __ Jurat 1 2 3 4	Survey Affidavit	__ Ack __ Jurat 1 2 3 4
Owner's Affidavit	__ Ack __ Jurat 1 2 3 4	Warranty Deed	__ Ack __ Jurat 1 2 3 4
Payoff Affidavit	__ Ack __ Jurat 1 2 3 4	Other	__ Ack __ Jurat 1 2 3 4

Vehicle Docs:

Duplicate Title	__ Ack __ Jurat 1 2 3 4	Odometer/VIN Verification	__ Ack __ Jurat 1 2 3 4
Lien Release	__ Ack __ Jurat 1 2 3 4	Title Transfer	__ Ack __ Jurat 1 2 3 4

Wills/Trusts/ POA:

Living Trust	__ Ack __ Jurat 1 2 3 4	Power of Attorney	__ Ack __ Jurat 1 2 3 4
Last Will & Test	__ Ack __ Jurat 1 2 3 4	Trust Certification	__ Ack __ Jurat 1 2 3 4

Medical Docs:

Advance Healthcare Directive	__ Ack __ Jurat 1 2 3 4	HIPAA Release	__ Ack __ Jurat 1 2 3 4

Other Non-listed Docs:

Document Title: _____ Act Type 1 2 3 4	Document Title: _____ Act Type 1 2 3 4
Document Title: _____ Act Type 1 2 3 4	Document Title: _____ Act Type 1 2 3 4
Document Title: _____ Act Type 1 2 3 4	Document Title: _____ Act Type 1 2 3 4
Document Title: _____ Act Type 1 2 3 4	Document Title: _____ Act Type 1 2 3 4

Date			Time		AM	PM

	Full Name ___ Signor ___ Witness	Verification Method DL PP Cred. Wit Other: _____ State: _____ Iss date: _____ Expiration: _____	Doc. Type ___ Paper ___ Electronic ___ Hybrid	Thumb Print
1	Address: _____			
	Signature	Screening ___ Coherent ___ Consenting	Phone I Email	

	Full Name ___ Signor ___ Witness	Verification Method DL PP Cred. Wit Other: _____ State: _____ Iss date: _____ Expiration: _____	Doc. Type ___ Paper ___ Electronic ___ Hybrid	Thumb Print
2	Address: _____			
	Signature	Screening ___ Coherent ___ Consenting	Phone I Email	

	Full Name ___ Signor ___ Witness	Verification Method DL PP Cred. Wit Other: _____ State: _____ Iss date: _____ Expiration: _____	Doc. Type ___ Paper ___ Electronic ___ Hybrid	Thumb Print
3	Address: _____			
	Signature	Screening ___ Coherent ___ Consenting	Phone I Email	

	Full Name ___ Signor ___ Witness	Verification Method DL PP Cred. Wit Other: _____ State: _____ Iss date: _____ Expiration: _____	Doc. Type ___ Paper ___ Electronic ___ Hybrid	Thumb Print
4	Address: _____			
	Signature	Screening ___ Coherent ___ Consenting	Phone I Email	

Signing Location:	Observers:	Signing Service:	Fee:

Appointment Notes:

Record of Signed Documents: Loan Documents

Borrower's Affidavit	__ Ack __ Jurat 1 2 3 4	Disbursement of Proceeds	__ Ack __ Jurat 1 2 3 4
Compliance Agreement	__ Ack __ Jurat 1 2 3 4	Errors & Omissions Agreement	__ Ack __ Jurat 1 2 3 4
Correction Agreement	__ Ack __ Jurat 1 2 3 4	Financial Affidavit	__ Ack __ Jurat 1 2 3 4
Indemnity Debt/Lien Affidavit	__ Ack __ Jurat 1 2 3 4	Grant Deed	__ Ack __ Jurat 1 2 3 4
Deed of Trust	__ Ack __ Jurat 1 2 3 4	Marital Status Affidavit	__ Ack __ Jurat 1 2 3 4
Mortgage	__ Ack __ Jurat 1 2 3 4	Quit Claim Deed	__ Ack __ Jurat 1 2 3 4
Mortgagor's Affidavit	__ Ack __ Jurat 1 2 3 4	Signature/Name Affidavit	__ Ack __ Jurat 1 2 3 4
Occupancy Affidavit	__ Ack __ Jurat 1 2 3 4	Survey Affidavit	__ Ack __ Jurat 1 2 3 4
Owner's Affidavit	__ Ack __ Jurat 1 2 3 4	Warranty Deed	__ Ack __ Jurat 1 2 3 4
Payoff Affidavit	__ Ack __ Jurat 1 2 3 4	Other	__ Ack __ Jurat 1 2 3 4

Vehicle Docs:

Duplicate Title	__ Ack __ Jurat 1 2 3 4	Odometer/VIN Verification	__ Ack __ Jurat 1 2 3 4
Lien Release	__ Ack __ Jurat 1 2 3 4	Title Transfer	__ Ack __ Jurat 1 2 3 4

Wills/Trusts/ POA:

Living Trust	__ Ack __ Jurat 1 2 3 4	Power of Attorney	__ Ack __ Jurat 1 2 3 4
Last Will & Test	__ Ack __ Jurat 1 2 3 4	Trust Certification	__ Ack __ Jurat 1 2 3 4

Medical Docs:

Advance Healthcare Directive	__ Ack __ Jurat 1 2 3 4	HIPAA Release	__ Ack __ Jurat 1 2 3 4

Other Non-listed Docs:

Document Title: _____ Act Type 1 2 3 4		Document Title: _____ Act Type 1 2 3 4	
Document Title: _____ Act Type 1 2 3 4		Document Title: _____ Act Type 1 2 3 4	
Document Title: _____ Act Type 1 2 3 4		Document Title: _____ Act Type 1 2 3 4	
Document Title: _____ Act Type 1 2 3 4		Document Title: _____ Act Type 1 2 3 4	

Date		Time	AM	PM

1

Full Name ___ Signor ___ Witness	Verification Method DL PP Cred. Wit Other: _____ State: _____ Iss date: _____ Expiration: _____	Doc. Type ___ Paper ___ Electronic ___ Hybrid	Thumb Print
Address: _____			
Signature	Screening ___ Coherent ___ Consenting	Phone I Email	

2

Full Name ___ Signor ___ Witness	Verification Method DL PP Cred. Wit Other: _____ State: _____ Iss date: _____ Expiration: _____	Doc. Type ___ Paper ___ Electronic ___ Hybrid	Thumb Print
Address: _____			
Signature	Screening ___ Coherent ___ Consenting	Phone I Email	

3

Full Name ___ Signor ___ Witness	Verification Method DL PP Cred. Wit Other: _____ State: _____ Iss date: _____ Expiration: _____	Doc. Type ___ Paper ___ Electronic ___ Hybrid	Thumb Print
Address: _____			
Signature	Screening ___ Coherent ___ Consenting	Phone I Email	

4

Full Name ___ Signor ___ Witness	Verification Method DL PP Cred. Wit Other: _____ State: _____ Iss date: _____ Expiration: _____	Doc. Type ___ Paper ___ Electronic ___ Hybrid	Thumb Print
Address: _____			
Signature	Screening ___ Coherent ___ Consenting	Phone I Email	

Signing Location:	Observers:	Signing Service:	Fee:

Appointment Notes:

Record of Signed Documents: Loan Documents

Borrower's Affidavit	__ Ack __ Jurat 1 2 3 4	Disbursement of Proceeds	__ Ack __ Jurat 1 2 3 4
Compliance Agreement	__ Ack __ Jurat 1 2 3 4	Errors & Omissions Agreement	__ Ack __ Jurat 1 2 3 4
Correction Agreement	__ Ack __ Jurat 1 2 3 4	Financial Affidavit	__ Ack __ Jurat 1 2 3 4
Indemnity Debt/Lien Affidavit	__ Ack __ Jurat 1 2 3 4	Grant Deed	__ Ack __ Jurat 1 2 3 4
Deed of Trust	__ Ack __ Jurat 1 2 3 4	Marital Status Affidavit	__ Ack __ Jurat 1 2 3 4
Mortgage	__ Ack __ Jurat 1 2 3 4	Quit Claim Deed	__ Ack __ Jurat 1 2 3 4
Mortgagor's Affidavit	__ Ack __ Jurat 1 2 3 4	Signature/Name Affidavit	__ Ack __ Jurat 1 2 3 4
Occupancy Affidavit	__ Ack __ Jurat 1 2 3 4	Survey Affidavit	__ Ack __ Jurat 1 2 3 4
Owner's Affidavit	__ Ack __ Jurat 1 2 3 4	Warranty Deed	__ Ack __ Jurat 1 2 3 4
Payoff Affidavit	__ Ack __ Jurat 1 2 3 4	Other	__ Ack __ Jurat 1 2 3 4

Vehicle Docs:

Duplicate Title	__ Ack __ Jurat 1 2 3 4	Odometer/VIN Verification	__ Ack __ Jurat 1 2 3 4
Lien Release	__ Ack __ Jurat 1 2 3 4	Title Transfer	__ Ack __ Jurat 1 2 3 4

Wills/Trusts/ POA:

Living Trust	__ Ack __ Jurat 1 2 3 4	Power of Attorney	__ Ack __ Jurat 1 2 3 4
Last Will & Test	__ Ack __ Jurat 1 2 3 4	Trust Certification	__ Ack __ Jurat 1 2 3 4

Medical Docs:

Advance Healthcare Directive	__ Ack __ Jurat 1 2 3 4	HIPAA Release	__ Ack __ Jurat 1 2 3 4

Other Non-listed Docs:

Document Title: _____ Act Type 1 2 3 4		Document Title: _____ Act Type 1 2 3 4	
Document Title: _____ Act Type 1 2 3 4		Document Title: _____ Act Type 1 2 3 4	
Document Title: _____ Act Type 1 2 3 4		Document Title: _____ Act Type 1 2 3 4	
Document Title: _____ Act Type 1 2 3 4		Document Title: _____ Act Type 1 2 3 4	

Date			Time		AM	PM
1	**Full Name** ___ Signor ___ Witness _____ Address: _____		**Verification Method** DL PP Cred. Wit Other: _____ State: _____ Iss date: _____ Expiration: _____		**Doc. Type** ___ Paper ___ Electronic ___ Hybrid	**Thumb Print**
	Signature		Screening ___ Coherent ___ Consenting		Phone I Email	
2	**Full Name** ___ Signor ___ Witness _____ Address: _____		**Verification Method** DL PP Cred. Wit Other: _____ State: _____ Iss date: _____ Expiration: _____		**Doc. Type** ___ Paper ___ Electronic ___ Hybrid	**Thumb Print**
	Signature		Screening ___ Coherent ___ Consenting		Phone I Email	
3	**Full Name** ___ Signor ___ Witness _____ Address: _____		**Verification Method** DL PP Cred. Wit Other: _____ State: _____ Iss date: _____ Expiration: _____		**Doc. Type** ___ Paper ___ Electronic ___ Hybrid	**Thumb Print**
	Signature		Screening ___ Coherent ___ Consenting		Phone I Email	
4	**Full Name** ___ Signor ___ Witness _____ Address: _____		**Verification Method** DL PP Cred. Wit Other: _____ State: _____ Iss date: _____ Expiration: _____		**Doc. Type** ___ Paper ___ Electronic ___ Hybrid	**Thumb Print**
	Signature		Screening ___ Coherent ___ Consenting		Phone I Email	

Signing Location:	Observers:	Signing Service:	Fee:

Appointment Notes:

Record of Signed Documents: Loan Documents

Borrower's Affidavit	__ Ack __ Jurat 1 2 3 4	Disbursement of Proceeds	__ Ack __ Jurat 1 2 3 4
Compliance Agreement	__ Ack __ Jurat 1 2 3 4	Errors & Omissions Agreement	__ Ack __ Jurat 1 2 3 4
Correction Agreement	__ Ack __ Jurat 1 2 3 4	Financial Affidavit	__ Ack __ Jurat 1 2 3 4
Indemnity Debt/Lien Affidavit	__ Ack __ Jurat 1 2 3 4	Grant Deed	__ Ack __ Jurat 1 2 3 4
Deed of Trust	__ Ack __ Jurat 1 2 3 4	Marital Status Affidavit	__ Ack __ Jurat 1 2 3 4
Mortgage	__ Ack __ Jurat 1 2 3 4	Quit Claim Deed	__ Ack __ Jurat 1 2 3 4
Mortgagor's Affidavit	__ Ack __ Jurat 1 2 3 4	Signature/Name Affidavit	__ Ack __ Jurat 1 2 3 4
Occupancy Affidavit	__ Ack __ Jurat 1 2 3 4	Survey Affidavit	__ Ack __ Jurat 1 2 3 4
Owner's Affidavit	__ Ack __ Jurat 1 2 3 4	Warranty Deed	__ Ack __ Jurat 1 2 3 4
Payoff Affidavit	__ Ack __ Jurat 1 2 3 4	Other	__ Ack __ Jurat 1 2 3 4

Vehicle Docs:

Duplicate Title	__ Ack __ Jurat 1 2 3 4	Odometer/VIN Verification	__ Ack __ Jurat 1 2 3 4
Lien Release	__ Ack __ Jurat 1 2 3 4	Title Transfer	__ Ack __ Jurat 1 2 3 4

Wills/Trusts/ POA:

Living Trust	__ Ack __ Jurat 1 2 3 4	Power of Attorney	__ Ack __ Jurat 1 2 3 4
Last Will & Test	__ Ack __ Jurat 1 2 3 4	Trust Certification	__ Ack __ Jurat 1 2 3 4

Medical Docs:

Advance Healthcare Directive	__ Ack __ Jurat 1 2 3 4	HIPAA Release	__ Ack __ Jurat 1 2 3 4

Other Non-listed Docs:

Document Title: _____ Act Type 1 2 3 4	Document Title: _____ Act Type 1 2 3 4
Document Title: _____ Act Type 1 2 3 4	Document Title: _____ Act Type 1 2 3 4
Document Title: _____ Act Type 1 2 3 4	Document Title: _____ Act Type 1 2 3 4
Document Title: _____ Act Type 1 2 3 4	Document Title: _____ Act Type 1 2 3 4

Date		Time		AM	PM

	Full Name ___ Signor ___ Witness	Verification Method DL PP Cred. Wit Other: _____ State: _____ Iss date: _____ Expiration: _____	Doc. Type ___ Paper ___ Electronic ___ Hybrid	Thumb Print
1	Address: _____			
	Signature	Screening ___ Coherent ___ Consenting	Phone I Email	

	Full Name ___ Signor ___ Witness	Verification Method DL PP Cred. Wit Other: _____ State: _____ Iss date: _____ Expiration: _____	Doc. Type ___ Paper ___ Electronic ___ Hybrid	Thumb Print
2	Address: _____			
	Signature	Screening ___ Coherent ___ Consenting	Phone I Email	

	Full Name ___ Signor ___ Witness	Verification Method DL PP Cred. Wit Other: _____ State: _____ Iss date: _____ Expiration: _____	Doc. Type ___ Paper ___ Electronic ___ Hybrid	Thumb Print
3	Address: _____			
	Signature	Screening ___ Coherent ___ Consenting	Phone I Email	

	Full Name ___ Signor ___ Witness	Verification Method DL PP Cred. Wit Other: _____ State: _____ Iss date: _____ Expiration: _____	Doc. Type ___ Paper ___ Electronic ___ Hybrid	Thumb Print
4	Address: _____			
	Signature	Screening ___ Coherent ___ Consenting	Phone I Email	

Signing Location:	Observers:	Signing Service:	Fee:

Appointment Notes:

Record of Signed Documents: Loan Documents

Borrower's Affidavit	__ Ack __ Jurat 1 2 3 4	Disbursement of Proceeds	__ Ack __ Jurat 1 2 3 4
Compliance Agreement	__ Ack __ Jurat 1 2 3 4	Errors & Omissions Agreement	__ Ack __ Jurat 1 2 3 4
Correction Agreement	__ Ack __ Jurat 1 2 3 4	Financial Affidavit	__ Ack __ Jurat 1 2 3 4
Indemnity Debt/Lien Affidavit	__ Ack __ Jurat 1 2 3 4	Grant Deed	__ Ack __ Jurat 1 2 3 4
Deed of Trust	__ Ack __ Jurat 1 2 3 4	Marital Status Affidavit	__ Ack __ Jurat 1 2 3 4
Mortgage	__ Ack __ Jurat 1 2 3 4	Quit Claim Deed	__ Ack __ Jurat 1 2 3 4
Mortgagor's Affidavit	__ Ack __ Jurat 1 2 3 4	Signature/Name Affidavit	__ Ack __ Jurat 1 2 3 4
Occupancy Affidavit	__ Ack __ Jurat 1 2 3 4	Survey Affidavit	__ Ack __ Jurat 1 2 3 4
Owner's Affidavit	__ Ack __ Jurat 1 2 3 4	Warranty Deed	__ Ack __ Jurat 1 2 3 4
Payoff Affidavit	__ Ack __ Jurat 1 2 3 4	Other	__ Ack __ Jurat 1 2 3 4

Vehicle Docs:

Duplicate Title	__ Ack __ Jurat 1 2 3 4	Odometer/VIN Verification	__ Ack __ Jurat 1 2 3 4
Lien Release	__ Ack __ Jurat 1 2 3 4	Title Transfer	__ Ack __ Jurat 1 2 3 4

Wills/Trusts/ POA:

Living Trust	__ Ack __ Jurat 1 2 3 4	Power of Attorney	__ Ack __ Jurat 1 2 3 4
Last Will & Test	__ Ack __ Jurat 1 2 3 4	Trust Certification	__ Ack __ Jurat 1 2 3 4

Medical Docs:

Advance Healthcare Directive	__ Ack __ Jurat 1 2 3 4	HIPAA Release	__ Ack __ Jurat 1 2 3 4

Other Non-listed Docs:

Document Title: _____ Act Type 1 2 3 4		Document Title: _____ Act Type 1 2 3 4	
Document Title: _____ Act Type 1 2 3 4		Document Title: _____ Act Type 1 2 3 4	
Document Title: _____ Act Type 1 2 3 4		Document Title: _____ Act Type 1 2 3 4	
Document Title: _____ Act Type 1 2 3 4		Document Title: _____ Act Type 1 2 3 4	

Date		Time		AM	PM

	Full Name ___ Signor ___ Witness	Verification Method DL PP Cred. Wit Other: _____ State: _____ Iss date: _____ Expiration: _____	Doc. Type ___ Paper ___ Electronic ___ Hybrid	Thumb Print
1	Address: _____			
	Signature	Screening ___ Coherent ___ Consenting	Phone I Email	

	Full Name ___ Signor ___ Witness	Verification Method DL PP Cred. Wit Other: _____ State: _____ Iss date: _____ Expiration: _____	Doc. Type ___ Paper ___ Electronic ___ Hybrid	Thumb Print
2	Address: _____			
	Signature	Screening ___ Coherent ___ Consenting	Phone I Email	

	Full Name ___ Signor ___ Witness	Verification Method DL PP Cred. Wit Other: _____ State: _____ Iss date: _____ Expiration: _____	Doc. Type ___ Paper ___ Electronic ___ Hybrid	Thumb Print
3	Address: _____			
	Signature	Screening ___ Coherent ___ Consenting	Phone I Email	

	Full Name ___ Signor ___ Witness	Verification Method DL PP Cred. Wit Other: _____ State: _____ Iss date: _____ Expiration: _____	Doc. Type ___ Paper ___ Electronic ___ Hybrid	Thumb Print
4	Address: _____			
	Signature	Screening ___ Coherent ___ Consenting	Phone I Email	

Signing Location:	Observers:	Signing Service:	Fee:

Appointment Notes:

Record of Signed Documents: Loan Documents

Borrower's Affidavit	__ Ack __ Jurat 1 2 3 4	Disbursement of Proceeds	__ Ack __ Jurat 1 2 3 4
Compliance Agreement	__ Ack __ Jurat 1 2 3 4	Errors & Omissions Agreement	__ Ack __ Jurat 1 2 3 4
Correction Agreement	__ Ack __ Jurat 1 2 3 4	Financial Affidavit	__ Ack __ Jurat 1 2 3 4
Indemnity Debt/Lien Affidavit	__ Ack __ Jurat 1 2 3 4	Grant Deed	__ Ack __ Jurat 1 2 3 4
Deed of Trust	__ Ack __ Jurat 1 2 3 4	Marital Status Affidavit	__ Ack __ Jurat 1 2 3 4
Mortgage	__ Ack __ Jurat 1 2 3 4	Quit Claim Deed	__ Ack __ Jurat 1 2 3 4
Mortgagor's Affidavit	__ Ack __ Jurat 1 2 3 4	Signature/Name Affidavit	__ Ack __ Jurat 1 2 3 4
Occupancy Affidavit	__ Ack __ Jurat 1 2 3 4	Survey Affidavit	__ Ack __ Jurat 1 2 3 4
Owner's Affidavit	__ Ack __ Jurat 1 2 3 4	Warranty Deed	__ Ack __ Jurat 1 2 3 4
Payoff Affidavit	__ Ack __ Jurat 1 2 3 4	Other	__ Ack __ Jurat 1 2 3 4

Vehicle Docs:

Duplicate Title	__ Ack __ Jurat 1 2 3 4	Odometer/VIN Verification	__ Ack __ Jurat 1 2 3 4
Lien Release	__ Ack __ Jurat 1 2 3 4	Title Transfer	__ Ack __ Jurat 1 2 3 4

Wills/Trusts/ POA:

Living Trust	__ Ack __ Jurat 1 2 3 4	Power of Attorney	__ Ack __ Jurat 1 2 3 4
Last Will & Test	__ Ack __ Jurat 1 2 3 4	Trust Certification	__ Ack __ Jurat 1 2 3 4

Medical Docs:

Advance Healthcare Directive	__ Ack __ Jurat 1 2 3 4	HIPAA Release	__ Ack __ Jurat 1 2 3 4

Other Non-listed Docs:

Document Title: _____ Act Type 1 2 3 4		Document Title: _____ Act Type 1 2 3 4	
Document Title: _____ Act Type 1 2 3 4		Document Title: _____ Act Type 1 2 3 4	
Document Title: _____ Act Type 1 2 3 4		Document Title: _____ Act Type 1 2 3 4	
Document Title: _____ Act Type 1 2 3 4		Document Title: _____ Act Type 1 2 3 4	

Date		Time	AM	PM
1	**Full Name** ___ Signor ___ Witness _____ Address: _____	**Verification Method** DL PP Cred. Wit Other: _____ State: _____ Iss date: _____ Expiration: _____	**Doc. Type** ___ Paper ___ Electronic ___ Hybrid	Thumb Print
	Signature	**Screening** ___ Coherent ___ Consenting	Phone I Email	
2	**Full Name** ___ Signor ___ Witness _____ Address: _____	**Verification Method** DL PP Cred. Wit Other: _____ State: _____ Iss date: _____ Expiration: _____	**Doc. Type** ___ Paper ___ Electronic ___ Hybrid	Thumb Print
	Signature	**Screening** ___ Coherent ___ Consenting	Phone I Email	
3	**Full Name** ___ Signor ___ Witness _____ Address: _____	**Verification Method** DL PP Cred. Wit Other: _____ State: _____ Iss date: _____ Expiration: _____	**Doc. Type** ___ Paper ___ Electronic ___ Hybrid	Thumb Print
	Signature	**Screening** ___ Coherent ___ Consenting	Phone I Email	
4	**Full Name** ___ Signor ___ Witness _____ Address: _____	**Verification Method** DL PP Cred. Wit Other: _____ State: _____ Iss date: _____ Expiration: _____	**Doc. Type** ___ Paper ___ Electronic ___ Hybrid	Thumb Print
	Signature	**Screening** ___ Coherent ___ Consenting	Phone I Email	

Signing Location:	Observers:	Signing Service:	Fee:

Appointment Notes:

Record of Signed Documents: Loan Documents

Borrower's Affidavit	__ Ack __ Jurat 1 2 3 4	Disbursement of Proceeds	__ Ack __ Jurat 1 2 3 4
Compliance Agreement	__ Ack __ Jurat 1 2 3 4	Errors & Omissions Agreement	__ Ack __ Jurat 1 2 3 4
Correction Agreement	__ Ack __ Jurat 1 2 3 4	Financial Affidavit	__ Ack __ Jurat 1 2 3 4
Indemnity Debt/Lien Affidavit	__ Ack __ Jurat 1 2 3 4	Grant Deed	__ Ack __ Jurat 1 2 3 4
Deed of Trust	__ Ack __ Jurat 1 2 3 4	Marital Status Affidavit	__ Ack __ Jurat 1 2 3 4
Mortgage	__ Ack __ Jurat 1 2 3 4	Quit Claim Deed	__ Ack __ Jurat 1 2 3 4
Mortgagor's Affidavit	__ Ack __ Jurat 1 2 3 4	Signature/Name Affidavit	__ Ack __ Jurat 1 2 3 4
Occupancy Affidavit	__ Ack __ Jurat 1 2 3 4	Survey Affidavit	__ Ack __ Jurat 1 2 3 4
Owner's Affidavit	__ Ack __ Jurat 1 2 3 4	Warranty Deed	__ Ack __ Jurat 1 2 3 4
Payoff Affidavit	__ Ack __ Jurat 1 2 3 4	Other	__ Ack __ Jurat 1 2 3 4

Vehicle Docs:

Duplicate Title	__ Ack __ Jurat 1 2 3 4	Odometer/VIN Verification	__ Ack __ Jurat 1 2 3 4
Lien Release	__ Ack __ Jurat 1 2 3 4	Title Transfer	__ Ack __ Jurat 1 2 3 4

Wills/Trusts/ POA:

Living Trust	__ Ack __ Jurat 1 2 3 4	Power of Attorney	__ Ack __ Jurat 1 2 3 4
Last Will & Test	__ Ack __ Jurat 1 2 3 4	Trust Certification	__ Ack __ Jurat 1 2 3 4

Medical Docs:

Advance Healthcare Directive	__ Ack __ Jurat 1 2 3 4	HIPAA Release	__ Ack __ Jurat 1 2 3 4

Other Non-listed Docs:

Document Title: _____ Act Type 1 2 3 4		Document Title: _____ Act Type 1 2 3 4	
Document Title: _____ Act Type 1 2 3 4		Document Title: _____ Act Type 1 2 3 4	
Document Title: _____ Act Type 1 2 3 4		Document Title: _____ Act Type 1 2 3 4	
Document Title: _____ Act Type 1 2 3 4		Document Title: _____ Act Type 1 2 3 4	

Date			Time		AM	PM

1

Full Name ___ Signor ___ Witness	Verification Method	Doc. Type	Thumb Print
_____	DL PP Cred. Wit		
Address: _____	Other: _____	___ Paper	
	State: _____	___ Electronic	
	Iss date: _____	___ Hybrid	
	Expiration: _____		
Signature	Screening ___ Coherent ___ Consenting	Phone I Email	

2

Full Name ___ Signor ___ Witness	Verification Method	Doc. Type	Thumb Print
_____	DL PP Cred. Wit		
Address: _____	Other: _____	___ Paper	
	State: _____	___ Electronic	
	Iss date: _____	___ Hybrid	
	Expiration: _____		
Signature	Screening ___ Coherent ___ Consenting	Phone I Email	

3

Full Name ___ Signor ___ Witness	Verification Method	Doc. Type	Thumb Print
_____	DL PP Cred. Wit		
Address: _____	Other: _____	___ Paper	
	State: _____	___ Electronic	
	Iss date: _____	___ Hybrid	
	Expiration: _____		
Signature	Screening ___ Coherent ___ Consenting	Phone I Email	

4

Full Name ___ Signor ___ Witness	Verification Method	Doc. Type	Thumb Print
_____	DL PP Cred. Wit		
Address: _____	Other: _____	___ Paper	
	State: _____	___ Electronic	
	Iss date: _____	___ Hybrid	
	Expiration: _____		
Signature	Screening ___ Coherent ___ Consenting	Phone I Email	

Signing Location:	Observers:	Signing Service:	Fee:

Appointment Notes:

Record of Signed Documents: Loan Documents

Borrower's Affidavit	__ Ack __ Jurat 1 2 3 4	Disbursement of Proceeds	__ Ack __ Jurat 1 2 3 4
Compliance Agreement	__ Ack __ Jurat 1 2 3 4	Errors & Omissions Agreement	__ Ack __ Jurat 1 2 3 4
Correction Agreement	__ Ack __ Jurat 1 2 3 4	Financial Affidavit	__ Ack __ Jurat 1 2 3 4
Indemnity Debt/Lien Affidavit	__ Ack __ Jurat 1 2 3 4	Grant Deed	__ Ack __ Jurat 1 2 3 4
Deed of Trust	__ Ack __ Jurat 1 2 3 4	Marital Status Affidavit	__ Ack __ Jurat 1 2 3 4
Mortgage	__ Ack __ Jurat 1 2 3 4	Quit Claim Deed	__ Ack __ Jurat 1 2 3 4
Mortgagor's Affidavit	__ Ack __ Jurat 1 2 3 4	Signature/Name Affidavit	__ Ack __ Jurat 1 2 3 4
Occupancy Affidavit	__ Ack __ Jurat 1 2 3 4	Survey Affidavit	__ Ack __ Jurat 1 2 3 4
Owner's Affidavit	__ Ack __ Jurat 1 2 3 4	Warranty Deed	__ Ack __ Jurat 1 2 3 4
Payoff Affidavit	__ Ack __ Jurat 1 2 3 4	Other	__ Ack __ Jurat 1 2 3 4

Vehicle Docs:

Duplicate Title	__ Ack __ Jurat 1 2 3 4	Odometer/VIN Verification	__ Ack __ Jurat 1 2 3 4
Lien Release	__ Ack __ Jurat 1 2 3 4	Title Transfer	__ Ack __ Jurat 1 2 3 4

Wills/Trusts/ POA:

Living Trust	__ Ack __ Jurat 1 2 3 4	Power of Attorney	__ Ack __ Jurat 1 2 3 4
Last Will & Test	__ Ack __ Jurat 1 2 3 4	Trust Certification	__ Ack __ Jurat 1 2 3 4

Medical Docs:

Advance Healthcare Directive	__ Ack __ Jurat 1 2 3 4	HIPAA Release	__ Ack __ Jurat 1 2 3 4

Other Non-listed Docs:

Document Title: _____ Act Type 1 2 3 4		Document Title: _____ Act Type 1 2 3 4	
Document Title: _____ Act Type 1 2 3 4		Document Title: _____ Act Type 1 2 3 4	
Document Title: _____ Act Type 1 2 3 4		Document Title: _____ Act Type 1 2 3 4	
Document Title: _____ Act Type 1 2 3 4		Document Title: _____ Act Type 1 2 3 4	

Date			Time	AM	PM

1	Full Name ___ Signor ___ Witness _____ Address: _____		Verification Method DL PP Cred. Wit Other: _____ State: _____ Iss date: _____ Expiration: _____	Doc. Type ___ Paper ___ Electronic ___ Hybrid	Thumb Print
	Signature		Screening ___ Coherent ___ Consenting	Phone I Email	
2	Full Name ___ Signor ___ Witness _____ Address: _____		Verification Method DL PP Cred. Wit Other: _____ State: _____ Iss date: _____ Expiration: _____	Doc. Type ___ Paper ___ Electronic ___ Hybrid	Thumb Print
	Signature		Screening ___ Coherent ___ Consenting	Phone I Email	
3	Full Name ___ Signor ___ Witness _____ Address: _____		Verification Method DL PP Cred. Wit Other: _____ State: _____ Iss date: _____ Expiration: _____	Doc. Type ___ Paper ___ Electronic ___ Hybrid	Thumb Print
	Signature		Screening ___ Coherent ___ Consenting	Phone I Email	
4	Full Name ___ Signor ___ Witness _____ Address: _____		Verification Method DL PP Cred. Wit Other: _____ State: _____ Iss date: _____ Expiration: _____	Doc. Type ___ Paper ___ Electronic ___ Hybrid	Thumb Print
	Signature		Screening ___ Coherent ___ Consenting	Phone I Email	

Signing Location:	Observers:	Signing Service:	Fee:

Appointment Notes:

Record of Signed Documents: Loan Documents

Borrower's Affidavit	__ Ack __ Jurat 1 2 3 4	Disbursement of Proceeds	__ Ack __ Jurat 1 2 3 4
Compliance Agreement	__ Ack __ Jurat 1 2 3 4	Errors & Omissions Agreement	__ Ack __ Jurat 1 2 3 4
Correction Agreement	__ Ack __ Jurat 1 2 3 4	Financial Affidavit	__ Ack __ Jurat 1 2 3 4
Indemnity Debt/Lien Affidavit	__ Ack __ Jurat 1 2 3 4	Grant Deed	__ Ack __ Jurat 1 2 3 4
Deed of Trust	__ Ack __ Jurat 1 2 3 4	Marital Status Affidavit	__ Ack __ Jurat 1 2 3 4
Mortgage	__ Ack __ Jurat 1 2 3 4	Quit Claim Deed	__ Ack __ Jurat 1 2 3 4
Mortgagor's Affidavit	__ Ack __ Jurat 1 2 3 4	Signature/Name Affidavit	__ Ack __ Jurat 1 2 3 4
Occupancy Affidavit	__ Ack __ Jurat 1 2 3 4	Survey Affidavit	__ Ack __ Jurat 1 2 3 4
Owner's Affidavit	__ Ack __ Jurat 1 2 3 4	Warranty Deed	__ Ack __ Jurat 1 2 3 4
Payoff Affidavit	__ Ack __ Jurat 1 2 3 4	Other	__ Ack __ Jurat 1 2 3 4

Vehicle Docs:

Duplicate Title	__ Ack __ Jurat 1 2 3 4	Odometer/VIN Verification	__ Ack __ Jurat 1 2 3 4
Lien Release	__ Ack __ Jurat 1 2 3 4	Title Transfer	__ Ack __ Jurat 1 2 3 4

Wills/Trusts/ POA:

Living Trust	__ Ack __ Jurat 1 2 3 4	Power of Attorney	__ Ack __ Jurat 1 2 3 4
Last Will & Test	__ Ack __ Jurat 1 2 3 4	Trust Certification	__ Ack __ Jurat 1 2 3 4

Medical Docs:

Advance Healthcare Directive	__ Ack __ Jurat 1 2 3 4	HIPAA Release	__ Ack __ Jurat 1 2 3 4

Other Non-listed Docs:

Document Title: _____ Act Type 1 2 3 4		Document Title: _____ Act Type 1 2 3 4	
Document Title: _____ Act Type 1 2 3 4		Document Title: _____ Act Type 1 2 3 4	
Document Title: _____ Act Type 1 2 3 4		Document Title: _____ Act Type 1 2 3 4	
Document Title: _____ Act Type 1 2 3 4		Document Title: _____ Act Type 1 2 3 4	

Date			Time	AM	PM

1	Full Name ___ Signor ___ Witness		Verification Method DL PP Cred. Wit Other: _____ State: _____ Iss date: _____ Expiration: _____	Doc. Type ___ Paper ___ Electronic ___ Hybrid	Thumb Print
	Signature		Screening ___ Coherent ___ Consenting	Phone I Email	
2	Full Name ___ Signor ___ Witness		Verification Method DL PP Cred. Wit Other: _____ State: _____ Iss date: _____ Expiration: _____	Doc. Type ___ Paper ___ Electronic ___ Hybrid	Thumb Print
	Signature		Screening ___ Coherent ___ Consenting	Phone I Email	
3	Full Name ___ Signor ___ Witness		Verification Method DL PP Cred. Wit Other: _____ State: _____ Iss date: _____ Expiration: _____	Doc. Type ___ Paper ___ Electronic ___ Hybrid	Thumb Print
	Signature		Screening ___ Coherent ___ Consenting	Phone I Email	
4	Full Name ___ Signor ___ Witness		Verification Method DL PP Cred. Wit Other: _____ State: _____ Iss date: _____ Expiration: _____	Doc. Type ___ Paper ___ Electronic ___ Hybrid	Thumb Print
	Signature		Screening ___ Coherent ___ Consenting	Phone I Email	

Address: fields appear under each Full Name row.

Signing Location:	Observers:	Signing Service:	Fee:

Appointment Notes:

Record of Signed Documents: Loan Documents

Borrower's Affidavit	__ Ack __ Jurat 1 2 3 4	Disbursement of Proceeds	__ Ack __ Jurat 1 2 3 4
Compliance Agreement	__ Ack __ Jurat 1 2 3 4	Errors & Omissions Agreement	__ Ack __ Jurat 1 2 3 4
Correction Agreement	__ Ack __ Jurat 1 2 3 4	Financial Affidavit	__ Ack __ Jurat 1 2 3 4
Indemnity Debt/Lien Affidavit	__ Ack __ Jurat 1 2 3 4	Grant Deed	__ Ack __ Jurat 1 2 3 4
Deed of Trust	__ Ack __ Jurat 1 2 3 4	Marital Status Affidavit	__ Ack __ Jurat 1 2 3 4
Mortgage	__ Ack __ Jurat 1 2 3 4	Quit Claim Deed	__ Ack __ Jurat 1 2 3 4
Mortgagor's Affidavit	__ Ack __ Jurat 1 2 3 4	Signature/Name Affidavit	__ Ack __ Jurat 1 2 3 4
Occupancy Affidavit	__ Ack __ Jurat 1 2 3 4	Survey Affidavit	__ Ack __ Jurat 1 2 3 4
Owner's Affidavit	__ Ack __ Jurat 1 2 3 4	Warranty Deed	__ Ack __ Jurat 1 2 3 4
Payoff Affidavit	__ Ack __ Jurat 1 2 3 4	Other	__ Ack __ Jurat 1 2 3 4

Vehicle Docs:

Duplicate Title	__ Ack __ Jurat 1 2 3 4	Odometer/VIN Verification	__ Ack __ Jurat 1 2 3 4
Lien Release	__ Ack __ Jurat 1 2 3 4	Title Transfer	__ Ack __ Jurat 1 2 3 4

Wills/Trusts/ POA:

Living Trust	__ Ack __ Jurat 1 2 3 4	Power of Attorney	__ Ack __ Jurat 1 2 3 4
Last Will & Test	__ Ack __ Jurat 1 2 3 4	Trust Certification	__ Ack __ Jurat 1 2 3 4

Medical Docs:

Advance Healthcare Directive	__ Ack __ Jurat 1 2 3 4	HIPAA Release	__ Ack __ Jurat 1 2 3 4

Other Non-listed Docs:

Document Title: _____ Act Type 1 2 3 4		Document Title: _____ Act Type 1 2 3 4	
Document Title: _____ Act Type 1 2 3 4		Document Title: _____ Act Type 1 2 3 4	
Document Title: _____ Act Type 1 2 3 4		Document Title: _____ Act Type 1 2 3 4	
Document Title: _____ Act Type 1 2 3 4		Document Title: _____ Act Type 1 2 3 4	

Made in United States
Orlando, FL
06 August 2024

49993479R00115